THE HERMETIC ORDER
OF THE GOLDEN DAWN

THE HERMETIC ORDER OF THE GOLDEN DAWN

MAGIC ARTS AND THE OCCULT REVIVAL

FELIX JOHN TAYLOR

For Damaris

Frontispiece: W. T. Horton, '*Assumptio*',
from W. T. Horton and W. B. Yeats, *A Book of Images*, 1898.

First published in the United Kingdom in 2026 by
Thames & Hudson Ltd, 6–24 Britannia Street, London WC1X 9JD

First published in the United States of America in 2026 by
Thames & Hudson Inc., 500 Fifth Avenue, New York, New York 10110

The Hermetic Order of the Golden Dawn: Magic Arts and the Occult Revival
© 2026 Thames & Hudson Ltd, London

Text © 2026 Felix John Taylor

All efforts have been made to trace the owners of the copyright and
reproduction rights for all of the quotations that appear in this book.
Thames & Hudson will be happy to rectify any omissions or errors
in future printings of this book.

All Rights Reserved. No part of this publication may be reproduced
or transmitted in any form or by any means, electronic or mechanical,
including photocopy, recording or any other information storage and
retrieval system, without prior permission in writing from the publisher.

EU Authorized Representative: Interart S.A.R.L.
19 rue Charles Auray, 93500 Pantin, Paris, France
productsafety@thameshudson.co.uk
interart.fr

A CIP catalogue record for this book is available from the British Library

Library of Congress Control Number 2025938785

ISBN 978-0-500-02918-3
01

Printed and bound in India by Replika Press Pvt Ltd

Be the first to know about our new releases,
exclusive content and author events by visiting
thamesandhudson.com
thamesandhudsonusa.com
thamesandhudson.com.au

CONTENTS

	Introduction: 'A Wild Performance'	6
1	'Metaphors for Poetry': W. B. Yeats	30
2	A Gift Given to the Wise: Florence Farr	59
3	The Twilight Star: A. E. Waite & Arthur Machen	97
4	Babe of the Abyss: Aleister Crowley	132
5	'The Spell of Sound': W. B. Yeats, Florence Farr & Pamela Colman Smith	164
6	Metaphysical Thrillers: Charles Williams & Dion Fortune	192
	'An Elaborate Appendix'	220
	Notes	232
	Bibliography	256
	Picture Credits	268
	Acknowledgments	270
	Index	272

Paul Hardy, 'It was a darkness shaping itself forth', from Algernon Blackwood, 'Smith: An Episode in a Lodging-House', *The Empty House and Other Ghost Stories*, 1906.

Introduction
'A Wild Performance'

Late in November 1891, in one of a cluster of small buildings known as Thavies Inn, south of Holborn Circus, London, a remarkable wooden structure was being painted. Seven-sided and eight feet tall, it had a coffin in the centre and, above that, a moveable altar. The painters – a tall, athletic man named Samuel Liddell MacGregor Mathers and a young woman, Moina Mathers – had been working for weeks on perfecting the grids of forty magical symbols that adorned each side. As the gas lamps were lit in the streets below and the distant rumbling of carriages on the busy London thoroughfare reached them through the open window, the couple murmured instructions to each other. Moina was an artist, having trained at the Slade School of Art from the age of fifteen, and had become invaluable to the Hermetic Order of the Golden Dawn as an in-house artist and designer. She played a vital role in carrying out her husband's design. For the past decade, meanwhile, Mathers had studied the occult symbolism of alchemy, astrology, tarot and the paths of the mystical Kabbalah, and had fashioned a system of correspondences that brought them all together. Even the colour scheme of the painted form was constructed according to the planets and the zodiac. Once the seven walls were complete, the magicians turned their attention to the coffin at the vault's centre.

The coffin was to be the centrepiece of the ritual to come. Mathers would play the dead Rosenkreutz, the mythical founder of Rosicrucianism, to be discovered in his tomb by the unknowing initiate. The Rosicrucian legend had begun in the seventeenth century with several anonymous manifestos that described the founding of a religious brotherhood by a German man named Christian Rosenkreutz, who had journeyed to the Arab world and returned with knowledge of science and the magical arts. Pledged to chastity, members of the new Brotherhood of the Rosy Cross healed the sick and spread wisdom through their books. When Father Rosenkreutz died, the location of his tomb was kept hidden, but the manifestos declared that it had recently been rediscovered, and that this signalled the birth of a new spiritual age.[1] This was what Mathers planned to replicate: the uncovering of Rosenkreutz's body in the seven-sided vault described in the manifestos. It would conclude the initiation of Candidates into the Second (or Inner) Order, a group newly devised by Mathers that would be known only to those who had attained the first four 'degrees' of the First Order of the Golden Dawn. There is no evidence that a Rosicrucian Brotherhood ever existed, or that the manifestos were intended to be taken seriously, but this did not stop Mathers from using the origin myth as a sensational metaphor for his students' magical advancement.

The vault was still not finished by the time the first initiation took place: the roof, to be washed a blinding white and inset with a rose of twenty-two petals, was not yet attached, and some of the paint was still wet. Nevertheless, on the evening of 7 December a group of men and women in ritual dress took their positions outside the structure, which had been hidden from sight by a curtain. Three Adepts (students of the Second Order), each in differently coloured robes according to their role, stepped behind the curtain and entered the vault. One woman was left behind, fingering the hem of her white robe. Against one wall was a tall wooden crucifix. She could hear that the opening ceremony had started, but could not make out the words; finally, she felt a sash being put over her shoulder from behind. She was given a sheet of paper. The Third Adept re-emerged and led her behind the curtain into the candlelit vault, an enormous circular altar positioned in its centre. The Second Adept stood beside her, but she could not see where the First had gone. After a signal, she read aloud from the paper:

> Hear ye all that I, the Honoured Soror 'Fortiter et Recte' stand before you, being a member of the 4° = 7° Grade of the First Order, Highest Grade of the Golden Dawn in the Outer, a Philosophus ... I am now come to demand my reception and acknowledgement as an Adeptus Minor of the 5° = 6° Grade of the Second Order.[2]

Annie Horniman had joined the Hermetic Order of the Golden Dawn in 1890 and was now bankrolling the Mathers' extravagant lives. She had paid for the oil paints and other 'personal expenses' of this current venture, and had secured a curatorial job for Mathers at her father's private museum in Forest Hill.[3] She had studied with Moina at the Slade, cut her hair short, and was to be seen cycling around London in bloomers: the ultimate sign of a radical New Woman.[4] Now, perhaps as a token of gratitude for her financial assistance, Horniman was to be the first Golden Dawn student initiated into the secret 'Adeptus Minor' grade. She would not have been told the intricacies of the ceremony before her, and would have had no idea that Mathers, in full regalia and clutching to his breast a crook and a scourge (a kind of whip), was now lying inside the coffin (or 'Pastos') beneath the altar.

After being questioned by the Adepts, Horniman was led out of the vault, her 'demand' symbolically rejected. She was quickly reclothed in a plain black robe and her hands tied behind her back: 'Let the Aspirant be bound to the Cross of Suffering'. Strapped to the wooden cross, she was taken through her Obligation by the Second Adept ('I will perform all practical work connected with this Order in a place concealed and apart from the gaze of the outer and uninitiated world') before being released.[5] Back in the vault, she watched in amazement as the altar was moved away, the lid of the Pastos removed. She was confronted by the body of Christian Rosenkreutz. 'In the alembic [distiller] of thine heart, through the athanor [furnace] of affliction, seek thou the true stone of the wise,' Mathers intoned. 'Quit then, this Tomb, O Aspirant, with thine arms crossed upon thy breast.'[6]

INTRODUCTION

The Hermetic Order of the Golden Dawn began life in 1888. It was the most sensational formal flowering of the nineteenth-century occult revival in Britain, and continued to exist in various mutations well into the next century. Its members studied a curriculum based on the Western hermetic tradition – Kabbalah, astrology, alchemical symbolism, tarot divination – and followed a hierarchical structure of grades and ritual ceremonies mostly borrowed from freemasonry, the three founding members having themselves been masons.

Schools of occult instruction had existed in England since at least the early 1800s, when Francis Barrett, compiler of a grimoire (magic book) called *The Magus* (1801), published an advertisement seeking 'those that are curious in the studies of Art and Nature, especially of Natural and Occult Philosophy'.[7] The Hermetic Brotherhood of Luxor, whose public work began in 1884 (though it claimed a far more ancient origin), provided practical training in occultism by correspondence course, predominantly in Britain and France.[8] The only group to call itself a Rosicrucian order was the Societas Rosicruciana in Anglia (the SRIA, or the Rosicrucian Society in England), an independent order based on an earlier society in Scotland and founded in the late 1860s by Robert Wentworth Little, a serial creator of masonic offshoots, for existing higher-grade masons with an interest in studying the magical tradition.[9] But the Hermetic Order of the Golden Dawn (GD) represented something new.

Its social values were progressive by comparison with similar organizations: 'We paid some small annual subscription, a few shillings for rent and stationery, but no poor man paid even that,' recalled W. B. Yeats.[10] An older generation of masons and clergymen ensured an element of Victorian traditionalism, but many of its young recruits were activists, involved in political movements outside the GD. Most significantly, women were permitted to join. Madame Blavatsky's Theosophical Society, founded in 1875, promoted a universal brotherhood 'without distinction of race, colour, sex, caste, or creed', as did other new religious groups, but it was common for masonic lodges to restrict membership to men, and 'loyalist, Protestant, respectable white men' at that.[11] The GD was responsible for creating a modern tradition of magic, connecting a 'rediscovered' ancient tradition to ideals of future promise and rebirth. It would go on to be a primary influence in twentieth-century magical practice.

But what did it mean to study the 'occult' in the late nineteenth century? What exactly was 'magic', and what could a person expect to achieve by joining societies like the GD and the Hermetic Brotherhood of Luxor? The occult (from the Latin *occulere*, to hide or to conceal) cannot be explained as a single belief or theological system, but has developed over time out of what Denis Saurat called the 'strange and monstrous alliances' of the 'conquered religions' – Neoplatonism, Hermeticism, Gnosticism, Zoroastrianism and the classical mystery cults.[12] Occultists have often claimed a historical continuity for these strands of eclectic knowledge or 'tradition', but in truth they have been subjected to reinvention and re-creation over and over again. The occultist is rarely theistic, but instead believes in a noumenal or 'astral' world, invisible to our physical senses, which can be accessed and communicated with. In this sense, the occult can be thought of as metaphysical speculation about the true nature of reality. The eighteenth- and nineteenth-century occult did not reject science, but typically used scientific language to attempt to prove what religion could not. As such, various belief systems and pseudosciences emerged – spiritualism, mesmerism, theosophy – claiming to bridge the divide between religion and science. With the rise of the initiatory society in the nineteenth century, however, came the promise of spiritual enlightenment through ritual and the revelation of secrets. Many candidates who joined these groups did so in the eventual hope of being reborn, like the mythical Rosenkreutz, into a new reality or 'Golden Dawn'.

With its magical books, illuminated grimoires, dramatic rituals and revealed texts, a self-conscious scholarliness naturally surrounds the occult. Its understanding of itself as the product of an arcane tradition and its emphasis on transmitted knowledge, symbols and creative correspondences unsurprisingly attracted many who were themselves poets, novelists, actors, painters and illustrators. The occult in the late nineteenth century was not merely an undercurrent adopted by eccentrics, cranks and those seeking alternatives to conventional religion. Art and literature in the *fin de siècle* was awash with occult ideas and images, and evidence continues to pile up to suggest that some of the giants of literary Modernism – T. S. Eliot, Hilda Doolittle (H. D.), Joseph Conrad, D. H. Lawrence and, most centrally to this book, W. B. Yeats – were under its disreputable spell. Only recently has it become academically acceptable to uncover these influences. Since the 1970s, the GD and its system of magic has been the subject of several comprehensive histories, its rituals printed, its teachings anthologized and annotated. Biographies of many of its creative members have been written, but there has not yet been an overview of the literary, artistic and scholarly environment generated by the society. How did the occult influence their individual work? How did the GD accord with their professional lives, how did it bring about opportunities and did their creative pursuits have a bearing on the workings of the Order itself?

Fittingly, the GD began with a fiction. In the early 1880s (so the accepted version of the story went), the coroner and freemason Dr William Wynn Westcott discovered – or was given – a collection of coded manuscripts of about sixty sheets. They may have been passed to him by fellow mason the Rev. Adolphus F. A. Woodford, who may have found them in a second-hand bookshop on Farringdon Road, London. Accompanying the Cipher Manuscripts, as they were known, was the name and address of a woman named Fräulein Sprengel, a Rosicrucian Adept living in Germany. On writing to Sprengel, Westcott received the information needed to decode the cipher and, more significantly, instructions to found an English Temple of Sprengel's European order, which was known as in German as 'Die Goldene Dämmerung' (Golden Dawn; in French, 'L'Aube Dorée'), or in Hebrew 'Chabrath Zerek Aour bokhr' ('Society of the Shining Light').[13] Westcott obediently translated the manuscripts into English, which revealed a basic syllabus for the study

William Wynn Westcott in Societas Rosicruciana
in Anglia (SRIA) regalia, before 1897.

of magic. After further correspondence with Sprengel, he received permission to appoint two other masons to complete the triad of founding Chiefs, and one of these, Samuel Liddell MacGregor Mathers, was tasked with working the outlines up into a full set of initiation rituals and teachings. The Isis-Urania Temple was born.

Unsurprisingly, there are various discrepancies to this story. The occult historian and GD student A. E. Waite identified the cipher as being merely an 'occult alphabet, the source of which is to be found no further off than the British Museum'.[14] The manuscripts themselves, supposedly centuries old, bore a watermark from 1809, and the content referred to information that would not have been available to someone writing so long ago. The grade structure seemed to have been lifted from the pages of a masonic encyclopaedia published in 1877. As for the Sprengel letters, they were written by someone with only a basic grasp of German. 'Everything points to their being fabrications,' Ellic Howe concluded in his 1972 history of the GD, and it is now thought that Westcott either forged the letters himself or had someone else do it for him.[15] Fräulein Sprengel was an invention, created to give the GD an authentic magical inheritance. But who wrote the Cipher Manuscripts in the first place? Frederick Hockley and Kenneth R. H. Mackenzie, two aficionados of the Rosicrucian-masonic tradition, may have had a hand in their creation; Hockley, a mystic and clairvoyant famous for his experiments with crystal gazing, left some of his papers to Woodford on his death in 1885.

The source for the Farringdon Road bookshop tale was probably a novel titled *Zanoni*, written in 1842 by the English politician Edward Bulwer-Lytton, which featured what many readers at the time considered an authentic account of a young man's initiation into an ancient Rosicrucian brotherhood. In true gothic style, its fictional introduction details the narrator finding a coded manuscript while rummaging through a bookstall in Covent Garden, hoping to discover information on the Rosicrucians. He makes the acquaintance of another customer, a man of 'venerable appearance' who reveals that this secret fraternity is 'ardent in Christian faith' and is 'but a branch of other yet more transcendent in the powers they have obtained, and yet more illustrious in their origin'.[16] The chance acquaintance dies soon after, bequeathing the narrator a sheaf of papers written in a cipher, and after two years the story of Zanoni is decrypted and published. Rumours have since swirled around Bulwer-Lytton, who was Secretary of State for the Colonies in the late 1850s, claiming that the baroque *Zanoni* and his other, similar fiction such as 'The Haunted and the Haunters' (1859) and *A Strange Story* (1862) were evidence for personal involvement in Rosicrucian societies. He had been researching the occult since the early 1830s, and experimented privately with mesmerism and held seances from his palatial residence in Hampshire, Knebworth House; one story has him walking through a roomful of guests as though he thought himself invisible.[17] He appeared to delight in the public reputation of his books to the extent that he spread the idea that *Zanoni* had come to him in a dream.[18] Whether the true sorcerer he was made out be, or merely an aristocrat who kept up with occult research, Bulwer-Lytton is an intriguing link between the early nineteenth-century stirrings of the occult revival and the explosive world of GD ritual magic in which the artists, poets and novelists of this book played a starring role.

One of the central theoreticians and communicators of magic during this period was a man named Alphonse Louis Constant, better known by his Hebrew pseudonym Éliphas Lévi. The son of a Parisian shoemaker, Lévi trained as a priest but was expelled from the seminary for 'holding opinions contrary to the Roman Catholic Church'.[19] Following a brief stint in prison for writing a *chanson* critical of Napoleon III, he launched a new career in the mid-1850s with *Dogme et rituel de la haute magie*, a guide to the Western magical tradition directed at a popular readership, covering the Kabbalah, necromancy, astrology and divination. A. E. Waite was the first English translator of Lévi, and his appraisal in the introduction to *Dogme et rituel* gives a clear picture of how he was regarded within esoteric circles: 'No expositor of occult claims can bear any comparison with Éliphas Lévi, and among ancient expositors, though many stand higher in authority and are assuredly more sincere, all yield to him in living interest, for he is actually the spirit of modern thought forcing an answer for the times from the old oracles.'[20] Lévi was often imprecise in his scholarship and sceptical of his own teachings, but he was an authoritative, literary voice and his presentation of magic as a new and complete system of knowledge that was possible to master proved a winning formula. He continued to write books – titles such as *The History of Magic* and *The Book of Splendours* – well into the 1870s. Significantly, Lévi visited England twice during the 1850s, and on both occasions met Bulwer-Lytton, later staying at Knebworth.[21] How this friendship came about is unclear, but it was possibly through Bulwer-Lytton that Lévi was introduced to the 'persons of eminence' who demanded he 'work wonders' and provide them with revelations from the astral world. Although initially reluctant, and doubtful that the result could not be explained by a 'drunkenness of the imagination', he eventually managed to invoke the spirit of the Greek philosopher and magician Apollonius of Tyana.[22]

In 1861 Kenneth R. H. Mackenzie, a twenty-eight-year-old freemason and student of the occult, travelled to Paris, where he visited Lévi in his lodgings on Avenue du Maine.[23] Recalling the encounter in an article for the magazine *The Rosicrucian*, Mackenzie remembered the French mage as congenial and chatty, willing to show his manuscripts and answer the starstruck pupil's questions. 'He spoke to me about his visit to England, stating his inability to speak English, a language he had in vain endeavoured to acquire – he rendered a tribute to the versatile knowledge of Lord, then Sir Edward Bulwer, Lytton, with emphasis.' This was a meeting of two different esoteric traditions. Freemasonry was, and remains, an international organization founded on liberal values and ideas of spiritual and moral enlightenment. Members participated in elaborate rituals that used the imagery of medieval craftsmanship, the masons symbolically taking on the identities of skilled artisans. Secrecy had been a structural principle of masonry since its formal beginnings in the early eighteenth century, the idea being that members had access to a body of 'privileged knowledge' that separated them from the rest of society and bound them together in brotherhood.

Freemasonry expanded alongside empire: merchants, politicians, soldiers and royalty all joined as a way to advance their social standing. While masonic lodges were rarely 'magical' or occult in their aims, the symbolism of Renaissance magic was nevertheless an important element of their activities, particularly in Britain, where Rosicrucian symbols (the rosy cross, a pelican feeding its young with its blood) had been included in rituals from early on. A group of Jacobite masons were reportedly working a 'Rosicrucian rite' by the 1740s, and in late eighteenth-century Germany a 'neo-Rosicrucian' order known as the Gold- und Rosenkreuz ('Gold and Rosy Cross'), interested in practical alchemy, was in operation. Both are examples of the esoteric current in freemasonry, as opposed to the traditional 'enlightened' mainstream.[24] It is easy to see the appeal of the Rosicrucian myth for masons, a fraternity 'bound by solemn obligations of mutual succour' who used their spiritual knowledge for acts of healing and humility.[25]

When Mackenzie knocked on Lévi's door in 1861, there were no masonic Rosicrucian societies active in Europe. Although A. E. Waite later accused him of 'recurring mendacity' on Rosicrucian subjects, Mackenzie would assure fellow masons that he had been initiated into one while studying in Vienna as a young man.[26] By 1870, however, he had become an early member of another masonic offshoot. The SRIA was ritual-based and ordered along the same hierarchical grade structure as traditional masonry. Sometime after 1862, its founder, Robert Wentworth Little, had unearthed in the library of Freemasons' Hall a manuscript translation of part of the *Geheime Figuren der Rosenkreuzer* (1785–88), originally three pamphlets of Christian theosophy containing a colourful trove of occult symbols and Kabbalistic maps. These had been compiled and edited by members of the Gold- und Rosenkreuz based on material from the sixteenth and seventeenth centuries, and so constituted a link, however slight, to that period of Rosicrucian activity. An excited Little seems to have used them as a basis for workable rituals in the SRIA.[27] The society's aim was to provide a forum for the discussion of the writings and activities of the Rosicrucians, but this was undermined by the fact that most of its original members were uninterested in the occult and had only joined because they knew Little. Further proof that the SRIA was dealing in fictions came in 1870, when Little declared Bulwer-Lytton an honorary member and 'Grand Patron', news of which apparently irritated him. The unaccepted patronage was advertised in *The Rosicrucian* until the author's death in 1873, at which point his name was removed from the masthead.

But the influence of Bulwer-Lytton's novels on the occult revival was not confined to the halls of esoteric masonry. A leading character in the repackaging of magical ideas in the nineteenth century was a Russian-born American émigrée named Helena Petrovna Blavatsky, a self-styled spiritualist authority who had travelled the world gathering wisdom from various religious traditions and co-founded the first Theosophical Society in New York in 1875. Blavatsky was one of many independent spiritual leaders to emerge in the Anglo-American world, but none has exerted more influence or attracted such a range of followers. Her father had been a baron of the Russian and German nobility, her mother the celebrated writer of romantic novels Elena Gan (translator of part of Bulwer-Lytton's *Godolphin* for a Russian literary magazine in 1835). As a child she read widely and used to 'dream aloud', taking her siblings into the family's museum, where she would narrate 'the most inconceivable tales about herself; the most unheard of adventures of which she was the heroine'.[28] This talent served her well in later years. Her ever-changing autobiography included high-profile lovers, participation in wars and a tour of Serbia as a concert pianist, all told with such persuasion that it is impossible to sort truth from fable. She claimed to have received many of her teachings from a pair of Tibetan Masters or 'Mahatmas', whom she apparently visited and studied with on an expedition in 1854 and again in 1867 (Tibet was at this time inaccessible to most travellers, so there is good reason to doubt her story).[29] The Mahatmas, named Morya and Koot Hoomi, were members of the 'Great White Brotherhood', a group of spiritually evolved Adepts who communicated with Blavatsky through visions and a series of letters.[30]

Her reputation was severely damaged when the Society for Psychical Research exposed her spiritualist activities – the letters, 'astral bells', and other supernatural phenomena – as a fraud while she was living in Adyar, India. The society's investigator Richard Hodgson denounced Blavatsky as 'neither the mouthpiece of hidden seers, nor as a mere vulgar adventuress', but simply an imposter.[31] The report led to infighting within the Theosophical Society, and her reputation as a clairvoyant never fully recovered.

From the earliest days of her theosophical career Blavatsky was indebted to the fiction of Bulwer-Lytton, whose novels she must have been introduced to by her mother. She absorbed the central ideas of occult adeptship and instruction directly from his books; the elaborate fictional worlds of *Zanoni* and *A Strange Story* taught her that hidden wisdom, even immortality, could be attained by studying Eastern mysticism and what she called the 'ancient sciences'.[32] *Zanoni* may also have been the source for the Mahatmas. Using a literary imagination, she plundered from the vast traditions of Rosicrucianism, masonry and world religions to produce a clever synthesis of spiritual systems that became her first book *Isis Unveiled*, published in two volumes in 1877. Her interest in ancient Egyptian civilization seems to have originated with Bulwer-Lytton's historical novel *The Last Days of Pompeii* (1834), and especially its blueprint of magic in Egypt as being either good or evil, 'theurgic' or 'goetic'. This became a theoretical basis for *Isis*, in which Blavatsky laid out her grand thesis: that every religion contains elements of a secret doctrine which has become obscured, but which may be uncovered through applied study and investigation.

Having passed through this backdrop of continental magic, esoteric freemasonry and theosophy, we now arrive at the very foundations of the Hermetic Order of the Golden Dawn, a society whose originators could not have escaped the influence of Bulwer-Lytton's novels if they had tried. Mackenzie, Westcott and others were at pains to establish a genuine connection between their Rosicrucian societies and ancient Rosicrucianism as they believed it to have existed, and in 1881 Mackenzie was urging Westcott to read 'H. Jennings again and *Zanoni*' to get a sense of how their degrees were constructed: 'Even Lytton who knew so much was only a Neophyte and could not reply when I tested him years ago. How could Little maintain he had them? I know how many real Rosicrucians there are in these islands.'[33] Hargrave Jennings had written a book in 1870 called *The Rosicrucians: Their Rites and Mysteries* (debunked by A. E. Waite in 1887 in *The Real History of the Rosicrucians*). Westcott went so far as to claim that Bulwer-Lytton had been initiated into a 'very old Rosicrucian Lodge' in Frankfurt, where he became 'imbued with the ideas he displayed in his novel *Zanoni*'. There is even a theory that Lord Lytton composed the Cipher Manuscripts himself before handing them over to Mackenzie by way of Frederick Hockley.[34]

The GD claimed Éliphas Lévi as a past member almost as soon as it began announcing itself to the world. Part of the history of the Cipher Manuscripts, according to a memo recording a conversation between Westcott and Woodford in 1886, was that the papers 'passed through Lévi's hands and indeed a loose page among them has a note signed A.L.C.'. The first Sprengel letter repeats this same fact, revealing that the Abbé Constant had lost them 'years ago'.[35] In February 1888 Mathers wrote to the editor of *Light*, the journal of the London Spiritualist Alliance, in response to an article that dismissed Lévi's abilities as a magician, declaring that Lévi had actually been 'an Initiate of the Kabbalah, a member of the Fraternity of the Rosy Cross, and of other kindred orders' (unconvinced, a note from the editor asked 'What is the proof?').[36] This was followed in a February 1889 issue of *Notes and Queries* by a response to a question asked two months earlier regarding the existence of a certain occult society: 'The order of mystics which have Eliphaz Lévi (Abbé Constant), his occult knowledge, and of which Johann Falk was at one time the Lecturer on the Kabbalah in London, is still at work in England ... and the few outsiders who have heard of its existence only know the society as "The Hermetic Students of the G. D.".'[37] Both the question and its answer seem to have been submitted by Westcott.

'Some ten or twelve years ago, a man with whom I have since quarrelled for sound reasons, a very singular man who had given his life to studies other men despised, asked me and an acquaintance, who is now dead, to witness a magical work,' W. B. Yeats recalled in his essay 'Magic'. 'He lived a little way from London, and on the way my acquaintance told me that he did not believe in magic, but that a novel of Bulwer Lytton's had taken such a hold upon his imagination that he was going to give much of his time and all of his thought to magic ... He expected nothing more than an air of romance, an illusion as of the stage, that might capture the consenting imagination for an hour.'[38] This was Mathers as Yeats remembered him sometime in the 1890s. Mathers was a fantasist who assumed various identities throughout his life, not least Imperator of the Isis-Urania Temple. Biographical detail is scant, and it is apt that two of the main sources that give an impression of his character are fictional: Yeats's unpublished novel *The Speckled Bird* and Aleister Crowley's libellous *Moonchild* (1929).

Born Samuel Liddell Mathers in Hackney in 1854, he attended Bedford School before moving to the coastal town of Bournemouth to live with his widowed mother. Freemasonry beckoned at an early age, and in 1877 he was initiated into a local order called the Lodge of Hengist, whose Brethren, while not strictly esoteric in their aims, had in recent years heard lectures on the history and 'occult symbolism' of the lodge's degrees.[39] A year later he had already ascended to Master Mason status, signing himself 'Comte de Glenstrae' on the certificate, evidence that even then he was fashioning for himself an aristocratic Celtic identity. There is no factual basis for Mathers's claim that the Scotsman Ian MacGregor of Glenstrae, an ardent Jacobite, had fought against the British in France in the 1750s and was made 'Comte' by Louis XV, or that Mathers had any relation to him, but he stuck to the story for the rest of his life.[40] Mathers also boxed and fenced, cultivating an athletic physique and an interest in military subjects.

It was during his years in Bournemouth that Mathers met Frederick Holland, whom he proposed as a member for the Hengist

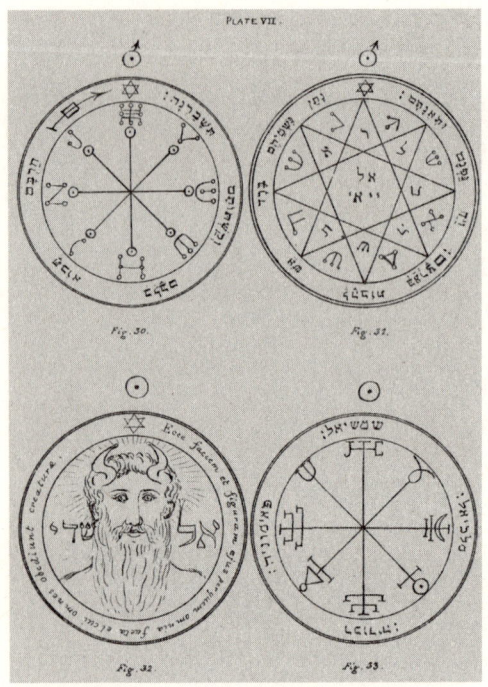

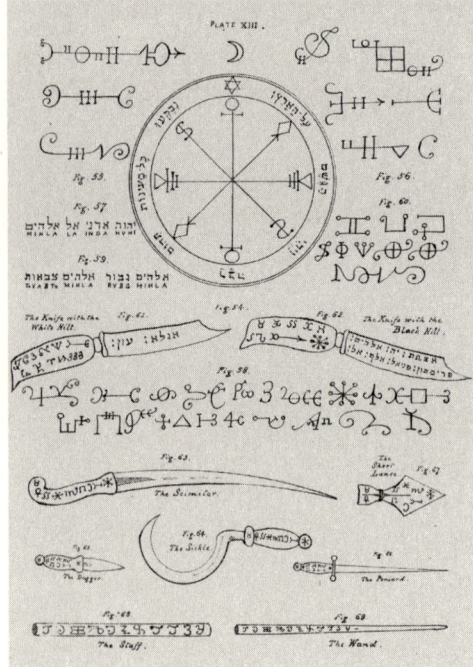

Plates from *The Key of Solomon* (*Clavicula Salomonis*), translated and edited by Samuel Liddell MacGregor Mathers, 1889.

Lodge. Holland in turn introduced Mathers to the Kabbalah, and the pair joined the SRIA – the obvious next step for two masons with occult leanings – in 1882. In 1885, when his mother died, Mathers moved permanently to London. He was in his element. The occult revival was blossoming, and Mathers threw himself at every opportunity, attending Rosicrucian meetings, theosophical lectures and the Hermetic Society, run by Anna Kingsford and Edward Maitland, both of whom he befriended and through whom he met Blavatsky. Mathers also discovered an enthusiasm for scholarship and translation. His first published translation, *The Fall of Granada: A Poem in Six Duans*, appended by three shorter poems, received no attention, but William Westcott, who had by then become a sort of mentor for Mathers in the SRIA, nonetheless encouraged him to produce an English-language edition of Christian Knorr von Rosenroth's *Kabbala Denudata* (1677–84).[41] First published in Latin, Von Rosenroth's book was itself a compilation and translation of important Kabbalistic sources from Hebrew, with accompanying essays by the philosopher Henry More and the Flemish mystic Franciscus Mercurius van Helmont. *The Kabbalah Unveiled*, Mathers's partial translation of the first volume, was issued by the antiquarian publisher George Redway in 1887. Mathers's scholarship was never particularly notable, but his verve and enthusiasm gave him status in the occult world. Yeats's later summation of the magus as having 'much learning but little scholarship, much imagination and imperfect taste' is borne out by reviews for *The Kabbalah Unveiled*: 'Mr Mathers's introduction is a wild performance from which we have been able to glean little knowledge of any kind,' advised the reviewer in *Notes & Queries*.[42] The *Saturday Review* was politely bemused, suggesting that maybe Anna Kingsford should have reviewed it instead. *The Kabbalah Unveiled* was followed in 1888 by an introductory volume on tarot; the short book, while showing off Mathers's readings of Lévi and other French scholars of cartomancy, was probably dashed off for him to remain afloat financially while he assembled his next big project. The earliest versions of *The Key of Solomon*, the *Key* or *Clavicula Salomonis*, had been written in Greek in the fifteenth century, but Mathers considered his English edition to be a 'pure' text, combining all the various Latin, French, Hebrew and English manuscripts he could find on the shelves of the British Museum. He sincerely believed that 'King Solomon' was its original author, and considered it a work of authentic Kabbalistic wisdom.[43] It was the first of the three grimoires that he would produce.

By this point Mathers was playing a series of roles with sincerity and imagination: military man, occult scholar, poet, Celt. His performance as a Scottish count was given additional Celtic glamour by his admiration for the mid-eighteenth-century Ossian epic of James MacPherson. Scholarly doubt had long been cast on MacPherson's claim that *The Poems of Ossian* were based on genuine Scottish Gaelic oral tradition; however skilfully, he had invented the whole thing.[44] But this did not matter to Mathers. He prefaced *The Fall of Granada* with a quotation from *Ossian* that urges the 'dim ghosts of my fathers' to 'behold my deeds of war'.[45] Yeats remembered that while living in Paris in the 1890s Mathers would alternate between reading Horus and MacPherson at the breakfast table: 'Once when I questioned that of Ossian, he got into a rage – what right had I to take sides with the English enemy – and I found that for him the eighteenth century controversy still raged.'[46] Perhaps unsurprisingly at this point, Mathers had also become obsessed by Bulwer-Lytton's *Zanoni*, and was apparently known as 'Zan' by his wife Moina after their marriage in 1890.[47]

Such early creative posturing was to prove useful when Westcott, by 1887 one of the ruling triad of the SRIA alongside William Robert Woodman and Mathers himself, approached Mathers with his Cipher Manuscripts: 'We have no doubt a rich treasure in poor old Woodford's MSS,' Westcott wrote in October. 'I hope you will accept co-equality with me, and write it up with all your erudition if I will do a simple translation of the cipher. We must then choose a 3rd and endeavour to spread a complete scheme of initiation.'[48] Westcott commissioned and paid Mathers to construct a set of ceremonial rituals for the first five grades of his magic school, based on the outlines in the documents. Later in life, Mathers would disavow this prosaic transaction as the reason behind his writing the GD rituals. At the beginning of March 1888, the warrant or 'charter' for the founding of Isis-Urania

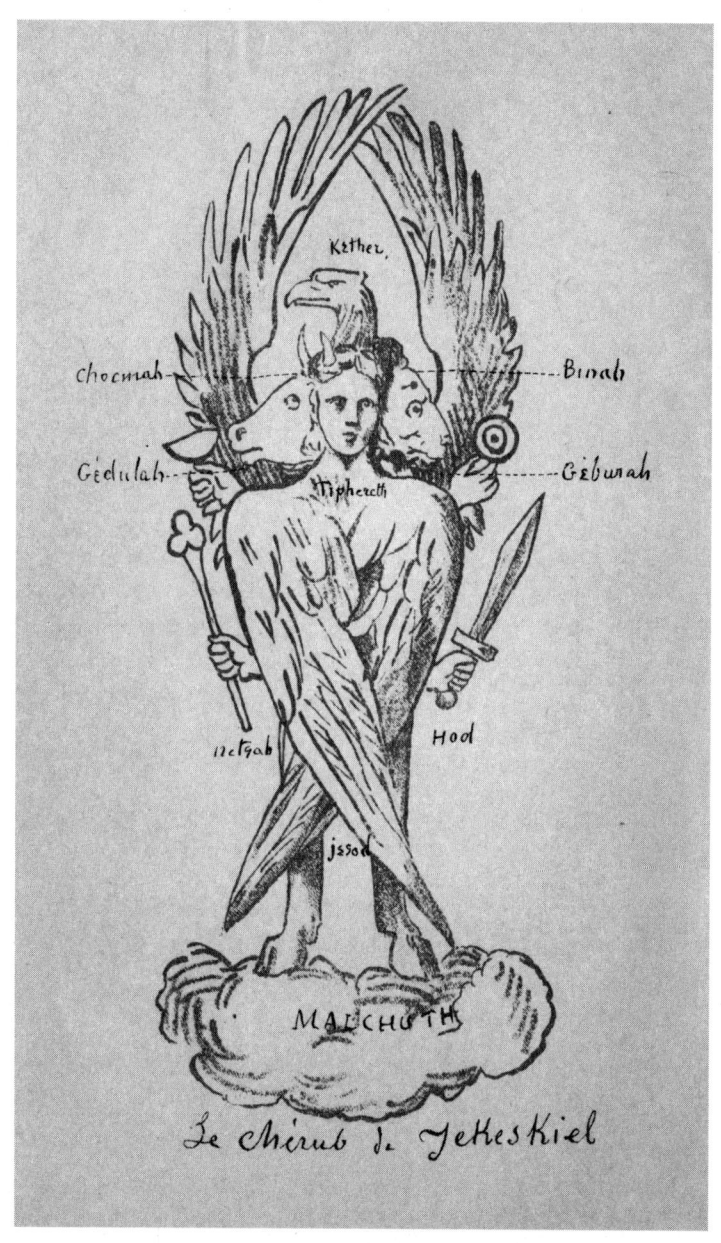

Plate from Éliphas Lévi, *The Magical Ritual of the Sanctum Regnum*, translated and edited by William Wynn Westcott, 1896.

had been signed; Westcott had again 'paid M for writing it', meaning that Mathers had drawn up the actual document, consisting of a dozen lines of text in scratchy, gothic lettering surrounded by line drawings of three animals and a woman's head. Moina may have been the artist, although the images were merely copied from a page in Lévi's *Dogme et rituel*.[49] The results were impressive: the curriculum and rituals devised by Mathers synthesized a large corpus of magical material into a coherent structure. The original five-grade structure of the GD's 'First Order' was based on that of the SRIA, which had previously been adapted by Little from the Gold- und Rosenkreuz's eighteenth-century system:

0° = 0°	Neophyte
1° = 10°	Zelator
2° = 9°	Theoricus
3° = 8°	Practicus
4° = 7°	Philosophus

Each grade represented a *sefira* or 'emanation' on the Kabbalistic tree, a diagram that symbolized the universe in classical Jewish esoteric tradition. The tree mapped a 'chain of being' expanding outwards from the godhead: at the bottom was the material world, represented mathematically by the number ten (*malkuth*, or 'the kingdom'), while the *sefira* closest to God was one (*kether*, or 'the crown'), indivisible and unchangeable. Westcott and Mathers included corresponding numbers for each degree (1° = 10°, 2° = 9°, instead of the masonic 1°, 2°, 3°, 4°), with the second number representing the candidate's distance from the godhead. As they passed their examinations and took the higher-grade rituals, candidates symbolically approached the top of the tree: a spiritual as well as academic ascension. The ten *sefirot* were also associated with individual planets, classical elements, angels and personal attributes; the twenty-two paths between the *sefirot* corresponded with the letters of the Hebrew alphabet, and in later traditions became linked to the twenty-two named tarot cards known as the Major Arcana. Each grade was therefore bursting with magical associations and imagery to be used in rituals and teaching. Westcott and Mathers also chose to include a probationary 'Neophyte' grade, which did not occupy a branch on the Kabbalistic tree and had not been present in the SRIA structure. The first five grades were expanded in 1891, when the idea of the 'Inner' or 'Second Order' was conceived; this marked the point at which students began to learn practical magic, rather than the merely theoretical study of the First Order. It became necessary to install a 'Portal' grade to act as a bridge between the two Orders, which involved the candidate waiting for a gestational period of nine months before beginning their ascent of the next three *sefirot*:

$5° = 6°$	Adeptus Minor
$6° = 5°$	Adeptus Major
$7° = 4°$	Adeptus Exemptus

The final three degrees in what would become the 'Third Order' that completed the Kabbalistic structure were essentially unattainable, for they were occupied by the supernatural Secret Chiefs, akin to Blavatsky's Mahatmas, who lived on the astral plane:

$8° = 3°$	Magister Templi
$9° = 2°$	Magus
$10° = 1°$	Ipsissimus

'Ipsissimus' was another addition. Westcott assigned himself, Mathers and Woodman to the Adeptus Exemptus ($7° = 4°$) grade, gaining written permission from the fictional Sprengel to allow the trio to initiate Candidates into the lowest five grades. They would assume different mottos and rule the GD as *de facto* Secret Chiefs: Mathers, for example, was ''S Rioghal Mo Dhream' ('Royal is my tribe') in the First Order, but 'Deo Duce Comite Ferro' ('With God as leader, the sword as companion') in his Second Order role. The three men appear in both of their guises on the warrant for Isis-Urania. Having fashioned a structure and a series of thrilling initiation rituals for a new magical order, Mathers was realizing his ambitions to become a Zanoni figure: the 'born commander' that Yeats had first considered him.

Two other temples sprang quickly into existence: Osiris, in the unlikely location of Weston-super-Mare on the Somerset coast, and Horus, in Bradford. According to the Isis-Urania membership roll, nine members were listed by the end of the GD's first month (including the three Chiefs and Fräulein Sprengel, still supposedly in Germany); at the end of 1888, this had risen to fifty-one across the three temples, a number not surpassed even when a further two temples were opened in the mid-1890s. Intrigued masons from the SRIA swelled the ranks, alongside women from the Theosophical Society (much to Blavatsky's annoyance). Early initiates included Alexandrina Aydon Mackenzie, the widow of Kenneth R. H. Mackenzie, William Crookes, the noted scientist and Fellow of the Royal Society, who was a Neophyte for only a few months, and the Irish writer Constance Wilde, wife of Oscar Wilde. Accompanying Constance in the Neophyte ceremony was her friend Anna Elizabeth, Countess de Brémont, an American poet and singer who was later expelled mysteriously from the Order without reason. 'I passed the ordeal quite composedly, but not so my companion,' Brémont remembered of the initiation. 'My sense of humour was secretly tried on that occasion, and I felt more inclined to laugh, although Constance Wilde's beautiful eyes were full of tears.' She was pleased to note that her grade examinations helped to develop her concentration, which in turn 'assisted me greatly in my literary career.'[50]

Moina, then Mina Bergson, a talented artist and the younger sister of French philosopher Henri Bergson, entered Isis-Urania in 1888, choosing the motto 'Vestigia Nulla Retrorsum ('No traces behind'). She had already encountered Mathers at the British Museum Reading Room the year before, and had introduced him to Annie Horniman as 'an interesting man whom she did *not* want to marry', but the two were soon engaged.[51] Beyond her artistic contributions to the GD, she acted as a kind of amanuensis and clairvoyant aide to Mathers, and guarded his literary and magical reputation after his death. Another important student to take the Neophyte ritual in 1888 was the Reverend William Alexander Ayton, who joined with Anne Ayton, his wife. Ayton was the Vicar of Chacombe, a village outside of Banbury, and having already been a mason for over twenty years, possessed remarkable knowledge of alchemy. He was instrumental in Mathers's marriage to Mina, not only officiating the ceremony but allowing the bride to stay at his vicarage (in the basement of which lay his alchemist's laboratory) for the 'time required by Law' for the publication of banns.[52] After the marriage, Mina assumed the Celtic variant 'Moina,' completing the transformation of her identity as she became legally bound to Mathers. The couple's new lodgings at Forest Hill were to be the unofficial meeting house for GD activities.

Many of the prominent occult teachers and scholars active during these few decades were also engaged in literary production: Mathers was a translator; Edward Maitland of the Hermetic Society had been a writer of popular romances in the 1860s and 1870s; Blavatsky worked on a collection of gothic tales up until her death; A. E. Waite wrote mystical verse and fairy tales. In the SRIA, Robert Wentworth Little was a poet, lyricist and founder of a masonic literary union; Kenneth R. H. Mackenzie had been a respected translator and biographer. The Scottish lawyer John Brodie-Innes, who would go on to found the GD's Amen-Ra Temple in Edinburgh in 1893, was the author of the serialized ghost story 'The Old House in the Canongate', an indication of the kind of supernatural-themed novels he would later write set in historical Scotland. The bookishness and scholarly creativity that the occult attracted was there for all to see; and yet the influx of writers and artists into the world of initiatory groups was only just beginning. With the arrival of Yeats and Florence Farr in 1890 and A. E. Waite in 1891, the GD was about to become the strangest society of the arts of its time.

1

'Metaphors for Poetry'

W. B. Yeats

I give permission to admit William Butler Yeats, who now loses his name and will henceforth be known among us as D.E.D.I., 'Demon Est Deus Inversus'.

W. B. Yeats was initiated into the Order of the Golden Dawn on a Friday evening, 7 March 1890. At the Isis-Urania Temple at 17 Fitzroy Street, the lodgings of Mina Bergson, the blindfolded twenty-five-year-old poet wore a black gown and red shoes. Three cords, signifying the bonds of the material world and the three sides of the white triangle, the Order's central symbol, were tied around his waist. He approached the altar to recite his oath: 'I solemnly promise to keep secret this Order ... to persevere with courage and determination in the labours of the Divine Science.' Yeats also acknowledged that if he broke this Magical Obligation that he would submit himself 'to a Stream of Power, set in motion by the Divine Guardians of this Order, Who live in the Light of their Perfect Justice, and before Whom my Soul now stands'.[1] A sword was placed on the back of Yeats's neck, and he was led to the Place of Forgetfulness, Dumbness and Necessity, where the Hierophant (the priest or officiator), in scarlet robes and crowned sceptre, welcomed him symbolically into the Light of Wisdom. His blindfold was removed. Signs were performed, benedictions delivered and his cords were untied and replaced with a sash. Following a symbolic meal of bread, wine and salt, the Kerux (herald or messenger) proclaimed 'It is finished!' Yeats had entered the 0° = 0° Grade: he was now a Neophyte of the Hermetic Order of the Golden Dawn.

Yeats's thread is perhaps the longest in the original Order's tapestry: Samuel Liddell MacGregor Mathers was forced out in 1900, after which he founded a group in Paris; Aleister Crowley lasted just over a year; but Yeats's involvement spanned almost three uninterrupted decades. He was already a member of several occult groups by the time he entered the Order, but it was the GD – and Mathers, who took over the role of Imperator of Isis-Urania after William Robert Woodman's death in 1891 – that prevailed as one of the enduring influences of the poet's life, and brought his previously unstructured magical activities to heel. Later contemporary poets such as W. H. Auden, while an admirer of Yeats's strength and clarity of language, dismissed out of hand his devotion to the 'mumbo-jumbo of magic and the nonsense of India'.[2] But ever since his occult papers were made more widely available to researchers in the late 1960s it has become plain that magic – and particularly the ritual magic learned at meetings of the GD and its later emanations, the Morgenröthe and the Stella Matutina – demands a place alongside his better known preoccupations. 'If I had not made magic my constant study,' he declared to the Irish separatist and old Fenian John O'Leary in his famous defence of the occult in 1892, 'I could not have written a single word of my Blake book, nor would *The Countess Kathleen* ever have come to exist. The mystical life is the centre of all that I do and all that I think and all that I write.'[3] Four years before his death in 1939, Yeats was writing disapprovingly of the occultist Israel Regardie's intent to publish core GD rituals, arguing that it would 'distress people to whom they are sacred, or endeared by early associations'.[4] He remained faithful to the secretive Order that had, in his words, 'shaped' and 'isolated' him.[5]

Born in the Dublin suburb of Sandymount in 1865 to an impoverished painter and the daughter of a merchant family, Yeats was a lanky and sensitive child prone to flights of imagination and a determined vagueness. As he matured, he became aware that his by then marginalized Protestant roots no longer afforded him the influence and wealth they once might have. The bustling, avant-garde world of secret societies brought about by the occult revival in Britain offered him an escape from what R. F. Foster terms his 'sense of displacement, a loss of social and psychological integration'; combined with his naturally superstitious personality, he was inevitably drawn to the esoteric.[6]

While at the Metropolitan School of Art in Dublin, he and his friends fell under the enchantment of the newest spiritual trend of the day: theosophy. Incited by a sense of youthful revolt and the discovery of A. P. Sinnett's *Esoteric Buddhism*, given to him by an aunt, by 1885 Yeats had formed the Dublin Hermetic Society, which was remoulded the following year into the Dublin Theosophical Society. The young men gave papers on the Vedas and the Upanishads and 'discussed great problems ardently and simply and unconventionally as men, perhaps, discussed great problems in the medieval universities'.[7] It was there that Yeats met Mohini Chatterjee, an Indian spiritual guru sent by Madame Blavatsky to sound out the new Irish recruits. He was especially attracted by the epistemological concept of *samskara*, a Sanskrit word referring to mental traits and behaviours ultimately linked to *karma*, and he also began attending animated, often frightening seances, including one in which he felt himself possessed by a violent impulse and was 'thrown backward on the wall'.[8]

In 1887, the Yeats family moved from Dublin to Bedford Park, a village-like suburb of west London described by G. K. Chesterton as 'a colony for artists who were almost aliens; a refuge for persecuted poets and painters hiding in their red-brick catacombs'.[9] Attracted by its clubhouse and School of Art, eminent residents included the Irish writer John Todhunter, the Oxford historian Frederick York Powell and the artist Henry M. Paget. The move offered connections and opportunities that Yeats had missed in Dublin. He was soon a recognizable personality on the London scene, moving seamlessly between supper with William Morris and the Socialist League in nearby Hammersmith, to coffee with the Welshman Ernest Rhys, with whom he would later found the Rhymers' Club. The British Museum Reading Room became his second home, from which he churned out reviews and political journalism for any paper that would accept them. Already he was turning his back on the classicism of the Pre-Raphaelites, instead finding in his Irish heritage a world of beauty and 'unpremeditated joyous energy' that he could funnel into his poetry and articles.[10] *Fairy and Folk Tales of the Irish Peasantry* appeared in 1888, a collection of retellings and remembrances from his family's home at Sligo that gave Yeats a reputation as a folklorist while also allowing him to lay claim to his own idea of Ireland. William Blake was another early love. With his rather dour neighbour, the poet Edwin Ellis, Yeats began to plot out a three-volume exegesis of Blake's prophetic works – albeit under the mistaken assumption that Blake was Irish. The pair even rediscovered the manuscript of 'Vala, or the Four Zoas', a late visionary poem that had been forgotten in an uncatalogued library. Characterized by friends and family as ethereal, absent-minded and desperate for literary recognition, Yeats was darting about town, shaping new identities and passions and, crucially, joining societies.

Complementing his interests in Blake, Ireland and Irish folktales, Yeats's passion for theosophy continued unabated; almost as soon as he arrived in London, he had called on Madame Blavatsky in her Upper Norwood rooms and found her surrounded by devotees, like an 'old Irish peasant woman with an air of humour and audacious power … a sort of female Dr. Johnson'.[11] Blavatsky, her influence waning following accusations of fraud by the Society for Psychical Research two years earlier, welcomed the poet, although her goodwill was not to last long. Yeats ultimately wanted to explore magic beyond the 'abstraction' of theosophy's teachings, and refused to submit to Blavatsky's cultish authority.[12] He seems to have petitioned her to form an offshoot of the Theosophical Society devoted to actual experiments in the occult, a suggestion previously made by the activist and fellow Society member Annie Besant. After some protest, Blavatsky gave in (probably due to her uneasiness that the newly established GD might poach her theosophists) and the Esoteric Section was brought formally into existence. 'About Xmas 1888' is the date recorded for Yeats joining the Section, which involved filling out separate application, obligation and 'pledge' forms. Yeats took issue with two clauses, one requiring members to 'work for theosophy', the other a more straightforward promise of obedience:

> I pledge myself to support before the world the Theosophical movement, and in particular to answer and obey, without cavil or delay, all orders given to me through the outer Heads of this School, in all that concerns my Theosophical duties and Esoteric work, so far as I can do so without violating my positive obligations under the moral law and the laws of the land.[13]

The 'outer Heads' referred to the human leaders like Blavatsky, while 'inner' heads were the mysterious teachers or 'Mahatmas' with whom she claimed to communicate. Yeats, along with others such as the leading theosophist Anna Kingsford, expressed doubts at signing this second clause in particular, arguing privately that while the teachers might in fact be 'living occultists', they might also be spirits or manifestations of Blavatsky's 'trance nature' to which he did not feel like submitting himself.[14] Though he relented after Blavatsky added a sub-clause asking for compliance 'subject to the decision of [the member's] own conscience', he resolved to keep a diary 'of all signings I go through and such like, for my future use, and always to state my reasons for each most carefully'.[15]

Yeats's observations on the group's membership underline an idea that became important to his political thinking later in this period: the belief that occult societies might in fact have the ability to influence society at large.

> They seem some intellectual, one or two cultural, the rest the usual amorphous material that gathers round all new things – All amorphous and clever alike have much zeal – and here and there a few sparkles of fanaticism are visible. This section will not in any way (I believe) influence educated thought – for this as yet unattempted propaganda the society has so far neither men nor method.[16]

The Section commenced meetings. Proposals for experiments were sent to Blavatsky for approval, but a resistance to magic continued among the ranks. Few experiments were ever carried out and not one

Lucifer: A Theosophical Monthly, edited by H. P. Blavatsky and Mabel Collins, September 1887.

produced results. In what might have been a last-ditch attempt, Yeats and some fellow members tried unsuccessfully to summon the ghost of a burnt flower. Unfazed, Yeats distributed a 'pure kind of indigo' to his colleagues, presumably in powdered form, and asked them to record their dreams after placing the indigo under their pillows. The instruction did not go down well with those present, and Yeats was taken aside and told that his experiment was 'not in agreement with their methods or their philosophy'.[17] Sometime after August 1890, Blavatsky's secretary demanded Yeats's resignation, and he gave it.

Before leaving the Theosophical Society, Yeats had been encouraged to find validation for his study of Irish folk customs in Blavatsky's teachings; in her view, the peasantry was more directly in contact with the 'Great Memory' of the world. Theosophy had also given Yeats a space to explore a curiosity that had only grown since the release of *Fairy and Folk Tales*. In an article for Blavatsky's journal *Lucifer* in January 1889, he announced that the examination and categorization of fairies was an important endeavour 'for the occultist ... as well as the folk-loreist', and expounded upon 'fairy doctors', 'social fairies' and 'solitary fairies'.[18] True to his word, a year later he recounted in the *Irish Theosophist* how he and Florence Farr, looking for something to occupy themselves while the kettle boiled, had performed a 'lunar invocation'. A queenly 'white woman' appeared to them and summoned 'a great multitude of little creatures ... with green hair like sea-weed and after them another multitude dragging a car containing an enormous bubble'.[19] Two more groups turned up to complete this elemental set, which the woman called the 'good fairies', followed by 'things like pigs only with shorter legs ... [and] flocks of cherubs and bats' accompanied by a snake named 'Grew-grew'. From this point on the Irish fairies, the *sidhe* of Celtic folklore, were recast by Yeats using a theosophical framework. In his poetry and later rituals they would become the diminished forms of the old Irish gods, representative of poetic 'moods' to serve his spiritual nationalism.

Alongside his occult exploration, Yeats was busy establishing himself as an important voice in the London literary scene. His Blake books would not be the 'red flag above the waters of oblivion' that he had first envisioned, but *The Wanderings of Oisin and Other Poems*, published to acclaim in 1889, did much for his reputation. Irishness, and Celtic literature in general, was in vogue. Framed as a conversation between Saint Patrick and Oisin, a poet and warrior-hunter in the Fenian cycle of Irish legend, the title poem allowed Yeats to foreground Irish tradition while disguising nationalist messages under a veneer of symbolism. 'The romance is for my readers,' he admitted in a letter to the writer Katherine Tynan. 'They must not even know there is a symbol anywhere. They will not find out. If they did it would spoil the art.'[20] The three sections relate Oisin's journey into Tír na nÓg, the Otherworld, led by the princess Niamh, and his eventual return to Ireland after three hundred years. Other poems in the collection look back to his fascination for Mohini Chatterjee, taking Indian mysticism as their subject. Elsewhere, the cash-strapped Yeats was still writing articles for periodicals, mostly on Irish themes or as a way of giving publicity to friends, such as in his 'Celt in London' column for the high-paying American Irish *Boston Pilot*. Magic, however, was calling, and rumours of the Golden Dawn had reached his ears.

What were Yeats's beliefs regarding magic by the time he left Blavatsky's circle? It seems likely that until his invitation to join Isis-Urania, and certainly before meeting Mathers, Yeats had no fixed idea about the reality of practical occultism. Every avenue of research, from Blake to Eastern mysticism, had opened up another world that required further exploration, and Yeats found this lack of easy coherence a frustration. The symbols in his art were potent devices, and his fairy summoning with Florence Farr had confirmed for him the power of imagination, but his experiments with friends and as part of the Esoteric Section had left him hungry for structure, hierarchy and the 'secret knowledge of the magical tradition' that the Theosophical Society was not able to provide.[21] To Yeats's mind, the GD of Mathers and Westcott might better deliver the answer.

'At the British Museum Reading-Room I often saw a man of thirty-six, or thirty-seven, in a brown velveteen coat, with gaunt resolute face, and an athletic body,' recalled Yeats of his first sightings of Mathers, 'who seemed, before I heard his name, or knew the nature of his studies, a figure of romance.'[22] By the late 1880s, Mathers was an authoritative personality and ritualist in the occult scene. He was not a member of the Theosophical Society, but he had lectured on the Kabbalah to Anna Kingsford's splinter group (when Yeats must surely have been in the audience) and his *Kabbalah Unveiled* was considered one of the seminal textbooks of the new revival.[23] There is some uncertainty about when the two men first met – Yeats remembered it as 1887, when Mathers asked him to join an 'Order of Christian kabalists, "the Hermetic Students"', either a more public-facing name for a proto-GD or an altogether different group possibly affiliated with Kingsford's Hermetic Society, and yet Yeats's formal initiation into Isis-Urania is recorded as happening in 1890.[24] Whatever the case, at this 'most receptive age' Yeats was attending small gatherings at the mage's 'romantic' lodgings in Forest Hill, and taking part in vision-based experiments.[25]

For all its theatrics, its Rosicrucian props and costumes, Yeats's initiation ceremony would have been a solemn and impressive occasion. The Candidate was met in the darkened, incense-filled Temple by the Hierophant, three Chiefs standing in the form of a triangle – Imperator (commander), Cancellarius (secretary) and Praemonstrator (responsible for overseeing the Order's teachings) – and other members lining the room. The officers spoke their appointed lines: 'Inheritor of a Dying World, arise and enter the darkness ... The Mother of Darkness hath blended him with Her hair ... The Father of Darkness hath hidden him under His wings ... His limbs are still weary from the wars which were in Heaven', and the Candidate was denied entry by the Kerux before his admission into the Hall of Truth and Justice. Yeats's choice of the motto 'Demon Est Deus Inversus' ('A demon is an inverted god') came from Éliphas Lévi, but he had probably found it in a passage in Blavatsky's *The Secret Doctrine*, where it demonstrates her contempt for the dualism she saw at the centre of Abrahamic religions. Henceforth, he would be known simply as 'Demon' or 'D.E.D.I.' in official documents and minutes.

As a Neophyte, Yeats attended a series of 'Knowledge Lectures' given by an Order member. The content ranged from basic occult terminology – the four classical elements, the signs of the zodiac, the Hebrew alphabet, the names of the ten *sefirot*, the principal alchemical symbols – to simple rituals and meditations. One of the first rituals taught was the Lesser Ritual of the Pentagram, a 'form of prayer' in which initiates invoked and then banished obsessive or disturbing thoughts by tracing a pentagram in the air using a steel dagger:

> Touch thy forehead
> and say ATEH (*thou art*)
> Touch thy breast
> and say MALKUTH (*the Kingdom*)
> Touch thy right shoulder
> and say VE-GEBURAH (*and the Power*)
> Touch thy left shoulder
> and say VE-GEDULAH (*and the Glory*)
> Clasp thy hands before thee
> and say LE-OLAM (*for ever*)
> Dagger between fingers, point up
> and say AMEN.[26]

For Yeats, having attended lectures at the Hermetic Society and researched much for himself, the tables of signs and symbols would have been familiar, probably even pedestrian, but the ceremonial aspect – the ritual with robes and daggers, the use of the pentagram – was like nothing he had tried before. It was, according to R. A. Gilbert, 'the nearest thing to a purely magical ritual found within the First Order curriculum'.[27] The Order was not technically a magical society when Yeats joined; only with the formation of the Second Order in 1892 did Mathers, supposedly with the approval of the mysterious 'Secret Chiefs', expand its purview to include the teaching of practical magic.

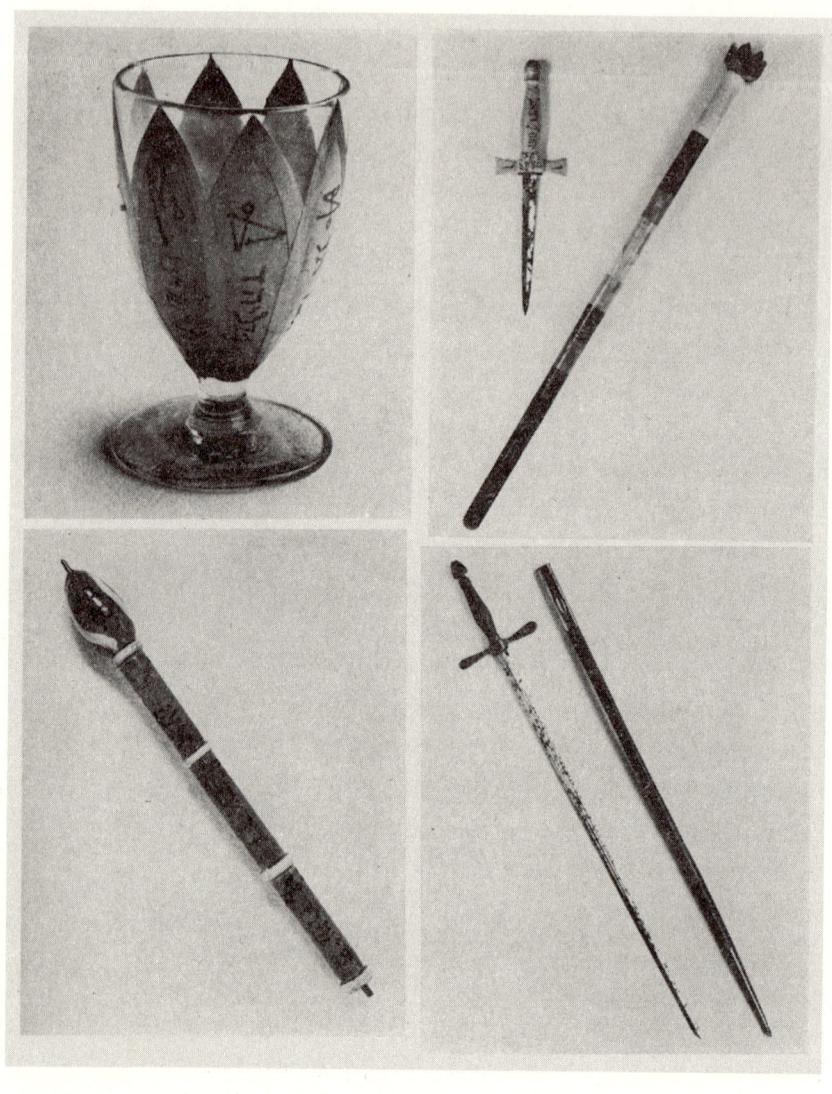

W. B. Yeats's four elemental weapons and consecrated sword, from Kathleen Raine, *Yeats, the Tarot, and the Golden Dawn*, 1972.

From 1890 onwards Yeats was committed to the GD's brand of ritual, and to Mathers as its orchestrator. As the seventy-eighth member of Isis-Urania, Yeats helped swell the ranks by recruiting from his own circles, bringing in Florence Farr just four months after his own initiation, John Todhunter in 1892 and his maternal uncle George Pollexfen, who practised from Sligo, in 1893. The Protestant freemason Pollexfen shared his nephew's interests in magic (unlike Yeats's more rationalist father) and transcribed careful copies of the Order's instruction manuals, becoming a reputable astrologer who sent out horoscopes to members when asked.[28] But the figure most important to Yeats was the Irish actress and nationalist Maud Gonne, whom he had met in 1888. He was captivated by Gonne's energy and beauty, her complexion 'like that of an apple-blossom through which light falls', and eventually supervised her preparations for entering the Order in November 1891.[29] Gonne had kept her relationship with the French journalist and right-wing politician Lucien Millevoye, who was married, a secret from Yeats. Millevoye and Gonne's young son Georges had died earlier that year, and it may have been her hope that Georges might be reincarnated that first stimulated her interest in the occult.[30] From her reflections on her involvement in the GD forty-five years later, she seems to have persisted so far as to pass three or four grades and to learn some basic Hebrew, but resigned soon after, very likely due to her belief in anti-masonic conspiracy theories. She also felt oppressed by the 'drab appearance' of her fellow mystics.[31]

GD meetings provided the opportunity for socializing with an array of creative and eccentric individuals, and for Yeats and many others this was one of the Order's major attractions. At Forest Hill he encountered the 'panic-stricken' Rev. W. A. Ayton, a practising alchemist who professed to have brewed the elixir of life in his laboratory in Oxfordshire: 'I put it away on a shelf. I meant to drink it when I was an old man, but when I got it down the other day it had all dried up.'[32] But what is perhaps most interesting about Yeats's activity with the Order in this period is its influence on his creative work. He had already harnessed the literary power of symbols in his verse (as in *Oisin*), but it was the extravagant Mathers who introduced him to their truly 'visionary' powers. At a small gathering of a dozen members at Mathers's Forest Hill residence, Yeats was given a piece of cardboard 'on which was a coloured geometrical symbol' and told to close his eyes. '[There] was not that sudden miracle as if the darkness had been cut with a knife,' he remembered, 'but there rose before me mental images that I could not control: a desert and a black Titan raising himself up by his two hands from the middle of a heap of ancient ruins.'[33] Once Yeats had related this vision to the group, Mathers explained that the black Titan had in fact been 'a being of the order of Salamanders', because he had shown Yeats their symbol. Yeats claimed soon after to have 'mastered' Mathers's symbolic system, enabling him after intense mental focus to replace his visible reality with the world of a particular symbol. Rituals such as these fired his imagination: 'I formed plans for deeds of all kinds,' he recalled much later, whereas his previous experiments with theosophy and the Esoteric Section had left him with 'no desire but for more thought, more discussion'.[34] He now lived in hope that these symbol-induced visions might lead to profound spiritual development.

How else did Yeats spend his time in these early years of the Order? Literary work and the desire to earn a steady living were his main preoccupations. *Oisin* had been published, which 'conferred prestige if not money', and in 1893 his second collection, *The Countess Kathleen and Various Legends and Lyrics*, followed. For reviewers this confirmed his image as a political poet whose lyrics combined nationalism with a mystical worldview.[35] Yeats's daring 'Apologia addressed to Ireland in the coming days' demands that he be considered among the great nineteenth-century Irish writers Thomas Davis, Clarence Mangan and Sir Samuel Ferguson, while stating:

> My rhymes more than their rhyming tell
> Of the dim wisdoms old and deep,
> That God gives unto man in sleep.
> For round about my table go
> The magical powers to and fro.[36]

'METAPHORS FOR POETRY'

Yeats had also entered the fraught battle to form a unified national literature. In 1891 he aided in the creation of the Young Ireland League following the death of Charles Stewart Parnell, a prominent Irish nationalist and former leader of the Irish Parliamentary Party, and that same winter the Irish Literary Society was founded in London, with Yeats pursuing linked projects such as an Irish magazine and a 'Library of Ireland' book series. But political differences in both Dublin and London made it impossible to progress his ideas. As he and Ellis continued their painstaking work on the Blake books, Yeats felt himself becoming increasingly isolated, cast by critics as either a neo-Fenian extremist or an Anglophone intent only on building up his own reputation.[37] This by turns depressed him and threw him into fits of rage. A welcome distraction from these messy conflicts came in the guise of an unforeseen development in his GD career: Yeats was invited to join the Second Order.

The Second Order had existed in name since the GD's foundation. When Yeats joined the Order, Mathers had only devised the grades up to an incomplete 5° = 6° (Theoricus Adeptus Minor), but in 1891 he made the decision to develop its hierarchy based on his magical research in France. Having lost his curatorial job, Mathers had moved to Paris, where Moina was studying art. The couple lived on a small allowance paid from the purse of Annie Horniman. Apparently dissatisfied with the Christian-focused Kabbalism of the First Order grades, Mathers developed the Second Order teachings with a stronger emphasis on ancient Egyptian tradition.[38] For this he had approached a 'Continental Adept' known only as Frater 'Lux e Tenebris' ('Light out of darkness'), and had studied new research in Egyptology.[39] According to Westcott, Mathers then 'brought from Paris the 5° = 6° ritual and said it was the culmination of G. D. 0° = 0° to 4° = 7°, and that it was to be known as the Ordo Roseae Rubeae et Aureae Crucis (R.R. et A.C., or Second Order).[40] As part of its teachings, the First Order would now prepare certain invited candidates for initiation into the Second Order, although the existence of the latter was to be kept secret from the former. 'Adepts,' declared the first R.R. et A.C. manuscript, 'must not tell First Order members: 1. that they have passed any further ceremony; 2. nor that they perform Practical Magic; 3. nor, when they meet; 4. nor where; 5. nor who is head of the Second Order.' The next step in Mathers's grand invention was the Portal ceremony, a connecting ritual between the First and Second, or Outer and Inner, divide in which the Chief Adept, wearing a yellow and white Egyptian headdress (or Nemes), officiated from behind the Veil of the Temple (a curtain).[41] This fantastic blend of Rosicrucian and Egyptian magic, communicated through imaginative stagecraft, produced what must have been a shocking and even transformative experience for candidates, and a series of rituals possibly unique within Victorian occultism.

By August 1892, the Second Order had taken the painted vault at Thavies Inn apart and rebuilt it in a house on Clipstone Street, Mayfair. It was there that Yeats was initiated.[42] He had been progressing steadily up the First Order grades until this point, dutifully taking the examinations after long periods studying what was essentially a curriculum of medieval occult science. When the invitation to join the Second Order came, it was accompanied by a document written by Westcott stressing the need for purity of thought and a grasp of the hermetic teachings beyond their mere facts:

> Intellectual grasp *alone*, will provide but a broken reed in your hands, in the higher grades: no real progress will be made unless you cultivate the ideals of objects rather than their materiality, and unless you can realise the forces which surround you, which you absorb, and which you may learn to wield. For this new development of yourself, two requirements are essential: a *Clean Life* and an *Indomitable Will*; if you have these two essentials all other things shall be added unto them.[43]

Inexplicably, Yeats was the only member to take the Second Order rituals on two separate occasions – the Portal ritual and the first

Adeptus ritual on Friday 20 January, and the remaining two Adeptus rituals the following evening. The entry in the Second Order diary (which acted as a form of attendance book) for the first night records Florence Farr leaving by 7pm, perhaps suggesting that something happened to cut short the proceedings, though it might have been that Yeats had needed to travel to Dublin at short notice.[44] 'Demon' or 'D.E.D.I.' is then recorded as paying visits to the vault throughout the summer of 1893, sometimes alone, often for many hours at a time, most likely working on personal talismans or using the space to induce visions: in July 'Flying Roll XII', one of a series of manuscripts containing the Second Order teachings, was presented to him by Westcott with several other Adepts in attendance. Mathers's instructions for working with 'Telesmatic Images' meant the employment of talismans or 'sigils' to invoke angelic forms.

That summer, Yeats was also 'up to [his] ears' preparing a second folklore-based collection, *The Celtic Twilight*, further solidifying his ideas about Ireland and the occult potential of its inhabitants.[45] In early 1894 he went to Paris and stayed with Mathers, who was now using his Second Order motto 'Deo Duce Comite Ferro', and Moina. While Yeats was chiefly there to revive his connection with Maud Gonne and network with the French literati, he was also developing a close bond with the Matherses, whom he perhaps considered occult mentors. In the evenings he and Moina played four-person chess against Mathers and a 'spirit' teammate (each player representing one of the four elements, the board based on the Enochian tablets of John Dee and Edward Kelley).[46] Yeats was striking an ostentatiously Celtic 'pose' around literary London and Paris, and Mathers, still several years away from being ousted from his own order, was also embracing a self-constructed Celtic identity. Now that he had become friends with this foremost writer of the Irish revival, he gave himself up to the Celtic movement. When Yeats returned to Paris in the winter of 1896, Mathers had assumed the title of his supposed Scottish ancestor Count MacGregor of Glenstrae, styling himself and Moina 'MacGregor Mathers': additional evidence to certain Order members that their Imperator was becoming 'unhinged'.[47]

CHAPTER 1

This change in Mathers's focus was fortunate, for as the 1890s progressed Yeats had begun to conceive of what was essentially an Irish counterpart to the GD. It was to be an Order of Celtic Mysteries, focusing on the evocation of the gods and heroes of Ireland's mythical past. Its intended setting was the ruins of McDermott's Castle, an island fortification rising dramatically out of Lough Key in County Roscommon. Yeats had visited the lake with Douglas Hyde in April 1895, and on seeing the castle fell into a reverie in which this 'Temple of Heroes' became the centre for a Celtic spiritual revival. Willing initiates were enlisted, chiefly his Dublin art school friend and mystic poet George Russell (known by the sobriquet 'AE'), the playwright and folklorist Lady Augusta Gregory and GD regulars Annie Horniman, Dorothea and Edmund Hunter, and Mathers. The GD provided much of the structure and ritual language for the project, and the Mysteries were to act as a development or emanation of its teachings. They were devised against a backdrop of millenarianism and visions of the end of the world. Yeats had concluded that 'true' Irishness could only be found in Ireland's (and the other Celtic countries') pagan past, an idea already explored in his poetry. The 'secret knowledge' inherent in the land and literature of pre-Christian Ireland was an antidote to sterile, modern religion. Magic was a way to access this ancient spiritual boon.

But the Celtic Mysteries concept was also a way to get nearer to Maud Gonne. Now an ex-Order member, over the latter half of the 1890s Gonne had been persuading Yeats to become more involved in Pan-Celtic and extremist nationalist projects, such as the centenary of the 1798 Irish rebellion. He complained to his new confidante Lady Gregory that the 'infinite triviality' of politics was exhausting and fracturing his mind, but nevertheless complied.[48] Gonne was still drawn to the esoteric, and by 1898 she was planning trips to Irish sites: 'Tomorrow I go down to New Grange with Miss Gonne to interview a god or two at the old pagan burial place there', Yeats wrote to Lady Gregory in June.[49] Though their trip was cancelled, Gonne visited later that summer and sent Yeats soil and bottles of well water that the poet used for talismans. At the end of the year she was still 'deep in occult science', and while in Dublin she and Yeats discussed astral travelling and attempted to communicate remotely with George Russell – on one night Yeats and Gonne were brought together in dream by the Irish deity Lugh, and they kissed.[50] Gonne complicated their relationship further by revealing to Yeats her past relationship with Millevoye and the existence of a second child, Iseult. The disclosure had the effect of binding Yeats in confidence, though she still refused to marry him. They continued to explore their chaste mystical connection, based on the bizarre assumption that they had been siblings in a previous life. For Yeats, the Order of Celtic Mysteries, however bound up with Pan-Celtic politics, gave him the pretext to continue seeing her. 'My own seership was, I thought, inadequate,' he recalled; 'it was to be Maud Gonne's work and mine. Perhaps that was why we had been thrown together ... I believed we were about to attain a revelation.'[51]

Yeats kept up with his Second Order activities alongside devising initiation rituals for the Celtic Mysteries, crafting its seven-grade structure over a series of letters. Just as the GD's First Order modelled its grade rituals on the four classical elements, corresponding with the *sefirot* on the Kabbalistic Tree of Life, Yeats matched his Celtic equivalents with the four treasures of the legendary Tuatha Dé Danaan: the Spear, the Cauldron, the Stone and the Sword. Eleusinian titles for ceremonial roles were retained at first, but in later versions they became professions honouring the Irish peasantry: the Candidate was instead 'Wayfarer', the Hierophant 'Herdsman'.[52] Now, Yeats could act out his romantic vision of Irish rural life while assuming control over the proceedings, an occult version of the Protestant Ascendancy wherein he was the Imperator and the teachings revealed to members were channelled through his own visionary experiences.

Not only was Yeats grafting the GD structure onto the Mysteries, but his methods of invoking the Irish gods used Mathers's vision system and the deployment of sigils and talismans. Much of the preliminary work was done at George Pollexfen's house and at Coole, Lady Gregory's imposing residence in County Westmeath. 'At every moment of leisure we obtained in vision long lists of symbols,' Yeats recalled, aided by Pollexfen's 'slow and difficult clairvoyance'. 'The forms became very continuous in my thoughts, and when AE came to stay at Coole he asked who was the white jester he had seen about the corridors. It was a form I associated with the god Aengus.'[53]

Letters flew between Dublin, London, Paris and Scotland as members updated one another on shared visions and spiritual activities. Often one member would be present as Yeats conjured up images of Irish deities and attempted to focus on them: Dorothea Hunter recorded him with Lug, whose red eyes revolved 'with a terrible rapidity', and Mannanán, rising from the ocean 'on a chariot formed of the crest of two meeting waves'.[54] At Yeats's suggestion, Moina contributed four oil paintings of Celtic deities, possibly modelled on Gonne and Florence Farr.[55] Much time was also spent composing rituals, usually with detailed Mathers-like stage directions.

Ultimately, activities relating to the Celtic Mysteries project dwindled and the Temple of Heroes remained unpurchased. In the years to come, Gonne would convert to Catholicism and marry a second time, leaving Yeats without his driving anima. His plans for an Irish National Theatre had begun to take shape, aided by Lady Gregory and his fellow Irish playwright J. M. Synge, and an increasingly absent Mathers meant that the GD was beginning to require Yeats's leadership to sustain itself.

Yeats's short stories and drafts of an unfinished novel from the 1890s particularly reflect the occult training he received from the GD and the developing ideas behind the Celtic Mysteries. With the exception of the naturalistic novella *John Sherman*, his very earliest stories were based on his research into Irish fairies and folklore, and were written for the *National Observer* between 1892 and 1894.[56] When these proved successful Yeats branched out into other newspapers, eventually collecting the stories into *The Secret Rose* in 1897. Although they were written over a number of years in different styles and manners, 'they have but one subject,' Yeats explained in his dedication to George Russell, 'the war of spiritual with natural order'.[57] They were Yeats's attempt to produce what he called an 'aristocratic esoteric Irish literature'; he had begun to shift his opinion that Irish literature must be for the common folk, instead seeing a need to 'convert the educated classes' to the national idea.[58] Though Ireland is the collection's chief setting, *The Secret Rose* was also a tantalising advertisement for the contemporary occult milieu, showcasing (though obscurely) the various cults and movements Yeats had encountered on his trips to Paris to see Maud Gonne and Mathers.

Yeats's initiatory experiences in the GD clearly influenced a triptych of stories written for *The Savoy* between 1896 and 1897: 'Rosa Alchemica', 'The Tables of the Law' and 'The Adoration of the Magi'. He had meant them to appear in sequence, but the publisher 'took a distaste' to the other two and only 'Rosa Alchemica' made it into *The Secret Rose*.[59] The tales feature three characters, some appearing in more than one, who are to differing degrees questing after esoteric knowledge. In 'Rosa Alchemica', the symbols of alchemy and Rosicrucianism represent the occult world that obsesses its narrator. A man named Michael Robartes (a blend of Mathers and George Russell) persuades him to join a society named the Order of the Alchemical Rose; at an ancient house on the west coast of Ireland, the narrator is led into a darkened room and given an ornate book to read, bound in vellum and with the alchemical rose on its cover. Its pages describe how the Order was founded by six students 'of Celtic descent' who discover that alchemy is the distillation of the soul:

> An owl passed, rustling among the vine-leaves overhead, and then an old woman came, leaning upon a stick, and sitting close to them, took up the thought where they had dropped it. Having expounded the whole principle of spiritual alchemy, and bid them found the Order of the Alchemical Rose, she passed from among them, and when they would have followed was nowhere to be seen. They formed themselves into an Order, holding their

W. T. Horton, *W. B. Yeats*, 1898.

goods and making their researches in common, and, as they became perfect in the alchemical doctrine, apparitions came and went among them, and taught them more and more marvellous mysteries.[60]

Might the old woman be a version of Blavatsky, or even the mythical Fräulein Sprengel? The occultists' ancestry coupled with the suggestion of animal transformation (had the woman been the owl?) provides the alchemical society with an origin story to rival the GD's, one that is markedly Celtic. Yeats also makes his case for the occult power of imaginative literature: Shakespeare, Milton and Dante adorn the narrator's shelves as magical grimoires in their own striking colour, and the temple contains Blake's prophetic books alongside Flamel, Lully and other alchemical writers. But throughout the three stories the narrator displays a hesitancy to fully commit to the supernatural and to the all-consuming life of an Adept. The narrator of 'Rosa Alchemica' writes a short work on alchemists, but receives letters from occultists upbraiding him for his artistic sympathy. The triptych reveals one of Yeats's key ideas about magic and art: that it was dangerous for one to be allowed to overcome the other.

The three occult tales were also 'preliminary studies' for a new novel that Yeats 'could never write nor cease to write', and would never finish. According to Yeats, its theme was 'Hodos Chameliontos', or 'the Path of the Chameleon'.[61] This was the name of a Kabbalistic manuscript shown to him by Mathers, which had come to represent the intellectual labyrinth of the occult revival. Like the chameleon, ever changing and adapting, Yeats struggled to create order out of the 'endless procession' of images passing before him.[62] The idea for expressing this helplessness in a novel first took shape in 1894 as *The Lilies of the Lord*, which in later versions became *The Speckled Bird*, in reference to the Bible verse from Jeremiah 12:9: 'Mine inheritance is as the speckled bird, all the birds of heaven are against it.' Financial worries drove its writing, but the book was also intended to function in service of an Irish literature Yeats considered denationalized, stripped of its core identity by England and by American influence. He hoped to produce books for the common Irishman that were 'radiant from the living heart of the day'.[63] It was the same motivation that had lain behind the founding of the Irish Literary Society and the Order of Celtic Mysteries. He did not begin writing properly until 1897; at the end of 1896 the promised novel had been bought by the publishers Lawrence & Bullen, with weekly instalments taking care of his money worries for the present. His writing was reliant on autobiographical detail, and in the pages of *The Speckled Bird*'s unfinished drafts – chiefly the 1900 and 1902 versions – we find characters based on people he knew in the Order, and who had aided him in establishing his Celtic ritual school. Jack Yeats, Annie Horniman, Maud Gonne ('Margaret') and Mathers ('Maclagan', or in an early draft 'Macgregor Martin') each cross the path of the hero Michael Hearne, embellished and altered for the purposes of fiction but close enough to their counterparts that they can be identified. The Celtic Mysteries is still envisaged as a society 'to bring back the gods', but recast as a series of rituals based on grail symbolism from the Arthurian legend, its 'manuals of devotion' found in imaginative literature.[64] The GD, already a product of competing fictions, was now being plundered for narrative and symbolism.

Later drafts share a basic sequence of events: early years spent in the Hearnes' aristocratic castle at Gleann-na-Gae (modelled on Yeats's friend and co-founder of the Irish Literary Theatre Edward Martyn's family home); Michael's attempts to form his grail order in London; his unrequited passion for the heroine Margaret. Michael's early encounter with Maclagan in the British Museum mirrors Yeats's own first sightings of Mathers, and is both a summing-up and affectionate characterization of the magician. Maclagan is found at work on his grimoire translations, forced, as in reality, to write a 'sixpenny book on fortune-telling by cards' to make ends meet.[65] The new acquaintances walk around the Museum and make their way through Bloomsbury together to Maclagan's lodgings, discussing alchemy: 'They had become as intimate as if they had known each other for years. They had awakened that intimacy which is only possible to lovers and to mystics. They had shared the hidden secrets of their lives.'[66] The semi-autobiographical episodes continue.

The Speckled Bird also provides a sense of the creative labour that went into the construction and design of the GD's rituals, an aspect rarely described in detail in Order records. With the help of art students, Michael works out ritual diagrams and plans for robes and 'draperies', until one day he comes across Holland, possibly modelled on Edmund Hunter, sketching by the river:

> Holland, for this was the name of the student, began to paint, design rather, an elaborate altar, on which he was [to] enamel patterns of the Grail, and to sketch out the designs of a forest [and of] the strange hieroglyphical animals and birds wandering over the grass and among the leaves, designs that were to be painted upon canvas and some day changed into embroidery. He made, too, two or three designs for the robes of the magical officers.[67]

Michael and Maclagan proceed to compose rituals using 'abstracts of various old methods of evocation or new methods made on the old plan', using symbols remembered in dreams or 'sudden waking illuminations'.[68] But these efforts expose a rift between the two men, and while at home in Gleann-na-Gae, Michael receives a letter from Maclagan informing him that due to Michael's artistic approach to magic he can no longer take part in the Order's management:

> You thought all of forms – I of the inner substance. When I was thinking about the gathering into the order of ancient tradition, you were thinking of making it the foundation for patterns.
> I have come to recognize that you are not a magician, but some kind of artist, and that the *summum bonum* itself, the potable gold of our masters, were less to you than some charm of colour, or some charm of words.[69]

Elsewhere, Maclagan criticizes Michael's attempts at writing rituals as 'too like a play'.[70] Yeats had always been aware that his attraction towards magic was motivated far more by its symbolic promise than genuine spiritual results; these passages, as in his earlier stories, underline his anxiety about the difference he presumably felt between himself and Mathers. The egomaniac Mathers thought, however sceptically, in terms of eras and epochs, of harnessing the powers of occult tradition to strive for a spiritual revolution in humankind, whereas Yeats made his living from art, and so was concerned with iconography, imagination and the 'ever shifting' borders of the mind.[71] 'What can Arthur's knights be to me,' Maclagan's letter continues, 'when compared with François de Brie [one of the 'original' Rosicrucians] … with the great masters who attained to all human wisdom and made death itself their servant.'[72] Like Mathers, Maclagan 'had ideas about the Celtic races', but their myths and folklore were not enough in the mage's mind to produce the outcomes he believed magic capable of.[73]

Yeats's closeness with Mathers around this time meant that he was witness, at least in part, to the GD's first real taste of the Imperator's tendency towards authoritarianism and paranoia. It began with money. By 1895 Annie Horniman had for several years been wiring the Matherses lump sums to fund their increasingly extravagant lifestyle in Paris, and while she did not at first appear discontent with these arrangements, it soon became clear that she was being taken advantage of. Without her knowledge, they had upgraded addresses to a flat on Avenue Duquesne with space enough for its own temple.[74] And now £100 was required for the entertainment of distinguished guests ('a duke and his suite'), so that the previous annual payment of £200 more than doubled.[75] Unwilling to supply the Matherses with such amounts any longer, Horniman's payments for the rest of the year were much smaller.

Horniman's state of mind was fragile. No doubt guilt at having withdrawn support from her mentor and friend was compounded by the suggestion of a new line of research among GD students back in England. The American spiritualist and religious reformer Thomas

Lake Harris had founded the Brotherhood of the New Life in the 1860s in New York State, and through his interpretations of Swedenborgian mysticism was advocating a type of 'conjugal' encounter with the divine that could only be achieved through a joint male–female 'inner transformation' (helped along, strangely enough, by fairies or 'elementals').[76] His teachings also drew on Western occult tradition, and were much debated in the occult community during the 1890s, as he and his followers published books and pamphlets. A. E. Waite's journal the *Unknown World* featured reprints of Harris's dogmatic poetry and a short series of articles outlining his views, written by the pseudonymous 'Respiro' (who may have been the GD's Edward Berridge, Sub-Imperator of Isis-Urania).[77] Yeats had been introduced to Harris's ideas in 1896, through his correspondence with the artist and 'Brother of the New Life' W. T. Horton, although he was not a convert.[78] Horton had been set to undergo the GD's Neophyte ritual, but ended up backing out due to his concern that the Order was 'nature-play through spiritism' and detracted from his relationship with Christ.[79]

A scene in a late draft of *The Speckled Bird* gives an indication of what GD meetings might have been like at the time of Berridge's articles: a group of Americans are present at a meeting of the Order, and conversation soon turns to the spiritual merits of Harris's Fountain Grove community in Santa Rosa, California, and the free love or 'sex fever' of the Oneida Community, a utopian Christian community in New York State. Yeats must have been aware of how uncomfortable Annie Horniman was with ideas of a sexual nature being discussed among GD members, as a later letter from Horton reveals: 'Another cause of my leaving is Miss H. to whom I feel strangely and most virulently opposed & antagonistic. She is my bete noire. I hope you have not shown her any of Harris' books.'[80] Horniman strongly expressed her discomfort to the Matherses, claiming that Berridge had 'issued a pamphlet' urging doctrines that the Second Order 'all thought impure and mischievous for the younger students to whom he offered them'.[81] It appears that she considered Mathers's lack of action a failure of leadership, an accusation that did not sit well with the Imperator. His responses to Horniman were indignant and chastising, bordering on manipulative: '*It is no pleasure for me to reprove your faults,*' he insisted. 'You have *every* right to your own opinion regarding *yourself* but what your *companions* do is another matter for *their* consideration and consciences.'[82] Interestingly, Mathers argued that in their roles as GD students, members took on a magical persona or 'mask', thereby leaving their outer personalities in the real world. This meant that Horniman's prudish anxieties about Harris's teachings were not relevant to her Order activities as 'Fortiter et Recte' ('Bravely and justly'), because they were a product of her non-occult personality. She had been told, essentially, that she needed to keep quiet.

Sometime in September 1896, Horniman, having caught wind of how other GD members were talking about her and suspecting that Mathers was using her money for political rather than magical purposes, suddenly resigned from her post as Sub-Praemonstratrix of Isis-Urania and cut off all funds to Paris. Her opinions about Berridge and his advocacy for Harris's teachings had in fact been shared by many other GD members, Westcott included. It transpired that Berridge had unwantedly kissed Helen Rand, a fellow Second Order member, after an astrology meeting, and was suspected of similar harassment of other, younger students.[83] But despite many members liking Horniman and sympathizing with her against Berridge, she was aware that she was not universally popular: besides Horton, the young chemist Allan Bennett was not impressed by her as an instructor, noting that he had been 'shocked at the casual and flippant treatment of the Spirit Vision' she had set forth.[84] Her complaints had shaken Mathers, and in October 1896 he circulated an imposition to his $5° = 6°$ Adepts that they formally submit to his authority:

> This Manifesto is to be placed in the hands of each Theoricus Adeptus Minor upon his or her attainment of that Grade. After he or she has carefully read the same; he or she must send a written Statement of voluntary submission in all points regarding the Orders of the G∴D∴ in the Outer and the R∴R∴ et A∴C∴ to G.H. Frater Deo Duce Comite Ferro before being permitted to receive any further instruction. Unless he or she is prepared to

do this, he or she must either Resign from the Order, or elect to remain a Zelator Adeptus Minor only. And he or she hereby undertakes to refrain from stirring up any strife or schism hereon in the First and Second Orders.[85]

It was the first real sign that Mathers was worried about challenges to his authority. He further claimed, as if to quash any resistance once and for all, that he had been in astral communication with the Secret Chiefs of the Order, who, he believed, took on human forms but possessed 'terrible superhuman powers'.[86] Horniman sent in her written statement, but Mathers pointed out that she had not deferred to him on the GD's '*workings*' (by which he meant administration). When she did not comply, and after Moina had sent a desperate plea for more funds, Mathers wrote to expel Horniman from the Order.

The attitude you have chosen to take leaves me no other alternative than (however unwillingly) to remove your name from the Roll of the Order; for I will not continue to teach one who persistently opposes my authority, and endeavours to influence others to do so.[87]

Despite these events, Yeats stayed on good terms with Mathers and Moina, and Mathers remained a central figure in the Celtic Mysteries until the allure of ancient Egyptian rites in Paris became a priority. Yeats seems to have resented this, but even so the two men remained in contact for several years. He and Maud Gonne may even have consulted Mathers on nationalist strategies.[88] Near the end of 1898, Moina was writing to Yeats about her attempt to translate *The Land of Heart's Desire* into French, but by the following year Yeats was seeing less of them, possibly because of animosity between Gonne and Mathers. Recovering from a heavy cold in February, Yeats reported to Lady Gregory that Gonne 'is quite convinced that it is the work of a rival mystic, or one of his attendant spirits. She points out that I went to see him [Mathers] without it & came back with it, which is circumstantial evidence at any rate.'[89]

The GD was to endure greater battles as the twentieth century drew nearer, but in the early years of the poet's career, Mathers and his society served Yeats admirably. Richard Ellmann describes Yeats as having 'lived several lifetimes in one', and the occult remained a major part in each of his many transformations.[90] He saw poetic composition as being akin to the practice of magic, and by 1901 his theory of symbols in art had reached an apogee in an essay titled 'Magic':

> I cannot now think symbols less than the greatest of all powers whether they are used consciously by the masters of magic, or half unconsciously by their successors, the poet, the musician, and the artist ... Whatever the passions of men have gathered about him, becomes a symbol in the great memory, and in the hands of him who had the secret it is a worker of wonders, a caller-up of angels or of devils.[91]

It was partly this dovetailing of poetry and the occult that encouraged Yeats to persist with the Order throughout the 1890s while others resigned (or, in some cases, were forced out). He looked to it for guidance, making use of its teachings in attempts to achieve his political, erotic and artistic ambitions. Once an Irish exile unsure of his position in London society, Yeats was now a core member of an inner circle in which he could learn and wield power to serve his cultural-nationalist ideals. Looking back on the GD in an early draft of his autobiography, the picture is wistful, placed in favourable contrast to his Esoteric Section days: 'One passes from degree to degree, and if the wisdom one had once hoped for is still far off there [is] no exhortation to alarm one's dignity, no abstraction to deaden the nerves of the soul.'[92]

2

A Gift Given to the Wise

Florence Farr

> Maclagan must be with a lady when he meets Michael. She goes away when they meet, but later on as they walk about the gallery they find her sitting with her eyes half-closed on a seat close to the Mut-em-menu mummy case, but Michael is not permitted to speak to her. Maclagan will not introduce him, she is at her meditation, she is doubtless conversing with Mut-em-menu.[1]

The actress and writer Florence Farr, the basis for W. B. Yeats's 'lady', had been a devout GD student since 1890. Beguiled by the magic systems of ancient cultures, she had written a short book on *Egyptian Magic* for William Westcott's series of hermetic tracts, and around 1900, when Yeats wrote this note to his novel *The Speckled Bird*, was under the impression that she had made contact with a mummified 'chantress' from the Ramesside period named Mutemmenu.[2] Yeats writes her into his novel as mysterious and unapproachable, almost a fixture of the gallery herself, to be observed but nothing more. In the same note, she is described by an indignant theosophist as a 'worshipper of devils', by others as an incarnation of Mary Magdalen and the Polish mystic Faustina, and is said to have lived many past lives, though her current incarnation is 'most innocent'.[3] Farr was absorbed by her studies even to the detriment of her professional career, writing in 1894, '*In* the world Adepts may be, but not *of* it.'[4]

By all accounts highly imaginative, an accomplished student of occultism and with a beautiful stage voice, Farr's life in the 1890s has been too easily categorized by her relationships with two Irish writers, Yeats and George Bernard Shaw. Shaw was the mentor and lover who propelled her to fame on the stage; Yeats introduced her to the Order of the Golden Dawn and encouraged her magical operations. At several points the two spheres overlapped, as when Farr appeared in Yeats's plays or collaborated with him in spoken word performances, though Shaw had no patience with her dabbling in fashionable magic, the 'changing your name and throwing a pinch of salt over your shoulder'.[5] She has been cast as a model for the early feminist 'New Woman', a mistress of Shaw and one of Yeats's poetic muses even after she had left permanently for Ceylon (now Sri Lanka) in 1917; but she was also a novelist, a scholar of magic, a playwright and an extraordinary influence on the fate of the original GD.

Her parents were Mary Elizabeth Whittal and Dr William Farr, a British epidemiologist and statistician whose friendship with Florence Nightingale following her return from Crimea provided him with a name for his youngest daughter, Florence Beatrice Farr, born in 1860. His death in 1883 left Farr and her siblings with enough money to live modestly without doing 'anything that was distasteful to her', as Shaw later put it, and so she pursued a career on the stage.[6] Already a pupil of the actor-manager J. L. Toole, she began to play small parts in new London comedies under the alias Mary Lester (her father had not wanted the Farr name associated with acting), and while on a provincial tour of *The Private Secretary* she met the actor Edward Emery. They were married in Chiswick on the last day of 1884. Whether out of a general antipathy for one another, or Farr's feeling constrained by matrimonial bonds, the marriage gradually fell apart over the next four years until finally Edward was 'sent away' to America, his fare paid by his sister, the actress Winifred Emery.[7] Finding herself suddenly unattached and happy to forget Edward, Farr moved to Brook Green, Hammersmith, to be nearer her sister Henrietta, who had married the artist Henry M. Paget.[8] She had 'given home and the family as much trial as seemed necessary'.[9]

Farr was living in Brook Green when the Yeats family were settling in Bedford Park, just a short walk away. Although they may have met as early as 1888, it was John Todhunter's *A Sicilian Idyll*, performed in May 1890 at the clubhouse there, that brought Yeats securely into Farr's orbit. Farr played the shepherdess to Edward Heron Allen's Daphnis, and Yeats was so entranced by her 'striking beauty and subtle gesture and fine delivery' (as he raved in the *Boston Pilot*) that when the other actors spoke he sat muttering insults under his breath until her next line.[10] Soon he was at her house constantly, seemingly to talk theatre but also, we can assume, to tell her about a society called the Order of the Golden Dawn. 'If she read out some poem in English or in French all was passion,' Yeats remembered, 'all a traditional splendour, but she spoke of actual things with a cold wit or under the strain of paradox.'[11] Two months after the clubhouse performance, Farr went through the GD's initiation ritual at Mark Masons' Hall in Great Queen Street, its spectacle surely not unfamiliar to one so used to stage artifice. As she later described in Flying Roll XIII, the ideals communicated in the 0° = 0° ceremony were of secrecy and fraternal love: 'Silence is in itself a tremendous aid in the search for Occult powers. In darkness and stillness the Archetypal forms are conceived and the forces of nature germinated.'[12] Her chosen motto, 'Sapientia Sapienti Dono Data', meant 'Wisdom is a gift given to the wise'.

Farr's relationship with George Bernard Shaw blossomed alongside her introduction to the occult, and almost as quickly. She and Shaw, who was four years older and a principled and attractive novelist and music critic, first met in the gardens of Merton Abbey, William Morris's textile workshop in Surrey. Farr was then engaged as an embroidery student of Morris's daughter May, alongside Yeats's elder sister Lily. Like Yeats, Shaw had been struck by her performance in *A Sicilian Idyll*, and as the pair saw more of each other they found that they were in love. 'This is to certify that you are my best and dearest love,' he wrote, 'the regenerator of my heart, the holiest joy of my soul, my treasure, my salvation.'[13] He seemed to like that she had separated from Emery, because it made her a liberated woman. Coupled with her feminist and socialist tendencies, she was an ideal match and an inspiration for some of his early plays. He sought to guide her acting career, and by late 1890 he was going over a new translation of Henrik Ibsen's *Rosmersholm* (1886) with her, eventually persuading her to take the part of Rebecca West, an exemplar of early New Womanhood, opposite the Shakespearean actor Frank Benson. It is also from Shaw that a picture of a sexually adventurous Farr emerges, someone who 'set no bounds to her relations with men whom she liked' and was so impatient with the formalities of flirtation that she would often kiss men to relieve the sexual tension.[14] In her own words, sex was good exercise and an enjoyable diversion, though Shaw's claim that she could list 'a dozen adventures' prior to their first meeting is suspect.[15] Shaw coached her according to his theory of the 'womanly' and 'unwomanly' woman, and in their shared view that the institution of marriage conditioned wives to sacrifice themselves in their husbands' interests and should be rebelled against.[16] A number of his letters to Farr early in the decade amount to a series of scoldings: she was an 'ill-starred woman', a 'will-less girl', a 'wretch'.[17] Around the time of her initiation into the GD he also chided her for her occult leanings, asking whether she knew of any 'subtle fluids' or 'telepathic wires' that would tell her when 'the chapter of accidents sets me free from my chains?' (i.e. when he would die).[18]

Not that Farr paid any attention to his taunts. Soon after her initiation she reported to Yeats that she had visited Mathers at one of his Forest Hill gatherings, where the magus had got her to focus on a certain symbol. 'By a process she could not describe', she had suddenly found herself on the seashore amid a flock of seagulls.[19] It was common for GD initiates to languish in the lower grades, or even resign from the Order after a year, but Farr, like Yeats, found it a pursuit worth sticking with. Following Mathers's Second Order revelation, twenty initiates seem to have been selected as honorary Adeptus Minors. The list included Moina, the Rev. Ayton and Anne Ayton, Edward Berridge – and Farr. According to A. E. Waite, Annie Horniman, the first to take the $5° = 6°$ vault ceremony, was 'preceding Sapientia', suggesting that Farr was expected to be next in line – whether by her own choice, or as the worthiest.[20] It was a remarkable ascent in so short a time. At this stage she was one of Isis-Urania's most devoted members, an acolyte of Mathers and privy to the temple's inner workings. It took Yeats until January 1893 before he was ready to enter the vault.

Second Order diaries show 'SSDD' participating in 5° = 6° admission ceremonies and 'invocating' in the vault.[21] Throughout 1892 and 1893 Farr attended various Adept Assemblies and Councils, at which members met to discuss matters such as the administration of other temples and to aid in the day-to-day upkeep of the Second Order rooms. There was also ample time for consecrating magical objects such as wands and talismans for ritual use. Unlike GD students in full-time employment (Edward Berridge, for example, was a practising physician), Farr and other 'lady' Adepts were able to devote more of their time to occult work — especially, for Farr, in the long gaps between acting roles. The differences in roles and experiences between male and female initiates, created in part by these differences in circumstance, is rarely examined in histories of the GD. Like many other women who had reached the Second Order grades, Farr was not obliged to work for a living, though she did have steady acting work during the period (several plays at the Royal Comedy Theatre throughout 1892). Chemist and fellow GD student Allan Bennett was later critical of the leisurely position afforded to Annie Horniman by her inheritance: 'I can see no great self-sacrifice involved in an evening or two a week for a woman who has practically nothing in the world to do.'[22] Evidently the Clipstone Street rooms were becoming too much like a social space for women during the day, because some kind of rule seems to have been imposed: 'What's the meaning of the new rule about Lady Students?', Farr recorded in the Clipstone diary.

Also in 1893, Farr contributed a Flying Roll, perhaps adapted from a lecture given at a meeting of Adepts. 'An Example of Mode of Attaining to Spirit Vision and What was seen by Two Adepti' recounted Farr and Elaine Simpson's ('Fidelis', or 'Faithful') experience of astral projection, achieved in November 1892 using a self-hypnotizing technique of the kind Mathers had taught at Forest Hill. The pair focused on the Empress tarot card, 'heightened in colouring, purified in design and idealised', until they found themselves 'in spirit' above a distant blue land:

> Effort to ascend was then made; rising to the planes; seemed to pass up through clouds and then appeared a pale green landscape

and in its midst a Gothic Temple of ghostly outlines marked with light. Approached it and found the temple gained in definiteness and was concrete, and seemed a solid structure. Giving the signs of Netzach Grade (because of Venus) was able to enter; giving also Portal signs and 5°=6° signs in thought form.²³

A month after recording this joint vision, Farr was on stage at the Royalty Theatre for two nights, starring as Blanche Sartorius in Shaw's first play *Widowers' Houses*. Structured as a traditional romantic comedy, the story was a startling critique of landlordism and the complacent middle class, who grow fat 'on the poverty of the slum as flies fatten on filth'.²⁴ The 'well-fed, well-dressed' Blanche, the daughter of the central entrepreneur, was a model for Shaw's developing brand of feminism, seeking to win control over her future with righteous anger and defiance. In one scene Farr had to throttle a serving maid. The audience was not pleased by *Widowers'* didactic tone (and lack of a happy ending), hissing and jeering at Shaw as he gave a closing speech. The reviews judged the play a 'faulty' Ibsen imitation, yet remarkable.²⁵ Shaw was pleased, but privately criticized Farr for a 'painfully amateurish' performance. Perhaps Farr was too busy to notice: she was appearing at the same time at the Royal Comedy in the lightly entertaining *To-day*.

The years 1893 to 1894 were some of the most professionally rewarding of Farr's early life. Far from restricting herself solely to GD matters, her social circle was expanding. She knew the Morrises at Kelmscott; through her friends at Bedford Park, she had ties to the Rhymers' Club, a group of male poets who drank at the Cheshire Cheese pub on Fleet Street; and by extension she had become acquainted with John Lane and Elkin Mathews, publishers at the Bodley Head, and the artist Aubrey Beardsley, then in his early twenties.²⁶ Shaw had been a prominent member of the Fabian Society since the mid-1880s,

Florence Farr, promotional photograph for *Arms and the Man*, 1894.

and may also have introduced her to his socialist collaborators. Yet it was her GD contacts who provided Farr with creative opportunity: Annie Horniman, already bankrolling the Matherses' Parisian lifestyle, offered Farr money, as she remembered it, 'to do anything I liked with the way of advertising myself', and Farr quickly set about soliciting material for a season at the Avenue Theatre, a music hall venue off Victoria Embankment.[27] While at the Pagets' Christmas party (with no doubt many GD members in attendance, her sister Henrietta, the host, included), Farr requested that Yeats write a one-act play for her eleven-year-old niece Dorothy. Yeats acquiesced, and finished *The Land of Heart's Desire* in early 1894. A vehicle for his continuing interest in folk tradition and with the 'Irish Theatre in mind', it was to be the first professional performance of Yeats's plays and the pair's first creative collaboration, with Farr as stage manager. Dorothy was cast as the Faery Child. Farr intended the main event to be a new 'romantic' play by Shaw, but by the start of the year he had made little progress and she was forced to begin rehearsing Todhunter's *A Comedy of Sighs*, with its Ibsen-esque Modern Woman themes and unfortunate lack of real plot.[28] Farr herself would play Lady Brandon. She asked Beardsley to design the poster for the season: another debut, as the artist's first, bold entry into 'public' design.[29] Featuring a sensual woman half-hidden behind gauze curtains, Beardsley's 'Japanese-Rossetti girl' poster drummed up significant interest for the opening night.

In Yeats's recollection of the evening, however, the audience had no patience for Todhunter's style:

> For two hours and a half, pit and gallery drowned the voices of the players with boos and jeers that were meant to be bitter to the author who sat visible to all in his box surrounded by his family, and to the actress struggling bravely through her weary part.[30]

For Yeats himself, described by the writer George Moore as having been 'on exhibition, striding to and forth at the back of the dress circle, a long black cloak drooping from his shoulders, a soft black sombrero on his head', *The Land of Heart's Desire* was at least a minor success.[31]

But the affair as a whole was, for this trio of GD students, a fiasco. Shaw wrote to a friend, distressed at how the 'amiable, clever' Farr had been metamorphosed into a Medusa, 'a cold, loathly, gray, callous, sexless devil ... What madness led Todhunter to write a part like that? – what idiocy has led me to do virtually the same thing in the play which I have written to help her in this hellish enterprise?'[32] He was called in to save the season (though it was his procrastination that had led Farr to fall back on Todhunter), and hurriedly finished his script for *Arms and the Man*, which opened in April with less than a week for the cast to learn their lines. Set during the Serbo-Bulgarian war of 1885, it was, in Shaw's words, 'an apparently insane success', although he felt that the clever audience had misunderstood his satire, constrained as he was by the rules of contemporary theatre and the inability to write a 'decent last act'.[33] He had written the main part of Raina Petkoff with Farr in mind, but in the end, following the Todhunter disaster, Shaw relegated her to the stock role of the serving girl Louka, 'the only part that plays itself'.[34] Farr's managerial career may have been rescued (*Arms* ran until 7 July), but her time on the stage had been slight, and to many critics, an utter failure, her performance in *A Comedy of Sighs* 'panic-stricken from the outset', in *Arms and the Man* unnoticed.[35]

Alongside the Avenue Theatre run and her esoteric studies, Farr had also been trying to start a career as a novelist. Shaw had begun a play for her 'in the style of Victor Hugo', but as he was not giving much time to it, she responded in May 1893 by reading him parts of what would become *The Dancing Faun*.[36] It was a society piece, its theme the inherent staginess of life. Her debt to Oscar Wilde was substantial – she may have begun writing after seeing *A Woman of No Importance* following its debut that April. A prefatory note admits that owing to circumstances which had arisen since finishing the novel, 'it seems necessary to state that it is purely a work of the imagination'. The 'circumstances' in question may refer to her Avenue run with Shaw, with which many readers might have drawn parallels. There is more than a hint that the events of the plot came from her own life. Its villain is the womanizer George Travers, a clear Shaw/Emery stand-in who has married the young actress Grace Lovell and keeps her hidden away while attempting to seduce the affluent Lady Geraldine. Elements of Farr's own history recur in both women, who are constrained by marriage and social expectation. Grace desires to return to the stage, where she hopes that women 'may be something more than waxen masks of doll-like acquiescence', and rediscovers her pleasure in reading aloud from Shelley's *The Cenci* (Farr and Shaw had worked together on a performance of *The Cenci* for the Shelley Society in 1892). Meanwhile, Geraldine's view of marriage may suggest Farr's own desire for a life unfettered by wedlock: 'I think it's a degrading bargain, which can only be carried out by unlimited lying on both sides.' Given how deep Farr was in the GD in this period, it is notable that there is nothing outwardly occult about the book, beyond a few references to Egypt and to Geraldine being the 'high priestess of humour'.[37] It is wholly in service of Farr's public persona, for while stage acting and hermetic ritual had much in common, *The Dancing Faun* makes plain that Farr still desired more conventional social and artistic recognition.

On the advice of the poet Edward Carpenter, Farr sent the finished manuscript to both Fisher Unwin and Heinemann with the intention of playing them off each other, but the idea fell flat.[38] Instead, she tried another friend, John Lane, who ran the Bodley Head out of premises in Vigo Street, near the British Museum. Lane had recently agreed to publish *Keynotes*, a collection of short stories by George Egerton (pseudonym of the writer Mary Dunne), and was looking for a second book to continue a series of the same name, a mouthpiece for new and countercultural topics. With the ex-Rhymers' Club poet Richard Le Gallienne as reader and Aubrey Beardsley supplying black ink illustrations and 'key' designs made up of each author's initials, it is not difficult to see why *Keynotes* titles became inseparable from the avant-garde 'Yellow Nineties' zeitgeist. Its first ten volumes were mostly by unestablished writers, among them Egerton, Dostoevsky (*Poor Folk*) and Arthur Machen, whose *The Great God Pan and the Inmost Light* scandalized the mainstream press. Whether out of friendship or genuine admiration for Farr's talents, Lane accepted *The Dancing Faun*. 'It is always very pleasant to accept the MS of a new riter [sic],' he replied in January, 'but it is a double pleasure when the book happens to be by a friend but when one adds by a woman it baffles so poor a creature as a publisher to express adequate delight.'[39]

When *The Dancing Faun* was published in *Keynotes* in the summer of 1894, Farr briefly entered the world of literary decadence. The inaugural issue of Lane's quarterly house journal, *The Yellow Book*, had come out in April, emblazoned with Beardsley's playful covers. The periodical was intended to give public voice to the avant-garde, its contents half-mockingly reflecting the current obsession with everything that was 'new'.[40] Beardsley was becoming a minor celebrity in the wake of his work for Lane and his illustrations for the English-language edition of Oscar Wilde's banned play *Salome* earlier that year, and he used the cover of Farr's book to continue his punk rejection of his Victorian elders. James McNeill Whistler's Anglo-Japanese style was a major influence, and for *The Dancing Faun*'s title page Beardsley drew a monocled satyr in red and black ink, horns poking through Whistlerish hair, a bow on its pointed hoof redolent of the painter's extravagant dress.[41] Farr's title and Beardsley's illustrations might have led readers to expect a tale on fashionable pagan themes (as with Machen the same year, or Kenneth Grahame's *Pagan Papers* in 1893). A backhanded writeup in *The Athenaeum* called the novel 'crude and spasmodic', but ultimately praised it for the 'lurid power in the very unreality of the story'.[42] *The Bookman* found much less to admire: 'The book is the symptom of a malady to which the weaker-fibred writers of the present day are peculiarly susceptible ... The malady is not wickedness, though it is distressing to have to say so, but is rather a hysterical desire to be accounted wicked.'[43] Farr wrote a cheerful note to Lane, asking whether he might advertise the book a little more to increase sales. She worked on other literary projects, but none came to fruition. Did Farr begin the intended 'epoch-making' book of 120,000 words that she mentioned to Lane, which was to be divided into three sections 'Hell', 'Purgatory' and 'The Gates of Paradise', or was the idea discarded? The first draft of Farr's essay, then titled *New Woman*, was sent by Richard Le Gallienne to the editors of *The Realm* magazine: they thought it 'very clever, but are disinclined to print' due to the market's oversaturation of New Womanhood.[44]

CHAPTER 2

In the year that *The Dancing Faun* was written, Farr was made Praemonstratrix to Isis-Urania after Wescott resigned from the role.[45] Praemonstratrix was not merely a ceremonial office, but made Farr a teacher and instructor to the entire temple, responsible for ensuring that initiates were equipped to perform rituals correctly and for maintaining discipline, 'seeing that in it [the working of the First Order] nothing be relaxed or profaned'.[46] She had to be present at all Neophyte ceremonies, and at the biannual Equinox rituals she was to announce the names of the Officers of the Temple selected for the ritual workings over the following six-month period. During these rituals she was now permitted to wear the White Cross and Triangle on her left breast (signifying purification by Water) and a blue 'lamen', a magical pendant worn about the neck. She could also, if she chose, wield a sceptre 'surmounted by a Maltese Cross in the Elemental Colours', an important symbol for the GD because it represented the harmonious balance between the four elements.[47] With these changes to duties and dress code, Farr began to supply written lectures to the First Order in the form of more Flying Rolls, these on the cultivation of will and hermetic love. She took the disciplinary aspect of the role seriously enough to urge students to memorize their lines, evidence that she recognized the theatrical nature of the ceremonies. She even organized understudies:

> If you propose to continue the studies of the rituals, I should be glad if you would learn by heart the part of the Kerux in the Ritual of the 32nd path of the [word illegible] so as to be able to take part in it without the aid of a book until the time when the lights are turned up. I am also writing to other members so that we shall have 2 officers at least ready for each part of this important ritual.[48]

The promotion was a curious example of how members' non-occult activities might have influenced how they were treated

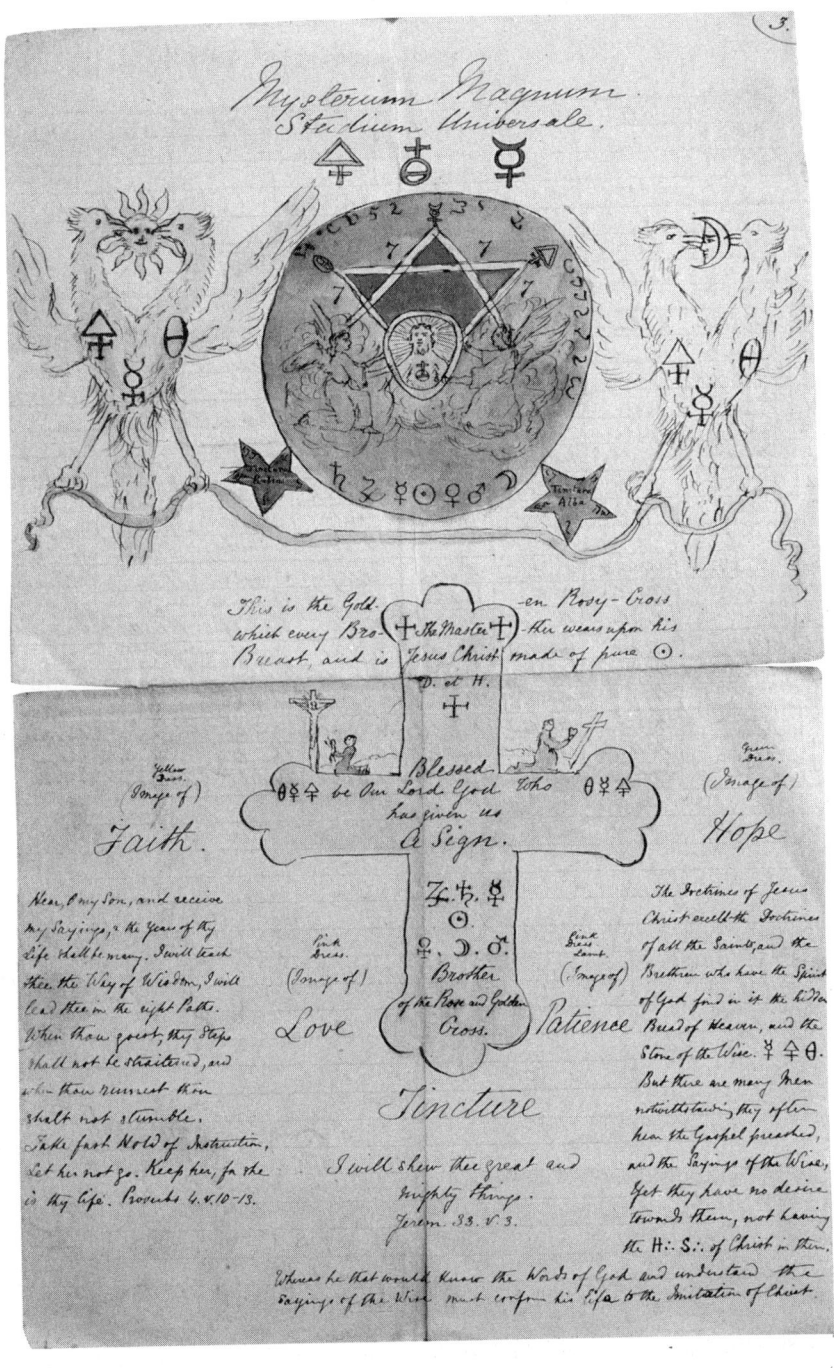

William Wynn Westcott, 'Rose-croix' lamen, 1888. Worn by adepts of the Second, or Inner, Order of the Golden Dawn.

within the GD. Had Mathers and Westcott observed Farr's management of the Avenue Theatre earlier that year and selected her for Praemonstratrix based on what they saw? It is not inconceivable: the two roles required instruction, direction and a central vision of how a scripted 'performance' was staged. Farr's public and esoteric lives were eliding.

Presumably motivated by her new role, Farr entered a fruitful period of hermetic scholarship. In 1893, under his masonic title 'Supreme Magus of the Rosicrucian Society', Westcott had begun editing a set of authoritative volumes on occult subjects, put out individually by the Theosophical Publishing Society. The series was called *Collectanea Hermetica*, and its authors used their GD mottos. Westcott authored most of the volumes himself, but allowed other students, including Percy Bullock (Isis-Urania) and Frank Coleman (Osiris), one book apiece. Farr produced three of the ten-volume set, a testament to Westcott's opinion of her abilities as a writer and teacher. Alchemy was her chosen speciality for a brief time: in October 1893, at the same time as transcribing Mathers's tract on Enochian magic *The Book of the Concourse of the Forces*, complete with watercolour illustrations of Egyptian deities, she was also finishing work (perhaps concurrently with *The Dancing Faun*) on what would become the third in Westcott's series, an edition of the 1714 alchemical text *A Short Enquiry concerning the Hermetic Art*.[49] Her introduction stressed the importance of imagination in the alchemical process, 'the development and intensification of an idea' strengthened into 'an act of Will'.[50] Farr's next contribution was a commentary on a seventeenth-century alchemical text by Thomas Vaughan, *Euphrates, or the Waters of the East*. Vaughan, claimed by Westcott in a preface as a 'Rosicrucian Adept', wrote *Euphrates* not as a how-to guide for what he called the 'torture of Metals', but rather as a reflection on nature and its relation to the spirit.[51] Farr had laboriously transcribed the 1655 manuscript and brought a breadth of scholarship to her commentary, teasing out what she saw as Vaughan's intrinsically Kabbalistic view of the universe. 'I have read many Alchemical Treatises, but never one of less use to the practical Alchemist, than this', she concludes in a final note.

'At the same time I have come across few occult works that have helped me more in my search for the secrets of these Great Adepts – who are the Masters of our Race.'[52]

The eighth volume of Westcott's *Hermetica* series, *Egyptian Magic* (1896), is the best and most extensive example of Farr's growing obsession with ancient Egyptian ritual and belief, which would continue to occupy her even after she had left the GD behind. Within the hermetic system, Egyptian magic was closely linked with the symbolism of alchemy, providing a natural intellectual path for Farr to follow. Its allure was irresistible to many esoteric movements of the late nineteenth century, triggered by exciting archaeological discoveries and given occult significance in books such as Éliphas Lévi's *Dogme et rituel* (1854–56) and Jean-Baptiste Pitois's *Histoire de la magie* (1870).[53] Both emphasized ancient Egypt's arcane importance to interpreting the secrets of the world. For theosophists especially, it was fundamental to the idea of a universal hidden doctrine: Blavatsky argued inventively that all magical sciences, including alchemy, Kabbalah and Neo-Platonism, could trace their origins to Egypt and the cult of the god Thoth. The Hermetic Brotherhood of Luxor also claimed to have ancient Egyptian roots. The GD, to some extent adopting the theosophical view, was itself steeped in rituals and symbolism adapted by Mathers from recent translations of funerary texts and C. W. Goodwin's study of the Greco-Egyptian magical papyri. Only one member, M. W. Blackden, ever actually went to Egypt to visit the archaeological sites there, having volunteered for the Egypt Exploration Fund during the early 1890s.[54]

Farr read widely in the new fields of British and continental Egyptology, and in 1895 was spending weeks in the British Museum Reading Room poring over recent scholarship, walking through the Egyptian Gallery and painting figures of gods and goddesses. Frederick Leigh Gardner, a friend and fellow GD member, had paid her to produce a set of four in the likenesses of those used in First Order ceremonies.[55] An appendix to *Egyptian Magic* provides a good indication of what Farr had been reading, ranging from more general works by the Egyptologist Flinders Petrie and the prolific but unreliable British Museum curator E. A. Wallis Budge, to in-depth studies of sarcophagi and the Gnostic gospels. Westcott's personal library for the use of GD members also contained several key works from earlier in the century, notably on the interpretation of hieroglyphics. The book focuses on an idea that was clearly very appealing to Farr, and which accorded with her understanding of the GD's own brand of hermeticism: that the physical and spirit worlds are linked by a system of correspondences. 'In studying Egyptian Magic one has at once a thoroughly scientific satisfaction,' she wrote. 'One is troubled with no vague theories, but receives precise practical details; we observe that every square inch of the Upper and Under Worlds is mapped out.'[56] It opens with a hand-drawn hieroglyphic chart detailing the parts of a human being and their symbolic counterparts: for example a fish (*khat* or *kat*) representing the body, and the radiating sun (*hammemit*) the unborn soul. Farr expanded on the concept of 'Ka', the principal aspect of the soul in ancient Egyptian religion (which she equates with Ego), a kind of spirit 'double' that could be perfected through the magical cultivation of Thought and Will.[57]

Egyptian Magic, with its obscure terminology and references to Westcott's Kabbalah research in the journal *Lucifer*, was directed first at GD students for guidance in their own practices, second at the wider occult community. It was not written with the general public in mind. It was Farr's manifesto, as Soror S.S.D.D., for the importance of Egypt in current ritualism. Beyond metaphysics, Farr was also concerned with more straightforward questions of what ancient Egyptian magic might have looked like. What kind of rituals had magicians performed? How did these correspond with the GD system of grades and initiation? To answer these questions, she quoted excerpts from translations of Egyptian stories by Flinders Petrie: his 'Tales of the Magicians' feature mages who channel the powers of the gods, whose words, for Farr, resembled present-day invocations or summonings.

Shaw had been trying with increasing desperation to steer Farr away from the 'unreality' of her occultism, but the publication of *Egyptian Magic* tipped him over the edge. 'And now you think to undo the work of all those years by a phrase and a shilling's work of exoteric Egyptology,' he wrote to her disbelievingly in October: 'I can no longer wait for you: onward must I go.'[58] His replies over the following two days suggest that Farr tried to win him back, but he condemns her for being irresponsible and living only for herself. 'I hereby warn mankind to beware of women with large eyes, and crescent eyebrows, and a smile, and a love of miracles and moonshees ... I renounce spiritual intercourse with you.'[59] But something had changed, too, in Farr's enthusiasm for her usual GD activities. It was around this time that she confided in Gardner that she was 'thinking of chucking the whole thing', and that he should let Westcott know.[60] 'I do not work on G.D. lines & I am only keeping on until I have seen one or two more people through 5=6.' Shaw's words may have made her think twice, or perhaps her managerial success with *Arms and the Man* had revitalized her aspirations for a proper career on the London stage. But Farr would not act in another of Shaw's plays: her time as his protégée had come to an end.

The research for *Egyptian Magic* led to two major developments in Florence Farr's career in the Order, both of which would lead to dissatisfaction and dissent among GD members. The first was the encounter with the Chantress. There were, and still are, an array of mummies on display in the Egyptian Gallery of the British Museum. Farr came to believe that she had made contact with Mutemmenu, Chantress of Amun, described by Wallis Budge in his catalogue of 1904 as a 'lady of the college of the God Amen-Ra at Thebes', mummified in around 100 BCE.[61] Scans of Mutemmenu carried out in the 1960s and more recently have revealed the mummy to be a man, heavy padding in the chest and thighs giving him a feminine appearance.[62] The coffin belonging to the Chantress of Amun had been reused during the Roman period, which explains the confusion.

While walking through the Third Egyptian Room, Farr would have seen the mummy through glass, positioned on its back, head resting on a pillow found with it in its coffin (the coffin itself, made of wood rather than the carved stone of sarcophagi, was displayed in the Second Room). How or why she was first drawn to the mummy is not

Isabelle de Steiger, 'A Neophyte in the Astral', from the *Unknown World*, 15 April 1895.

known, but it led to a communication with a personality she would later refer to as the 'Egyptian Adept'. Writing to John Brodie-Innes during the later GD crisis, Farr explains how she had sent a 'charged drawing' of the Egyptian figure to Mathers, along with an account of her experience with Mutemmenu. Farr asked him whether she had not been deceived by the Adept, who had claimed to be 'equal in rank to an 8–3 of our order' and had provided her with numbers that she had later calculated to be 'correct for that grade'.[63] Mathers had apparently replied at length in January confirming the Adept's status and approving Farr's request that she might begin magical work with her (the Adept). Farr should also make offerings to her, Mathers suggested, so that 'all would be well'.[64] To discover what kind of offerings she was to make to Mutemmenu, she placed two watercolour and pastel portraits of the Egyptian inside a decorated wooden box. 'She was the keeper of Documents connected with the Mystic Order and was in a position of authority,' Farr recorded in March 1896 during a scrying session with Westcott and Annie Horniman. 'She will not be of so much use to me in my mental Studies as in Magical Physical work.'[65]

To make contact with an Adept was an important revelation for Farr, for the Magister Templi (8° = 3°) grade was attainable only by a magician who had surpassed the Second Order and now occupied the astral plane: this meant that she had communicated with a Secret Chief of the Third Order. Whatever evidence she had offered to Mathers had been sufficient to overcome what might have been viewed as an attempt to override his authority. So far in the GD's short history, only the conveniently dead Fräulein Sprengel and the Matherses had claimed to have received instructions from the Secret Chiefs. While Farr's Egyptian Chantress was on the lowest rung of the Third Order ladder, it was nevertheless a major step.

With Mathers's permission attained, possibly in January 1896, Farr assembled a group of three Second Order members of the Theoricus grade, Allan Bennett, Charles Rosher and Frederick Leigh Gardner, each of whom she knew would be amenable to Egypt-based magic (Gardner especially; like Farr, he was a theosophist, interested in alchemy and Egyptian symbolism). This was the first of several iterations of an Egypt sub-group spearheaded by Farr, a secret society within the already secret Second Order that experimented in spiritual invocations using Farr's astral contact. The twenty-three-year-old Bennett ('Iehi Aour', 'Let there be light'), an intense and experienced GD student who was often ill, was keen to use the opportunity to write his own occult formula; several years later he would become Aleister Crowley's roommate and tutor. Bennett and Farr conceived of a plan to invoke Taphthartharath, the spirit of the planet Mercury. Bennett composed the ritual with care; apparently aware of the potential danger of such a summoning, he also prepared in advance a 'Hellbroth' as 'physical pabulum [food]' for the spirit, 'which will more than double our chances of getting him materialized'. 'If you could bring that snake and some of the other ingredients to Headquarters [Clipstone Street] Friday afternoon when the Council is to be held,' Bennett instructed Gardner in early May, 'I will be there to receive them. You know that you must not *talk* to anyone save us three of the work we are about to do. It would greatly weaken us.'[66] His shopping list also included half a pound of spermaceti with which to fashion a 'Magic Candle', so that he would be able to read in the darkened room. Then, several days later, he conveyed the alarming news that 'S.S.D.D. Rosher and myself' had been struck down by 'grim and horrible' diseases, though he did not elaborate and Farr made no mention of the setback.[67] Was this Taphthartharath preventing the group from summoning it? The invocation itself was to be performed 'on the day and in the hour of Mercury', most likely Wednesday 13 May, a little after 8.30 pm. During the ceremony Farr, in her chief role as 'Magus of Art', wielding an Ibis wand and an Ankh of Thoth, took on the 'godform' of Thoth, and with the same impassioned delivery that had once enraptured Shaw and Yeats in Bedford Park, recited the lines written for her by Bennett:

'The Sign of Silence (Harpocrates)',
from *The Equinox*, vol. I, no. 1, 21 March 1909.

CHAPTER 2

O thou Great Potent Spirit Taphthartharath, I do command and very potently conjure thee by the Majesty of Thoth, the Great God, Lord of Amenta, King and Lord Eternal of the Magic of Light:

> That Thou do teach us continually the Mysteries of the Art of Magic, declaring unto us now in what best manner may each of us progress towards the accomplishment of the Great Work. Teach us the Mysteries of all the Hidden Arts and Sciences which are under the Dominion of Mercury, and finally swear Thou by the Great Magic Sigil that I hold in my hand, that Thou wilt in future always speedily appear before us ... to the end that thou mayest be a perpetual link of communication between the Great God Thoth and ourselves.[68]

According to Bennett's script and account, the entirety of which appeared in Crowley's magazine *The Equinox* in 1910, the Angel of Mercury was conjured and bound within the 'magical figures' traced on the floor. The spirit was then threatened with curses, and subjected to a 'Stronger and More Potent Conjuration' while Bennett drew symbols using the Hell-broth.[69] After many more pages (at which point the spirit, who had come and gone several times, had fully materialized), Farr 'formulate[d] the desires' and offered a final admonition while Rosher burned incense in the corner. It was complete. Taphthartharath departed.

Just how 'Egyptian' was this ritual? Thoth is clearly an important figure throughout the invocation, though it is difficult to see how Farr might have been working with her Adept, if at all. It may have been that she believed it to be working *through* her. It is also hard to guess just how much of her research into Egyptian magic Farr had passed onto Bennett while he was writing the conjuration, but it seems that she inserted passages from *The Book of the Dead*.[70] Other Egyptian deities besides Thoth are invoked – 'I am Ra incarnate,' Farr declaimed at one point, 'Kephra [a scarab god] created in the flesh!' – alongside archangels, Odin and Hermes, indicating the usual GD hermetic approach of compounding Hermes/Thoth into the Hermes Trismegistus avatar of occult history. Whether or not the group felt they had succeeded, the ritual was an impressive act of creative imagination based on Farr's research and Bennett's talent for composition.

Westcott withdrew completely from the GD in 1897 after his ritual activities were made known to 'State officers', almost certainly by a paranoid Mathers, thereby threatening his professional career as a coroner.[71] Following this Mathers promoted Farr once again, this time to his chief representative 'in Anglia'.[72] The unexpected move was surely a sign of Farr's loyalty to the Imperator, a way for Mathers to maintain control over the British temples from abroad. After their summoning of Mercury and perhaps other, similar experiments that were not recorded, the make-up and purpose of the Egypt group changed. Farr's account, related to Brodie-Innes in 1901, suggests that she continued to work with the three Theorici in secret, perhaps with renewed vigour now that her role was secured, and that they resolved to carry out a plan suggested to them by the Adept. Meditating on the symbol of the 'globular sephiroth' (the Kabbalistic Tree of Life), Farr's design was for the group to mentally project the *sefirot* once every Sunday, first placing it 'over the Order', then the planet, growing steadily larger until it became like a constellation 'on the visible universe'. Invoking the light from the topmost *sefira* of the tree, known as *kether*, the crown, they would proceed to direct this guiding light towards every sphere that had been formulated, reversing the process and thus bathing each astral plane in *kether*'s 'spirit of light and growth'.[73] Her Egyptian Adept would occupy the centre. At this point the membership of the 'Sphere' group seems to have expanded to a round dozen, although on a list provided by Robert Felkin in 1902 the names of Bennett, Gardner and Rosher are distinctly absent (Farr and Gardner had fallen out after she accused him of undignified and rude behaviour during rituals, and he resigned from Isis-Urania in 1897). It may in fact have been a different group altogether; but much like the Egypt group, it was clearly an extremely ambitious and time-consuming project away from strict GD ritual, and one whose aims were not shared by certain other members of the Second Order. While these astral practices were going on, Farr began to detect 'a considerable prejudice against Egyptian symbolism' among the other GD students and decided not to advertise her group any further. This did nothing to curtail the coming storm.

The second major creative exposure for GD members occurred in 1899, with the first public performance of Yeats's *The Countess Cathleen*, which was part of the opening season of the Irish Literary Theatre in Dublin. The original verse drama, set during a famine in rural Ireland, tells of a wealthy countess who sells her soul to a group of demons to save the peasantry from starvation. She dies, her soul borne away by angelic spirits to the 'floors of peace'.[74] The play had gone through two iterations since 1889, when Yeats had first read a draft of it aloud to Farr, and now Yeats's fellow playwright Edward Martyn, whose *The Heather Field* was to be staged alongside *Cathleen*, was concerned that audiences' potentially allegorical reading would stir controversy: the demons as scheming Protestant Englishmen, the countess the sacrificial redeemer of a starving Ireland.[75] In the end this aspect was to the play's advantage, and helped drum up anticipation. Yeats appointed Farr general stage manager for the run and cast her as Aleel, a poet. Cathleen (originally written with Maud Gonne in mind) would be played by the West End actress May Whitty. George Moore, who had been in attendance five years before at the Avenue Theatre first night, was now a reluctant sponsor, and took a very dim view of Farr during rehearsals. 'I found Yeats behind some scenery in the act of explanation to the mummers, whilst the lady in the green cloak [Farr], seated on the ground, plucked the wires, muttering the line "Cover it up with a lonely tune".' He recalled derisively the way she lay down on the floor mid-scene and began speaking through the floorboards: 'I had to ask her what it was, and learnt from her that she was evoking hell.'[76] As satirical as Moore's account is, it is also further evidence for

Farr's appearance of otherworldliness and seeming disconnection from those who encountered her, her mystical approach to her work evident even outside the confines of the GD.

'Miss Florence Farr was a charming Aleel. Hers is the best delivery of verse that we have heard upon the modern stage; and Miss Dorothy Paget, who was the Sheogue, also spoke the prologue tastefully,' wrote the *Irish Daily Independent* in what turned out to be the dissenting voice in a sea of negative reviews.[77] Yeats's intention with the Theatre had been to 'spiritualise the patriotism' of Ireland, and as such, *Cathleen* was dragged into debates about Fenian nationalism and Pan-Celticism. The audience, however, had been broadly enthusiastic, and spurred Yeats and Martyn on to start planning a second production. Yeats was contented: his new collection *The Wind among the Reeds*, replete with magical symbolism and motifs from Irish legend, had been published that same year by Elkin Mathews, and he continued to find hope in his astral-infused relations with Maud Gonne. But fresh conflict in the GD was brewing, and both he and Farr (who now felt that the Irish Theatre project was 'depressing her energy') were about to become main actors in the ensuing drama. Annie Horniman had been expelled in 1896, following Mathers's demand for complete submission from his Adepts, and although he took Annie's side, Yeats had continued to visit Paris to formulate rituals relating to the Celtic Mysteries with the Imperator.[78] The Matherses, however, were becoming increasingly distracted by the possibilities of Egyptian magic (unconnected with Farr's group), and their project to build and decorate a new Temple of Isis in Paris was their chief focus. Yeats remembered Mathers at this time as living 'in a world of phantoms', and wrote that his ritual activities appeared to take a physical toll: 'Every Sunday he gave to the evocations of spirits, and I noted that upon that day he would spit blood.'[79] He also drank too much brandy, performed sword dances as part of his Jacobite posturing and began to prophesy seismic changes in global politics, learning 'ambulance work' in preparation for a war he considered imminent.[80] His various peculiarities were mostly tolerated by the Order, seen as 'necessary' to its workings, but following his expulsion of Horniman, Mathers's

Moina Mathers as the High Priestess Anari,
from the Ritual of Isis, Paris, 1899.

Samuel Liddell MacGregor Mathers as the Hierophant Rameses, from the Ritual of Isis, Paris, 1899.

hold on the GD was in danger of slipping. It was Farr who eventually forced his hand.

In January 1900, now back in England, Farr sent Mathers a letter (unfortunately lost) that seems to have included a request that the Isis-Urania Temple be dissolved and Farr allowed to resign from her position as his representative in England. Mathers responded a month later with a long, itemized letter, firstly accusing her of discussing his private affairs with GD members and secondly refusing both her resignation and her request to close Isis-Urania. His reply suggests, rather astonishingly, that Westcott was claiming to have made contact with the Secret Chiefs (either recently, or at the same time as Mathers), and that a new secret group or 'schism' had been formed under his leadership. 'For this forces me to tell you plainly,' wrote Mathers, evidently hoping that what he had to say would quash Farr's plans for dissent:

> He [Westcott] has NEVER been *at any time* either in personal or in written communication with the Secret Chiefs of the Order, he having *either himself forged or procured to be forged* the professed correspondence between him and them, and my tongue having been tied all these years by a previous Oath of Secrecy to him, demanded by him, from me, before showing me what he had either done or caused to be done or both ... I again reiterate that *every atom* of the knowledge of the Order has come *through me alone* from 0–0 to 5–6 inclusive.[81]

To a reader unfamiliar with the hierarchies of occult orders, Mathers's accusation may not seem existential in its effect. But to Order members it amounted to the shattering of the GD's very basis. The originating documents, the letters from Fräulein Sprengel containing permissions for the creation of the Isis-Urania Temple, had been faked. It was as if a religious leader whose cult had been founded on divine revelation had just exposed that revelation as a sham. Mathers did not pull the entire rug out from under the GD, however: the Secret Chiefs still existed, but they relayed their instructions through him alone. This was designed to suppress any uprisings or attempted magical offshoots. If the (already retired) Westcott's occult authority was removed, then Mathers would have absolute power over the Order. The ensuing letters between Farr and Mathers further convey the Imperator's state of mind. In most accounts of this short period he becomes a bodiless voice of paranoia, a spirit from the astral plane attempting to play students off one another and to preserve allegiances. Farr showed other Second Order members his letters, and a committee made up of Farr, Edmund and Dorothea Hunter, Yeats, M. W. Blackden and Percy Bullock was formed to investigate Mathers's shocking claims. A letter from Bullock ('Levavi Oculos', 'I lift up my eyes') to Mathers describes their motive:

> We find ourselves in the position of having lent ourselves – and such influence as our long connection with the Order may constitute – to the dissemination of ideas, traditions or actual teaching to others who have come into the Order after us, and it is consequently with deep concern that we now gather reflection is cast on some of them.[82]

Mathers wrote to Farr forbidding the committee and removing her from her position as his representative, 'for I can no longer feel confidence in you as such'.[83] The committee approached Westcott several times about the Sprengel letters, but the venerable mason deflected their enquiries: he could not legally prove anything, he said, because his witnesses from that time (chiefly William Woodman) were dead.[84] They also requested Mathers's attendance at a meeting of 24 March, but he would not come. Without evidence to the contrary, Bullock was forced to conclude that the Sprengel documents had indeed been forged, and that Mathers, having been aware of this fact, had himself 'condoned a felony'.[85]

The improbable events which occurred over the next several weeks are commonly referred to as the Battle of Blythe Road, and mark the point at which a young Aleister Crowley enters the main GD narrative. 'I have had a bad time of it lately,' Yeats confided in Lady Gregory in late April. 'I told you I was putting MacGregor out of the Kabbala.

Aleister Crowley as Osiris, n.d.

Well last week he sent a mad person – whom we had refused to initiate – to take possession of the rooms and papers of the society.'[86] Crowley, a wealthy Cambridge graduate, poet, mountaineer and aspiring student of black magic, had taken the Neophyte ritual in late 1898 under Farr's guidance, but had been denied entry into the Second Order because of his reputation for arrogance and rumours of sexual liaison with GD students (including with Farr herself, though there is no evidence to back this up). He was not the kind of person they wanted to be training as a magician. It soon transpired, however, that he had befriended Mathers and been permitted to take the vault ceremony at the Ahathoor Temple set up by the Matherses in Paris in 1894. His advancement not recognized by Isis-Urania. In early 1900 he pledged himself to Mathers, and together they formulated a plan to send Crowley to London as an 'emissary' to retrieve what Mathers regarded as stolen property, including manuscripts and temple furniture, from 36 Blythe Road in Hammersmith. Crowley would then summon each rebel Adept to be interviewed, and interrogate them about their allegiance to Mathers. Events never progressed this far. After managing to break into the Second Order rooms on 16 April with the aid of Elaine Simpson (Farr's old astral projection partner and his then-lover) and changing the locks, Crowley returned two days later to the scene of the crime 'in Highland dress, a black mask over his face, and a plaid thrown over his head and shoulders, an enormous gold or gilt cross on his breast, and a dagger at his side'.[87] He had paid a bouncer from a Leicester Square pub as intimidation, but before the man could show up Crowley was confronted by Yeats and Edmund Hunter. Farr rented the Blythe Road rooms, but it was Yeats who lay in wait for Crowley and called the police. A frantic Crowley took the matter to the courts, but promptly withdrew the case and was obliged to pay legal fees of five pounds. Thus the battle, described by Hunter as Mathers's 'contemptible theatrical farce', was ended.[88]

Mathers had to go. A meeting was held on 21 April at which it was decided that the GD would no longer recognize him as Chief of the Order.[89] A reformulation of the structure of the Second Order followed, with Farr elected as 'Moderator', Edmund Hunter as 'Warden' and Annie Horniman brought back as 'Scribe' (each position to be nominated annually). Seven Adepti Litterati were also appointed, a team of scholars that included Yeats as instructor in mystical philosophy. Despite a long month of occult crises, Yeats was back at work on *The Speckled Bird* by the end of April, adding more characters resembling GD students, and forming future plans for the Irish Literary Theatre, including editing issues of its accompanying journal, *Beltaine*.[90] His ritual-based poem *The Shadowy Waters* was going to be published by Hodder & Stoughton. Farr was also continuing her creative and hermetic endeavours. Without *Collectanea Hermetica* to showcase her treatises (an unfortunate casualty of Westcott's retirement), her elucidation of the Hebrew alphabet was released instead by the occult publisher J. M. Watkins as a small pamphlet titled *The Way of Wisdom*. Based on her research into Near Eastern civilizations other than Egypt, Farr's study suggested a Chaldean source for the meaning behind Hebrew letters. In preparation she may have read the archaeologist François Lenormant's *Chaldean Magic: Its Origin and Development*, which discussed the Assyrian-Babylonian cuneiform tablets known as Evil Spirit texts; it is also likely that she followed Westcott's 1895 edition of *The Chaldæan Oracles of Zoroaster* (*Hermetica* vol. VI, with an introduction by Percy Bullock comparing Chaldean and Kabbalistic philosophies).[91] But neither Farr nor Yeats had much time to breathe after Mathers's expulsion: further crises within the Second Order were already on the horizon.

Without the guiding figurehead of Mathers, whose 'artificial support' and 'vigorous and imaginative personality' Yeats had once considered essential to the GD's existence, the Order was now struggling to maintain its unity of purpose.[92] Annie Horniman was on the prowl to detect further wrongdoing and dissent from the official GD line. She had become aware of Farr's sub-group during her exile, and of another group formed for different purposes by Brodie-Innes in Edinburgh, and she considered them potentially harmful to the Order's workings. In 1898 an unnamed Soror of the Zelator (1° = 10°) grade had approached Horniman with one of the 'Sphere' diagrams, asking for help in interpreting its meaning. Recognizing that the diagram did not come from the GD teachings, Horniman identified an error in its composition, as well as 'one most serious omission': the symbol let in an imbalance of force (rather than spreading it out across the higher and lower spheres). In Horniman's eyes, this amounted to 'faulty' ritualism to the extent that 'evil forces' would gain entry, and she wrote to Farr with her misgivings. Farr, presumably in a bid to flatter Horniman into silence, offered her a central role if she would join the group. Horniman declined. 'Much later when in the British Museum I had by chance felt a force which was not harmonious to my nature coming from a small statue which I found to be that of their Adept.'[93] She concluded that Farr's Egyptian contact was a harmful influence – for both disciplinary and occult reasons – and that the astral symbol, should it be allowed to remain active, was 'still capable of injuring and perhaps destroying the Order'. Horniman had also cast a scrutinizing eye over the administration of the GD and found it to be falling short of Mathers's usual rigorous standards. As Chief Adept Farr had allowed unconstitutional changes to Portal ceremonies, had failed to properly record examinations and membership lists and had approved the design of an alternative Tree of Life diagram (or 'Minitum Mundum') for the convenience of the Egypt group. She had also made arrangements for a candidate to be initiated privately, in a location other than the Order rooms.[94] Most outrageous to Horniman, besides the existence of the Egypt group, was the apparent abandonment of the 5° = 6° Adeptus Minor examination. It was Mathers who had ordered this change sometime in 1897, because he claimed to have seen the 'practical imperfection of the system in dividing the fit from the unfit', so in this respect at least Farr was not entirely culpable.[95]

Why had Isis-Urania been allowed to fall into such disarray under Farr's leadership? Before his retirement Westcott had performed all clerical duties, mostly out of personal enthusiasm, and Farr, it seems, had been unwilling or unable to follow his example. Perhaps it was unfair of Horniman to find fault in every aspect of an organization whose three founding chiefs were dead, inactive or out of the country, but Farr's idea of an ethereal Adeptship '*in* the world ... but not *of* it' was also to blame. Farr now had much to answer for. Horniman kept demanding new information in individual letters: in 1900 Farr complained of having to go through the Examination Books on four separate occasions 'for information which anyone could have got from the Roll and at an address book at one sitting'.[96]

Meanwhile, Yeats's efforts to establish the Irish Literary Theatre were proving an uphill struggle, pulled as he was in different directions by Maud Gonne's anti-imperial politics (including her pro-Boer campaign) and the uncertainty of the theatre's financial backers.[97] He had also continued to write drafts of *The Speckled Bird* and to revise *The Countess Cathleen*. Early in 1901, after his return from Ireland, Horniman confronted Yeats, imploring him to support her in the conflict. Yeats, who considered Horniman a potential backer for his Irish theatre, sided with her. Official statements were written and frantic letters of justification were circulated. Henceforth the Egyptian 'Sphere' students were referred to collectively as the 'group' in GD documents. Farr found herself the target of a slew of accusations, mostly levelled by Horniman and most of which seemed like mere bureaucratic nit-picking (for instance the rooms at Blythe Road being always in use by the 'group'), but which in the case of the faulty diagram amounted to aspersions of allowing *evil* to penetrate the GD. In a defiant conclusion to a letter to Brodie-Innes, Farr doubled down:

> SSDD wishes to say that any Member of the Order who feels sympathy either for the study of the Egyptian Book of the Dead or for the symbolism of the Tree of Life projected onto a Sphere will be very welcome to join her group on their attainment of the grade of Theoricus. Yours under the wings of the eternal O.[98]

Horniman felt herself betrayed once again, after all she had been through with Mathers. Since Farr and Yeats were now on opposing sides, both their theatrical and esoteric relationships threatened to snap. 'We can make great movement and in more than magical things,' Yeats was writing to a resolute Farr, possibly sometime in January 1901, 'but I assure you that if (through weak vitality, through forgetfulness or through any other cause) you make it difficult for us to rely upon one another perfectly you make all of this impossible'.[99]

Officiously detailed, Horniman's account of the Council meeting which took place on 1 February 1901 is a heavily biased source, but it nevertheless offers a visceral picture of the animosity on display that evening between the pro-group Council members on the one hand, and Horniman and Yeats on the other. Its tone, and the actions of participating members, resemble the petty squabbles of a parish council or Parent–Teacher Association meeting. Horniman had brought a resolution for a scheme whereby the Council would nominate their own replacements, inspired by the Fabians, but this idea was contested by Blackden and Robert Palmer Thomas (Sub-Imperator). Horniman considered this an 'organised attack' egged on by Farr and other pro-groupers. The agenda then turned to the main item in hand. Horniman asked the room where her suspicions had come from, to which in the ensuing babble of replies she heard Farr call out 'They came from your own mind, Fortifer'. Horniman was asked to defend the charge that she had accused Farr's 'group' of harbouring evil intentions. At this juncture Yeats rose and made a speech 'which by its beauty enforced silence but it fell on the ears of an audience who were on a different plane of thought'. It was Farr whose turn it was to speak next and, according to Horniman, she demanded of Yeats 'who and what are *you* in the Order', perhaps meaning to accuse the poet of disloyalty. The meeting came to an end after a motion was put forward as to whether the 'groups' should be legalized and allowed to continue – that 'no one of any seniority or grade is to be allowed to make any enquiries or to see after the working of members in any way'. Groups were now to be encouraged and, in Horniman's words, 'the Order merely used as a screen' for their unorthodox activities. She and Yeats lost the vote 2–6, and a second meeting was scheduled for three weeks' time.

Yeats had sided with Horniman not simply out of financial canniness, but because he too disapproved of the way Farr had been running things in Mathers's absence. Yeats naturally wanted to uphold the strict hierarchy of the GD's grade system, to separate the lower students from the higher with a veneer of secrecy. To his mind the Egypt groups allowed members who were not yet Adepts to influence the wider GD without being beholden to its codes. He considered them a hangover from Mathers's authoritarian rule and a threat to the revelatory structure of the Order. The day after the Council meeting he wrote the first in a series of three open letters addressed 'to the Adepti of R.R. et A.C. upon the Present Crisis', in which he gave an account of the situation as he saw it, condemning Palmer Thomas for his behaviour towards Horniman and asking for his resignation. With this letter and the later two, he hoped to encourage non-Executive Second Order members to express their own objections to the groups. In a shorter note distributed to the Twelve Seniors on the same day, he effectively resigned from his position on the Council: 'I am ready to teach anything I know of magical philosophy to any fratres and sorores who may desire; but I shall take no other part in the business of the Second Order until its moral health has been restored.'[100]

Yeats's last attempt to bring the rebel majority around to his view was to privately print and distribute the pamphlet *Is the Order of R.R. et A.C. to remain a Magical Order?* to all Second Order members in April. In it he continued to argue for the importance of the ascending grade system, running from Neophyte to the highest degrees, and its correspondence with the descent from above 'symbolised by the Lightning Flash among the sacred leaves'. It was an elaborate restatement of his and Horniman's position, but it was also Yeats's defence of a society that had absorbed him for the past decade, that had supplied him with structure and ritual for his Celtic Mysteries and brought him closer to Maud Gonne. His conception of the GD as a working whole is conveyed by the effective (and hermetic) symbol of the body: the Order was an 'Actual Being', and to weaken its structure by the existence of dissenting 'groups' was 'to dislimn, to disembody' and 'to cut this being in two':

To do this last thing is to create an evil symbol, to make the most evil of all symbols, to awake the energy of an evil sorcery. On the other hand, to create within this Order, within this Actual Being formal 'groups', centres of astral activity, which are not the Degrees of this Order, the organs of this Being, is to create centres of life, which are centres of death, to this greater life; astral diseases sapping up, as it were, its vital fluids.

The year 1902 was to produce a wave of GD resignations, but not for reasons of infighting. Two years previously, Mathers had been visited in Paris by three American occultists who had borrowed rituals and books and had attended Ahathoor Temple meetings. One of the group, a woman calling herself Mrs Horos, managed to convince Mathers that she was channelling the dead Madame Blavatsky and perhaps may even have been the real Fräulein Sprengel.[101] Mrs Horos and her husband then appeared in London, where they tried unsuccessfully to infiltrate Isis-Urania. In September 1901, they were finally arrested on charges of 'procurement for immoral purposes' of three young women. Theo Horos was charged with raping one of the women, a sixteen-year-old who believed that she was being initiated into the GD.[102] The couple had the Neophyte Initiation ritual in their possession at the time of their arrest, and as a result the Order of the Golden Dawn name appeared in newspapers for weeks, linked with their criminal activities. Many students, including John Todhunter and Henrietta Paget, seem to have left the Order as a direct result.

Farr also resigned, but the Horos scandal may not have been the only cause. Sometime in 1901, as Robert Felkin later recalled, Farr explained to the twelve group members that her Egyptian had withdrawn from them, 'the reason being that he was changing his place on the higher planes and could no longer work with us'.[103] Instead, in a move from Farr towards the Arthurian tradition, the group's 'sphere' symbol was replaced by an image of the Holy Grail – the legendary cup superimposed onto the Tree of Life. But tired of the internal politics, unwilling to fight any longer for what seemed a reduced reward, Farr eventually jumped ship. 'I joined the Theosophical about a fortnight ago,' she wrote on 8 July 1902.[104] The Theosophical Society must have seemed tame compared to Farr's final years in the Order, but the change of pace was probably welcome. Although 1902 marked the end of her involvement with the GD, she would not leave the occult behind. Happily, her relationship with Yeats survived the turmoil – 'an enduring friendship that was an enduring exasperation'.[105] The pair had already begun to collaborate in a very different kind of art.

1 Moina Mathers, portrait of Samuel Liddell MacGregor Mathers, *c.* 1895.

11 Symbolic design for the lid of the Pastos in the vault of the Adepts, c. 1895

III Divination wheel used by William Wynn Westcott, 1892.

IV Warrant of the Isis-Urania Temple, London, c. 1888. Illustrations by Moina Mathers.

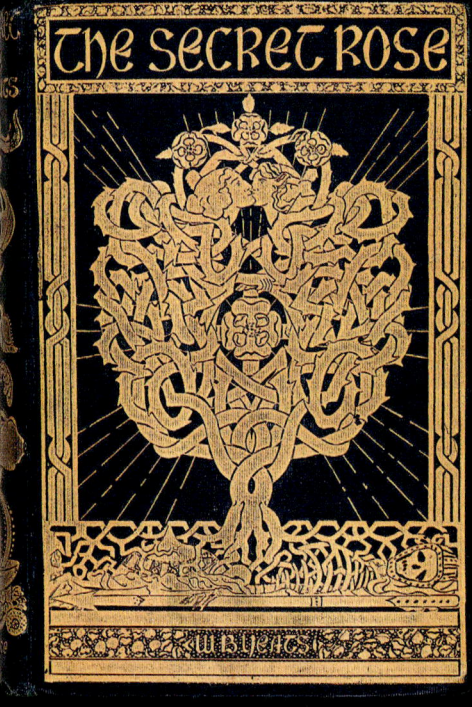

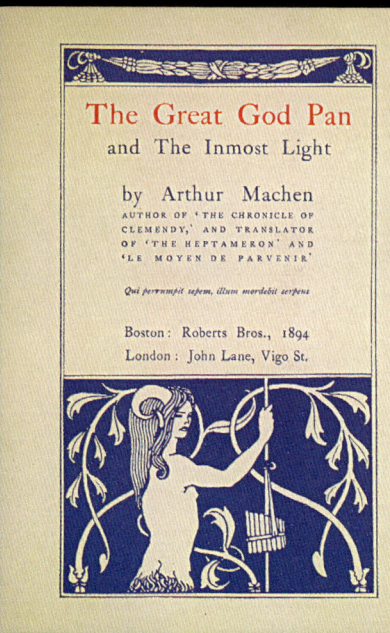

CLOCKWISE, FROM TOP LEFT: **V** Althea Gyles, cover of W. B. Yeats, *The Secret Rose*, 1897.
VI Aubrey Beardsley, cover of Florence Farr, *The Dancing Faun*, 1894.
VII Aubrey Beardsley, design for Arthur Machen, *The Great God Pan and The Inmost Light*, 1894, from *20 Miniature Posters drawn by Aubrey Beardsley*, 1896.
VIII Isabelle de Steiger, cover of *The Unknown World*, 15 October 1894.

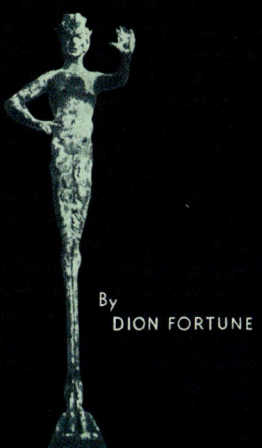

CLOCKWISE, FROM TOP LEFT: **IX** *A Broad Sheet* 2, June 1902. Illustrations by Pamela Colman Smith and Jack Butler Yeats.
X Aleister Crowley, *The Equinox* 3.1, 1919.
XI Beresford Egan, cover of Aleister Crowley, *Moonchild*, 1929.
XII Cover of Dion Fortune, *The Goat-Foot God*, 1936.

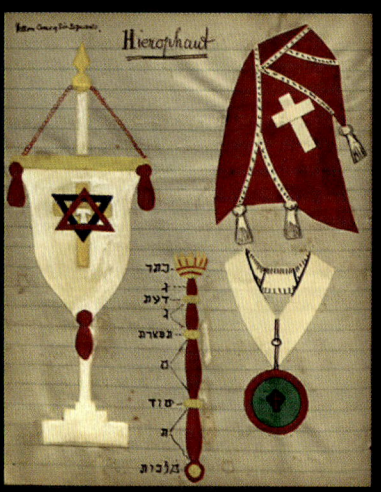

XIII Pages from W. B. Yeats's Golden Dawn notebooks, 1890s–1910s.

XIV Aubrey Beardsley, poster for John Todhunter, *A Comedy of Sighs*, 1894.

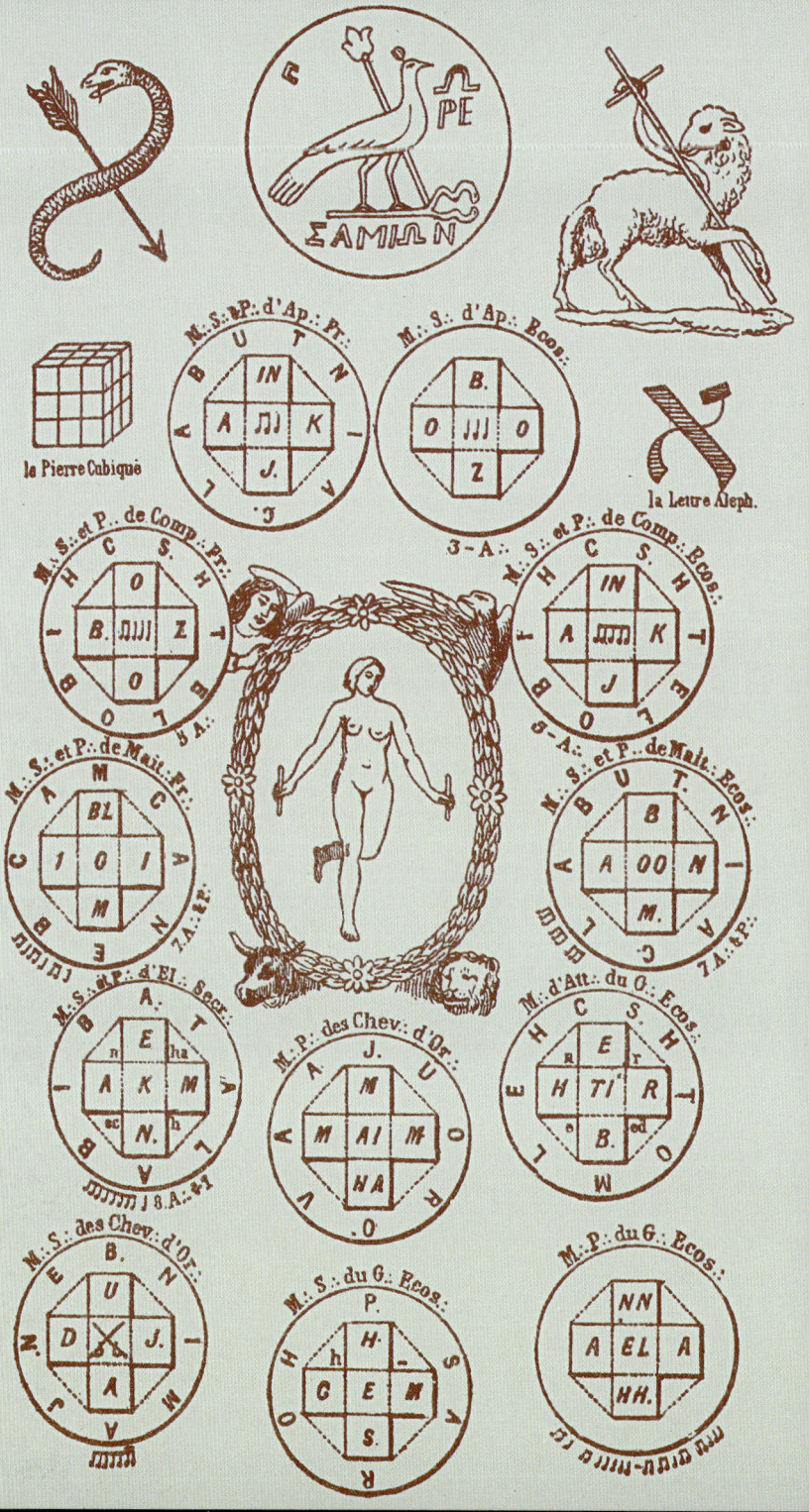

xv Twenty-first key of the tarot, from Eliphas Lévi, *The History of Magic*, translated by Arthur Edward Waite, 1922.

3

The Twilight Star

A. E. Waite & Arthur Machen

> Belief in a Supreme Being, or Beings, is indispensable. In addition, the Candidate, if not a Christian, should at least be prepared to take an interest in Christian symbolism.[1]

Before a prospective candidate for the Order of the Golden Dawn could be accepted, they were given a copy of the First Order By-Laws and asked to sign its Pledge Form. As the form made clear, only a broad theism was required of GD students. The symbolism of Christian tradition was nevertheless an important component of the rituals devised by Mathers – the masonic SRIA, from whom the membership of the GD was initially formed, was described by Westcott as a 'Christian order'– but unlike in masonic ceremonies, several other traditions took centre stage: Egyptian, Chaldean and the hermetic Kabbalah. Still, Christianity did play an important role in the GD's transmission of magical tradition, and many of the Order's members held Christian beliefs, not least the elderly Rev. W. A. Ayton, whose position in the Church of England was no hindrance (at least in his mind) to his study of alchemy.

The occult revival was not a wholesale rejection of religion, but rather a dramatic turn away from Victorian orthodoxy. Many of the unconventional strains of Christianity operating at the tail end of the nineteenth century might be termed 'esoteric' – groups willing to promote and study revived occult ideas as part of their faith. The activist and theosophist Annie Besant described Christianity as having a

A. E. Waite, n.d. (top) and Arthur Machen, c. 1900 (left).

'hidden side' whose profound inner knowledge could only be attained through 'mystic teaching'.[2] This, too, was the common belief in societies such as Thomas Lake Harris's Brotherhood of the New Life, who developed their peculiar mysticism from the writings of spiritual philosophers Emanuel Swedenborg and Jakob Böhme. Others, such as the SRIA, advanced the ideals of the legendary Rosicrucians and their founder Christian Rosenkreutz and were more academic in their aims. In *The Perfect Way; or, the Finding of Christ* (1882), the theosophists Anna Kingsford and Edward Maitland sought, like Besant, to restore and explain the hermetic truths of an 'ancient' Christianity.[3] Mathers himself was clearly impacted by the book – he dedicated his *Kabbalah Unveiled* to its authors. In Europe, the Austrian occultist Rudolf Steiner encountered theosophy at the end of the 1890s and began to spread his own mixture of Gnosticism and German idealism. Steiner eventually founded the Anthroposophical Society, which aimed to conduct a 'scientific exploration of the spiritual world'.[4]

Two GD students who stuck by their Christian faith as they navigated the hidden byways of the *fin de siècle* were Arthur Machen and A. E. Waite. Waite was one of the great occult expositors of the nineteenth and early twentieth centuries. He published scholarship and magical handbooks, and it was under his auspices that the Independent and Rectified Rite, also known as the Independent and Rectified R.R. et A.C., surfaced in 1903 as an outgrowth of the derelict Order. The writer Gerald Yorke considered this the beginning of the GD's Christianization.[5] Machen, an Anglo-Welsh writer who became known for his gothic and supernatural tales, was a member of the GD in its initial form for only a year. He was sceptical of its claims, and differed with Waite in his opinions of the Order's usefulness. 'Of course, an enormous mass of occultism, ancient and modern, may be brushed aside at once without the labour of any curious investigation,' he reflected many years later, but this did not prevent him from transforming that 'mass' (often communicated to him by Waite's writing) into saleable fiction.[6] In fact, both Arthurs used literary methods to grapple with their spirituality – Waite mainly in poetry, Machen in prose.

CHAPTER 3

Arthur Edward Waite was born in Brooklyn in 1857 to a New England sea captain father and an English mother. His father was 'buried at sea' the following year, and Arthur and his newborn sister Fredericka were brought to London, where the family settled near Hampstead and later Bayswater. His mother's conversion to Catholicism in 1863 alienated her from her immediate relations. Waite was rechristened; he obediently served as an altar boy at St Joseph's Retreat, Highgate, and attended a Catholic boys' school until an increase in fees brought his formal education to an end. To make matters worse, Fredericka died at the age of fifteen after a bout of scarlet fever. 'The sorry dream of being was now a more sorry nightmare,' Waite remembered, 'while as to my poor Mother the hopeless days of mourning went on for years.' The event complicated the boy's religious life. Although he continued to attend mass and in 1877 began contributing essays to *The Lamp*, a weekly Catholic magazine, Waite had also begun seeking out leading spiritualist figures and attending their seances.[7] He ingested the entire literary output of the transatlantic spiritualists, and after obtaining a reading ticket for the British Museum (entry was at the age of twenty-one), made his early steps into 'lore occult'. Edward Bulwer-Lytton's magic-infused romances were his first encounters with the world of secret brotherhoods, yet all, he felt, were 'false beacons' when it came to revealing genuine information.[8] A second-hand volume of *Isis Unveiled* produced better results: Waite disliked Madame Blavatsky for her anti-Christian bias, but appreciated the book's wide-ranging subject matter as offering an accessible 'miscellany of magic' and, most significantly, references to Éliphas Lévi's *Dogme et rituel*. He visited the London Lodge of the Theosophical Society, where he conversed with A. P. Sinnett, who had just recently published the influential *Esoteric Buddhism*.[9] Waite was quickly in thrall to Lévi's writings and proceeded to read everything he could find in the British Museum under his name. By 1884 he was compiling and translating the first edition of Lévi into English, a digest of his major works titled *The Mysteries of Magic*, marking the beginning of a career writing and editing occult books for a popular audience.

Alongside this scholarship, however, Waite saw himself as a poet, and it was through poetry that he was better able to express his spiritual aspirations. An early enthusiasm for 'old boys' stories and lurid 'Penny Dreadfuls' had inspired early short tales for *The Idler* with titles like 'Tom Trueheart; or, the Fortunes of a Runaway'; but from the age of seventeen, Waite's attention turned to writing verse.[10] 'A hunger and thirst after glory in the craft of song possessed my whole being,' and he read nothing but poetry 'and the lives of those who had achieved a name in rhyme'.[11] This compulsion produced a lyrical drama in the style of Shelley and a pair of eulogies for Fredericka. Two more dramas followed, both published in journals under the pseudonym Philip Dayre, and several times in the late 1870s he wrote to the poet Robert Browning for instruction in how to advance his literary career. Browning, whose celebrity had grown since writing *The Ring and the Book* (1868–9), responded by telling the precocious Waite to get a job:

> But, if you permit me to advise you, do *anything* rather than attempt to live by literature, anything good and reputable, I mean. An ungenial situation – such as you seem to have retired from – would send you to your studies, and, subsequently, to a proper use of them – with a sense of relief and enjoyment you will never obtain from 'singing' all day long.[12]

Browning urged Waite to be a 'brave fellow' and resist publishing for the time being, but Waite paid him no heed.[13] He put out a few short pamphlets, which were mostly ignored by critics. Finally, he settled on fairy poetry as a road to public recognition. Walter Scott and the British Romantics had rehabilitated fairies as literary subjects earlier in the century, and now children's stories and the large, theatrical paintings made by Richard Dadd (a troubled artist who had stabbed his father to death in 1843 and spent most of his life in asylums) had captured the public's imagination. As a reaction to the industrial age and an expression of nostalgia for simpler times, fairy poetry became a familiar mode for writers like Ruskin and even Browning himself to grapple with changing perceptions of the natural world.[14] Waite's

Illustration from A. E. Waite, *Songs and Poems of Fairyland*, 1888.
From a drawing by C. E. Brock.

A Lyric of the Fairyland and other poems, a gloomy pamphlet of Poe-esque verse, appeared in 1879. Within a decade, Waite had met the Scottish writer William Sharp and was commissioned to edit an anthology of English fairy poetry as part of Sharp's series *The Canterbury Poets*. It was published in 1888, first as *Elphin Music*, then in an extended version as *Songs and Poems of Fairyland*.[15] 'This little volume is devoted to a sweet and delightful section of poetic fancy,' wrote Waite in the introduction, preparing readers for the book's twee contents, 'and not to the lofty flights of inspired imagination.'[16] He rounded off the collection with a poem of his own under the Dayre pseudonym; titled 'An Invocation', its language was influenced by his recent diet of occult and spiritualist literature:

> Purest thoughts are brightest chrism
> In the mystical baptism,
> Which to those elected duly
> Lifts the veil, revealing truly
> Elfin worlds in 'rapt clairvoyance,
> Elfin marvels, Elfin joyance,
> Elfin vistas, Elfin vision,
> Elfin voice, dreams Elysian,
> Fay-built isles and seas that be
> Glamour all and gramarye.[17]

The *Spectator* praised the anthology as a 'charming volume', while questioning the lack of chronology and Waite's choice to include Poe's 'Fairyland' ('scarcely one of his happiest efforts').[18] Fairy tales became a regular type for Waite. The allegorical novel *Prince Starbeam: A Tale of Fairyland* (1889) was deemed 'too long and diffuse' and unsuitable for children, but *The Golden Stairs: Tales from the Wonderworld* (1893), printed by the Theosophical Society, was commended for its biblical phrasing.[19] As the 1890s drew on, however, his focus was directed almost exclusively by occult study.

Waite's style was effusive, his introductions scattered with asides criticizing the errors of his predecessors. His scholarship became so famous that Aleister Crowley could caricature him in his novel *Moonchild* as Edwin Arthwait, a 'stupid pedant' who 'made sentences so complicated that the complete works of George Meredith, Thomas Carlyle, and Henry James, tangled together, would have seemed in comparison like a word of three letters'. Crowley spent much of his time libelling Waite in the pages of his journal *The Equinox* (see his column 'My Crapulous Contemporaries'), though he admitted to admiring his poetry.[20]

Waite's major project, which fed into and energized his activities with the GD and its later iterations, was an attempt to resolve the dilemma that he had first encountered in Lévi's writings and saw reflected in his own life. Lévi consistently asserts that he has uncovered the great secrets of occult and spiritual wisdom, reducing all religions to mere 'puppets', but Waite found a gaping flaw in this proposition: his Catholic faith.

> Now, in attempting to estimate the value of this gigantic claim, and of Éliphas Lévi's contributions to the elucidation of occult science, we are brought face to face with that fact, that after posing as an initiate in possession of the Great Arcanum, he has done his best to stultify himself by attempting to pose himself as a faithful and humble child of the Catholic Church, and this without abandoning his previous position. Such a course has naturally led him into grave and numerous contradictions, which cannot but scandalize his students in proportion to their personal earnestness, and are calculated to make many reject his claims to secret knowledge as utterly unfounded.[21]

In 'limpid French', Lévi's books expressed to Waite such a conflicting intellectual viewpoint that he could no longer read them with any academic seriousness.[22] Neither, Waite discovered, had Lévi read all the texts he claimed to have read: barely any of Rosenroth's *Kabbala Denudata* and almost nothing of the alchemical corpus. But while Waite saw through the vagaries and inaccuracies of popular occult writing, he still sustained a hope that there was something behind it all: a 'Church behind the Church' or 'some Holy of Holies undreamed of by the so-called Supreme Magus and the High Council of the Soc ∴ Ros ∴'.[23] Thereafter he devoted his studies to illuminating the history of what he referred to as the 'Secret Tradition', a body of spiritual knowledge that contains 'firstly, the memorials of a loss which has befallen humanity; and, secondly, the records of a restitution in respect of that which was lost'. He looked for this tradition in masonic rituals, Rosicrucianism, alchemy and the Holy Grail, his eventual aim being to find evidence of its survival in modern Christianity – in particular the 'Instituted Mysteries and cryptic literature' of Catholicism.[24] His quest was set.

While Waite had fought hard to fashion an identity for himself in adverse circumstances, Arthur Machen's childhood was a source of relative stability and comfort. Proudly 'three-quarters Celt', he was the son of a Welsh clergyman, John Edward Jones, and Janet Robina Machen, his Scottish wife, whose last name the reverend adopted to benefit from a will. Arthur was born in 1863 in the South Wales town of Caerleon-on-Usk, legendary seat of King Arthur in Geoffrey of Monmouth's *Historia Regum Britanniae*, and spent a solitary childhood in his father's nearby rectory at Llanddewi Fach, surrounded by 'woods and deep lanes and wonder'.[25] Wentwood, the Soar Valley, Mynydd Maen – the young Machen romanticized the local landscape and its history, combining evidence of Roman occupation and warnings of malicious fairies into a dream of dark enchantment. Books were an early comfort and obsession, and the 'hugger-mugger' of his father's collection kept him occupied through long winters. He read indiscriminately from the Brontës, George Borrow, Dickens, his grandfather's Hebrew grammar and – the crown jewel – a translation of *Don Quixote*, borrowed from Mrs Gwyn of Llanfrechfa Rectory.[26] Perusal of the magazine *Household Words* led Machen to a series of articles on alchemy, and the names of Nicolas Flamel and other practitioners were soon familiar to him. Aged eleven, Machen was sent to board at Hereford Cathedral School, where in 1881, with financial assistance from obliging family members, he published his first (and only) long poem, based on an encyclopaedia entry for the Eleusinian Mysteries. The agricultural depression meant he was denied the Oxford education once afforded to his father, and after several false starts, including a failed attempt to train as a surgeon, Machen found himself in London, pursuing a career as a writer.

Isolated by his own stubbornness, Machen experienced the miseries of poverty. Subsisting on a diet of green tea, stale bread and tobacco, he earned a living teaching Euclid and in his free time went 'tramping, loafing, strolling' out into the city's borderlands, dreaming of books he did not dare write.[27] But it was his burgeoning curiosity about the occult that led to his first foray into the literary world. Machen read Hargrave Jennings's *The Rosicrucians: Their Rites and Mysteries* (1870), the same work of 'sham learning' that had for years been read by SRIA members to bolster their genuine backstory.[28] Finding a significant omission in the book's account of the Egyptian Mysteries, Machen wrote to Jennings directly, pointing to a section of Herodotus that he hoped would interest the author. No reply came, but Jennings apparently passed Machen's name and address to the publisher George Redway, because Machen received Redway's prospectus through his door. Machen responded by sending Redway the manuscript of a book, *The Anatomy of Tobacco*, a short treatise on pipe smoking that mimicked the scholastic logic of the seventeenth century.

Redway was one of several publishers of occult books in London during the 1880s; overseeing Madame Blavatsky's journal *Lucifer* and titles by A. P. Sinnett and Henry Steel Olcott had given him influence in theosophical circles, and he continued to put out Jennings's increasingly eccentric studies of phallic symbolism. He agreed to publish *The Anatomy of Tobacco* only if Machen paid for printing (this time the funds were supplied by goodhearted Llanddewi neighbours), and in 1885 offered him employment at his offices in Covent Garden, which Machen accepted. Machen recalled all sorts of 'odd jobs and queer jobs' being delegated to him, but his main task was to sort through and catalogue a library of occult books which Redway had stored in a 'sumptuous and rich' garret on Catherine Street. For a pound a week, he went about his task, imagination aflame. 'It was as odd a library as any man could desire to see,' Machen remembered vividly:

> Occultism in one sense or another was the subject of most of the books. There were the principal and the more obscure treatises on Alchemy, on Astrology, on Magic; old Latin volumes most of them. Here were books about Witchcraft, Diabolical Possession, 'Fascination', or the Evil Eye; here were comments on the Kabbala. Ghosts and Apparitions were a large family, Secret Societies of all sorts hung on the skirts of the Rosicrucians and Freemasons, and so found a place in the collection.[29]

Among the more desirable titles listed were a rare first edition of Francis Barrett's *The Magus* from 1801 and the *Mysterium Magnum*, a major work by the Christian mystic Jakob Böhme. Popular grimoires featured in the section on 'Magic and Magicians', including *Le Petit Albert* and the *Grimoire du Pape Honorius* ('Contains incantations and directions for raising spirits'), alongside a 'fine set' of Éliphas Lévi's best known works.[30] Assuredly Machen did not have the time to read a whole garret's worth of books cover to cover, but he must have learned enough to be able to assess their merits and give a good summary of their contents. Beyond Thomas Vaughan's alchemical writings and Jennings's Rosicrucian fantasy, Machen had not read much about magic; for an aspiring writer who was drawn to the study of life's mysteries, the project was an education in the contemporary trends of occult society. It also meant that he probably had a much broader idea of the occult sciences than many of the GD's first students, who were to be initiated only a year later.

When news of his mother's death reached him, a grieving Machen retreated to Llanddewi Fach to write his next book, a medieval frame-tale called *The Chronicle of Clemendy*, again in the seventeenth-century style. By 1887 he was in Bloomsbury and once again employed by

Redway, who had begun to oversee Edward Walford's journal *Walford's Antiquarian Magazine and Bibliographical Review*, a periodical catering to a range of historical interests. He made Machen its *de facto* editor. Machen was also responsible for writing the catalogue prospectus for the library of the clairvoyant Frederick Hockley, who had departed the material world two years earlier.[31] Hockley had been a member of the SRIA, and it was part of the GD's origin story that the Cipher Manuscripts had passed from his collection to his friend Kenneth R. H. Mackenzie. Hockley had worked for another occult bookseller, John Denley (whose office had also been on Catherine Street), copying manuscripts for Denley's clientele, and had accumulated a vast library of esoteric literature. Spiritualism, mesmerism, masonry, folklore, alchemy and astrology were represented in Machen's catalogue alongside far more unusual documents, many transcribed by Hockley himself: among them were an account of a witch trial held at Bury St Edmunds in 1682, a sixteenth-century freemason's manual and a collection of alchemists' horoscopes. The catalogue related only to a fraction of Hockley's original collection, but once again Machen found himself exposed to a vast array of 'odd' subjects, some of which he would go on to use as material for his supernatural tales.

Machen and Waite both had professional ties to Redway, but the two men were only brought together through a mutual friendship. Amy Hogg, the eldest daughter of Anglo-Indian parents, enjoyed a bohemian existence living opposite the British Museum, 'mixing with authors, artists and actors'.[32] She also 'frequented restaurants and aerated bread shops,' her friend Jerome K. Jerome remembered, 'and had many men friends, all of which was considered very shocking in those days'.[33] Waite had befriended Amy in 1886 on a visit to Worthing, and it was she who insisted that the two Arthurs meet, for she knew that the men shared an interest in the occult. Their meeting was delayed until January 1887, but immediately a friendship was formed. Waite, or 'the High Class Gypsy' as Machen called him in letters, was a man 'incapable of any kind of affectation' who talked in the same 'slightly archaic fashion' in which he wrote his books and was a perfect fit for Machen's inquisitive and ponderous mind.[34] Together the two bibliophiles explored the London nightlife and went in search of Edgar Allan Poe's old school, which they believed to be somewhere in Stoke Newington, all the while debating furiously points of spiritual importance. Machen encouraged Waite to contribute a handful of articles to *Walford's* and angered Hargrave Jennings by getting Waite to review the third edition of *The Rosicrucians* ('simply a mass of ill-digested erudition').[35] Together they also compiled several issues of *George Redway's Literary Circular*, an advertising leaflet distributed inside Blavatsky's theosophy magazine.[36]

Rationally, Machen did not believe in the occult – at least not in the quasi-scientific showiness of mesmerism and spiritualism – and for the most part remained attached to his Anglican roots. He had no experience of ritual magic and had resisted involving himself in any of the occult movements *du jour*, seeming content with solitary study and conversations with Waite. He was not tempted by meetings of the Theosophical Society – Blavatsky and her Mahatmas he considered 'rubbish, not worth a moment's consideration' – and the rappings and knockings of the seance tables were equally uninteresting. Waite, by contrast, was a Catholic and a spiritualist, and his faith was undeniably of the 'esoteric' variety. By 1887 he was to be found 'slogging away at his Lives of the Alchemists' in the British Museum, intent on uncovering his idea of the Secret Tradition.[37] But Machen was still guided by his curiosity, and his early interest in alchemical systems of spirituality is surely one of the reasons he eventually entered the GD. His attitude towards magic during this period can be summarized by his description of a character in *The Great God Pan* (published 1894):

in his sober moments he thought of the unusual and eccentric with undisguised aversion, and yet, deep in his heart, there was a wide-eyed inquisitiveness with respect to all the more recondite and esoteric elements in the nature of men.[38]

At the time that Waite met Machen, he had also fallen deeply in love with Theodora ('Dora') Lakeman, whom he had encountered at a series of 'haphazard' and uneventful seances hosted by the spiritualist Granville Stuart-Monteith. But Dora was soon betrothed to the wealthy Stuart-Monteith, leaving Waite to settle for her younger sister Ada (or 'Lucasta', as he called her). Their wedding took place in January 1888, just five months after Machen and Amy Hogg's, and their only daughter, Sybil, was born in October. In 1889 Waite accepted an offer from A. P. Sinnett, by now a partner of Redway, to edit the *British Mail*, the journal of 'the Chambers of Commerce in the United Kingdom', which provided a meagre salary. He was also making failed attempts to form his own society: an association for the study of mystical philosophy that would at first be 'of a literary character'. He wrote a letter to this effect to *Light* magazine in 1888, laying out his grand theory that the material processes the alchemists had written about were in fact metaphors for the evolution of the soul, but this seems to have attracted no interest. He would later outline this hermetic interpretation in astonishing detail in *Azoth; or, the Star in the East* (1893), but he first began to write more about his alchemical theories in edited books for Redway, including *Lives of the Alchemystical Philosophers* (1888) and *The Magical Writings of Thomas Vaughan* (1888).[39]

Waite was acquainted with William Westcott, whom he described as 'like a dull owl, hooting dolefully among cypresses over tombs of false adepts', and Mathers, whom he had encountered (as many members seemed to) in the British Museum Reading Room in 1883 and characterized as 'a strange person, with rather fish-like eyes'. 'I suppose that we must have spoken of occult books or subjects in one of the corridors, for he said to me in a hushed voice and with a somewhat awful accent: "I am a Rosicrucian and a Freemason; therefore I can speak of some things, but of others I cannot speak".'[40] Waite was particularly friendly with Mathers, who was three years his elder, but he perceived correctly that his eccentric style and scholarly aspirations were part of a posture designed to draw in the 'unversed' (one of Waite's terms for people without specialist knowledge of the occult).

Writing in 1938, long after the structural split within the Order, Waite claims that it was what Westcott called his 'codification of Lévi' that had prevented him from attaining any reputation within occult circles: Lévi was revered by all, and Waite's critical introduction to *Mysteries of Magic* had apparently struck a sour note.[41] His later estimation of Mathers's grimoire translations is best summarized by the preface to *The Wordsworth Book of Spells*, or *Book of Ceremonial Magic* (1911), in which Mathers, the expounder of 'the more arid and unprofitable side of Kabbalistic doctrine', is cast as a '*mentor stultorum* [teacher of fools]'.[42]

Waite continued to see Mathers, who was then hard at work on *The Kabbalah Unveiled*, at the occult gatherings they both attended. He had also begun to hear rumours of a mysterious hermetic society. In an overdramatic recollection, he notes: 'Obscure persons were placing cryptic sigils after their names in unexpected communications, as if to test whether I was already a Member. Dark hints were conveyed in breathless murmurs.'[43] The real existence of the GD, however, proved impossible to discover until Westcott revealed himself to be Praemonstrator in an issue of *Lucifer*, and a determined Edward Berridge (a student since May 1889) persuaded Waite to apply for membership. Surprisingly, it was Berridge, not Mathers or Westcott, who recommended Waite to the Order. The prompt rejection of his application might have had something to do with Waite's treatment of Lévi, or a spat with Westcott several years previously: in 1887 he had printed the SRIA's *Rules and Ordinances* in a chapter of *The Real History of the Rosicrucians*; embarrassed that the documents were not under copyright, Westcott had asked Waite for an apology, which was duly given.[44] Whatever the reason for the rejection, Waite half-heartedly applied again, and was accepted.

He was a reluctant candidate. His admission as Neophyte took place at Forest Hill, where Mathers was still in residence, in January 1891, and he adopted the motto 'Sacramentum Regis' ('The Sacrament of the King'). He was disappointed, however, to be met 'with nothing worse than a confounding medley of Symbols, and was handed a brief tabulation of elementary points drawn at haphazard from familiar

'Edward Kelley, a magician in the act of invoking a spirit', frontispiece to A. E. Waite, *The Wordsworth Book of Spells*, or *Book of Ceremonial Magic*, 1911. From a drawing by Ebenezer Sibly.

occult sources: on these I was supposed to answer given questions, did I wish to proceed further'. His reaction mirrors Crowley's seven years later: already well established as a historian of the occult, Waite had no trouble whatsoever with the first lessons of the First Order's curriculum, and contrasted them with the more 'profound' information given out by the eighteenth-century Gold- und Rosenkreuz. He convinced Ada to join with him, though she only attended a single meeting.

Around this time, Waite would have met the novelist and spiritualist Emily Katharine Bates, who entered Isis-Urania several months after him. Bates had travelled widely throughout the 1880s, attending her first seance in Boston, and had returned to England to mix with occult society. She would leave the GD in 1894, after being cautioned by a spirit contact that ritual studies would damage her psychical growth. Similarly, by April 1892 Waite had risen to $4° = 7°$, recognizing at the time that he 'stood on the threshold of the Second Order', but for reasons never fully explained he went no further and resigned in 1893. It seems that he thought that he was about to be threatened with legal action: 'I began to hear things which, in my several positions at the moment, told me that I should be well out of the whole concern [i.e. the GD] ... It was a question of things which had an equivocal legal aspect and in which leading Members of the Order should not have been concerned.' It may have had something to do with the demise of Sinnett's Hansard Publishing Union, which suddenly 'fell to pieces', and with it Waite's many projects, among them the *British Mail* and the *Municipal Review*.[45] He found himself out of the GD and, for the time being, unemployed.

By the early 1890s the Waites were living at Gunnersbury, West London, not far from the Bedford Park community of Florence Farr, John Todhunter and Yeats. Arthur and Amy Machen had moved from Buckinghamshire to an upper-floor apartment on Great Russell Street, down the road from the British Museum. Since 1889 Machen had made the transition into writing short essays known as 'turn-overs' for *The Globe* and *St James's Gazette*, and in a mirroring of Waite's correspondence with Browning, had been prompted by none other than Oscar Wilde to begin writing short stories for magazines. Wilde, whose wife Constance was at that time a regular student of the GD, had just published *The Picture of Dorian Gray*. He and Machen met for dinner, where he related the 'wonderful' plot of a story that Machen thought he could rival.[46] His stories were 'society pieces' at first, set in the London social scene and intended to entertain, but during that summer Machen turned to darker subject matter: the occult and nefarious societies. Resulting from this period was 'The Lost Club', an effective mimicry of Robert Louis Stevenson's 'The Suicide Club', and 'The Great God Pan', both of which were accepted by *The Whirlwind*, a magazine with sympathies toward 'Jacobite' causes. In 1891 Machen decided to expand the 2,000-word 'Pan' to a full eight chapters.

The Great God Pan was Machen's attempt to put into words the feelings of wonder and terror the South Wales landscape had inspired in him in his youth. Writing in 1916 about *Pan*'s conception, Machen recalls the image of a white farmhouse set 'in the awe of the forest and the breath of the winding river' joined with his impressions of Caerleon-on-Usk, the ruins of its city wall 'as the sun set red over Twyn Barlwm'.[47] The mechanics of the story rely on the view of reality expressed in Neo-Platonism, an ancient school of philosophy that posited a series of spiritual planes, or 'Hypostases', beyond the sensible world, which connect man with God. Machen had surveyed the central texts of Neo-Platonist and mystic literature in his cataloguing work for Redway, and knew how their ideas had been integrated into magical and occult systems (chiefly alchemy) throughout the school's various revivals. *Pan* opens with the scientist-occultist Dr Raymond explaining to his friend Clarke how he intends to make 'a slight lesion in the grey matter' of his young ward Mary in order to 'lift the veil' from her eyes. The Greek god Pan acts a symbol of the unknowable terror experienced when an individual is confronted with the 'spirit-world', known as 'seeing the god Pan'. Raymond quotes the historical alchemist and Neo-Platonist Oswald Crollius to illustrate his thesis: 'In every grain of wheat there lies hidden the soul of a star.'[48] The operation results in Mary's insanity. The story's remainder is a bricolage of memoir, newspaper reports and first-hand encounters that, when pieced together by Clarke and his associates, describe the scandalous and ultimately tragic life of Helen Vaughan, the daughter conceived by Mary in her union with Pan.

Attracted by the *Keynotes* series of the Bodley Head, Machen had sent the manuscript of *The Great God Pan* to John Lane in 1893, around the time that Florence Farr's *The Dancing Faun* had been accepted. The reader's report by Richard Le Gallienne considered it 'a clever story of horror on the Edgar Poe or Sheridan Le Fanu pattern', but went on to say that Machen relied too much on 'ghastly interjections ... horrified notes of exclamations'.[49] Lane asked for changes and requested a shorter tale to bulk out the text, and Machen provided 'The Inmost Light', a piece originally commissioned by the novelist Mary Elizabeth Braddon for an anthology but rejected for its unsuitable content. *The Great God Pan and the Inmost Light* was eventually published as the fifth title in *Keynotes* in December 1894, generating a wave of bad reviews. Many of these attacked *Pan*'s sexual overtones and vivid body horror (the book ends with Helen's transmutation 'from sex to sex, dividing itself from itself' and finally to a 'substance as jelly').[50] Nevertheless, *Pan* was Machen's first major success at writing in 'the modern way': he was with a fashionable publishing house, and critics were taking notice. Lane would print a second edition early the following year, confirmation for Machen that he had found an audience for his own occult-infused brand of gothic literature.

Robert Louis Stevenson remained the model for Machen's next book, *The Three Impostors; or, The Transmutations*, published in 1895 as the nineteenth volume in *Keynotes*. It employs the same story-within-a-story framing device as Stevenson's *New Arabian Nights* (1882) and *The Dynamiter* (1885). Through a string of haphazard encounters on the streets of central London, Mr Dyson and Mr Phillips try to piece together a mystery involving an individual known only as 'the Young Man in Spectacles'.[51] Though Machen was not yet part of the Order, *The Three Impostors* is notable for its references to GD members, stories of whom Waite may have passed on. Yeats can be seen as the spectacled man, pale and 'of somewhat timid bearing'; the society to which he is introduced, while criminal in intent, is occult in its operations. He is guided to 'secret rooms' north of Oxford Street by a Dr Lipsius, a

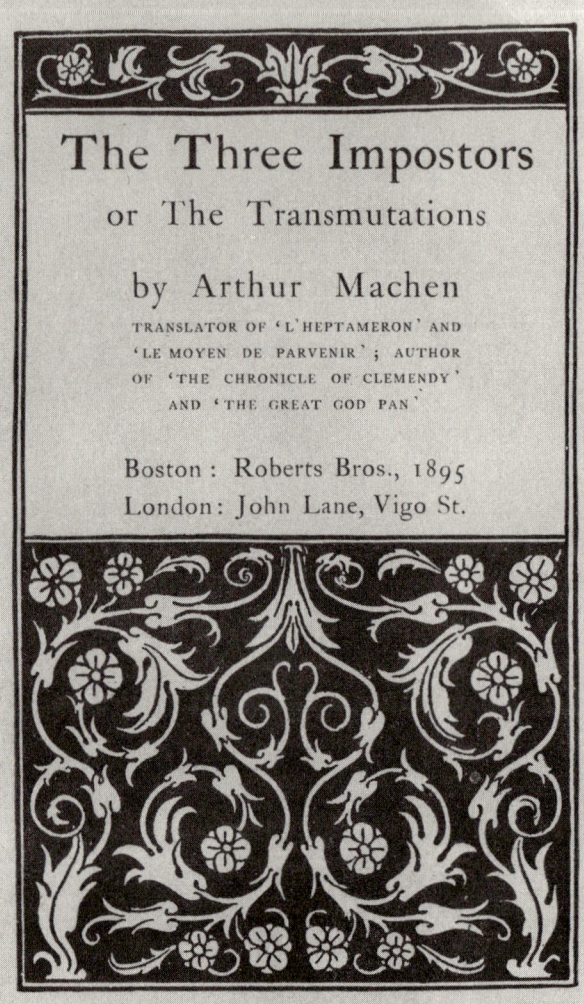

Aubrey Beardsley, design for Arthur Machen's *The Three Impostors*, 1895, from *20 Miniature Posters drawn by Aubrey Beardsley*, 1896.

blend of Westcott and Berridge, and there his 'initiation' begins: 'I was no longer a thinking agent, but at once subject and object,' he recalls: 'I mingled in the horrible sport, and watched the mystery of the Greek groves and fountains enacted before me.'[52]

Machen also took the opportunity in one tale to kill off his ex-employer, Edward Walford of *Walford's Antiquarian*, in the guise of the old and cantankerous James Headley, 'the well-known antiquary'.[53] He is led to his death by the unknowing man in spectacles, his mutilated body gruesomely disposed of in an antique sarcophagus to be displayed in a local museum. On its publication, *The Three Impostors* made a similar splash to *The Great God Pan*; Machen's writing was increasingly cast as 'decadent' in its style, helped along by the Beardsley frontispieces that adorned each *Keynote* release. Like Waite, Machen was aware of the spiritual underpinnings of medieval alchemy, and it is significant that many characters who fall foul of occult powers go through a physical dissolution, embodying the process of *nigredo*: the alchemical 'blackening' or cleansing process required to attain the *Magnum Opus* (Philosopher's Stone). A year later, in his 'Rosa Alchemica', Yeats would himself come to a similar conclusion that the alchemists' doctrine 'was no mere chemical phantasy, but a philosophy they applied to the world, to the elements and to man himself'.[54] The fact that both *Pan* and *The Three Impostors* were eventually donated to the GD's Second Order library suggests that they were of some occult value to the society's students.[55]

Periodicals on esoteric themes flourished in the 1880s and 1890s as part of a diverse London publishing scene, among them magazines catering to astrologers (*The Future*), spiritualists (*Light* and W. T. Stead's *Borderland*) and theosophists (*Lucifer*, later the *Theosophical Review*). The Hermetic Brotherhood of Luxor published the *Occult Magazine* monthly from 1885 to 1886.[56] August 1894 saw the publication of the first issue of the *Unknown World*, a monthly magazine devoted to the 'whole circle of the Occult Sciences'. Its editor was A. E. Waite.[57] The new venture was the result of James Elliot & Co. agreeing to reissue many of Waite's books; Elliot, then on the brink of ruin, was transformed into an occult publisher almost overnight.[58] A magazine edited by Waite thus seemed to be the logical next step, and was also a good opportunity to advertise his back catalogue. A high proportion of its contents was unsigned, most likely because it was written by Waite himself, whose turns of phrase make him easy to identify. Beyond frequent reviews of Westcott's *Collectanea Hermetica* series, Waite's desire to maintain a link with the GD was clear in his publication of Edward Berridge, whose articles praising Thomas Lake Harris and his Brotherhood of the New Life were to be partly responsible for Annie Horniman's expulsion from the Order. Under his GD motto 'Resurgam' ('I will rise again'), Berridge also penned pieces hinting at a contemporary order of Rosicrucians, gloating that their mysteries could not be uncovered by mere book-learning or membership of 'bogus societies' and 'will never be lightly revealed to the world'.[59] In a later issue Waite was forced to distance himself from Berridge's advocacy of the death penalty for initiates who betray Rosicrucian secrets, reassuring readers that his 'considerable acquaintance' with the author allowed him to say that Berridge did not mean it.[60] The writer Edward Maitland also contributed articles, as did the spiritualist and barrister Charles Carleton Massey.

The *Unknown World*'s frontispieces and black-and-white cover, which depicted a pentagram surrounded by a band of lacklustre fairies, were the work of Isabelle de Steiger, an artist and theosophist who had studied alchemy as a GD student since 1888.[61] The magazine also allowed Waite to repay Machen's earlier kindness at *Walford's Antiquarian* (although Machen was also doing Waite a favour by filling the pages). In December 1894, *The Great God Pan* was advertised as a work of genius, and Machen's 'The Shining Pyramid' was serialized over the May and June 1895 issues, the third in his triptych of 'Little People' stories from that period. Set in the thinly disguised 'grey hills' of Machen's Gwent, the tale is full of alchemical imagery and would prove to be one of his most anthologized works over the next several

Isabelle de Steiger, 'The Spirit of the Crystal', from the *Unknown World*, 15 September 1894.

decades. Waite's magazine expired with its eleventh issue – not, as he was quick to emphasize, because it was a failure, 'but because there was no money for Elliot to carry it on'.[62]

Perhaps due to his continuing contact with Berridge, Waite was drawn back into the GD's circle. Sometime before 1896, he was meeting regularly with Robert Palmer Thomas, a railway officer and enthusiastic freemason who later became a participant in Farr's Egypt group and Sub-Imperator during the 1901 crisis. Palmer Thomas sought information on the Rosicrucians, having read Waite's *Real History*. Waite gave up what secrets of the GD he was permitted to reveal, and several years later had a letter from his friend to say that he was now a member of the Second Order.[63] Palmer Thomas assured Waite that he was 'missing things' that he would value in the higher degrees, things that Waite would not have known about from his time in the First Order. 'I made an application to rejoin,' Waite recalls, 'feeling, and perhaps mischievously hoping to hear in due course that, having turned my back on the light, I was doomed to remain in darkness.'[64] But he was summoned to a meeting with Westcott in February 1896 and, to his surprise, his membership was restored.

Machen's time in the Order was preceded by an event that had for a long time threatened to upend his life and plunge him into psychological stasis – the death of Amy in 1899. She had been diagnosed with breast cancer earlier in the decade but did not have surgery, and it was only a matter of time before the disease overcame her. At the start of that year Machen, energized following his resignation from *Literature* (the literary arm of *The Times*, where he was forced to review favourably books he did not like), had sat down to write what he hoped would be his 'Great Work'. This was not to be; he produced only single stones 'instead of a whole house'.[65] But among these stones was the long essay *Hieroglyphics*, which argued that for a book to be considered 'fine literature' it must contain 'ecstasy', and the long tale 'The White People', one of Machen's best-known works. It is an account of a young girl's indoctrination into a witch cult, told in a dreamy, stream-of-consciousness style and full of Celtic and other folktales reminiscent of the Brothers Grimm. Annotations in

Crowley's personal copy of *The House of Souls* (a collection of Machen's work published in 1906) suggests that Crowley considered 'The White People' a perfect representation of the magical experience.[66] Amy's death, however, put a stop to this creative outpouring. Her friend Jerome K. Jerome recorded his impressions of her final days:

> The windows looked out on to the great quiet garden, and the rooks were cawing in the elms. She was dying, and Machen, with two cats under his arm, was moving softly about, waiting on her. We did not talk much. I stayed there till the sunset filled the room with a strange purple light.[67]

Machen lingered in his 'house of mourning' at Gray's Inn after Amy had passed away, unable to write, the manuscript for another story set aside in a desk drawer. Perhaps recognizing in Machen's grief his own pain from the death of his sister, Waite rushed to his friend's aid. 'Amy was older than her husband by quite a few years, and much as he felt her loss there is a not unreal sense in which – consciously or unconsciously – it acted as an open entrance to a new epoch,' Waite remembered. 'Another phase of life, almost a new world, was destined to unfold about him.'[68] Waite presumably recommended Machen for membership of Isis-Urania, and Machen, hoping that the GD might assuage his pain, underwent initiation on 21 November 1899. He was a student in the original Order for just over a year, selecting the motto 'Avallaunius' ('Man of Avalon') in reference to a novel he had just written. In his autobiography, which pseudonymizes the GD as the 'Order of the Twilight Star', he admitted to having joined the society not 'merely in quest of odd entertainment'. He had experienced 'strange things' following Amy's death, and 'I supposed that the Order, dimly heard of, might give me some light and guidance and leading on these matters. But, as I have noted, I was mistaken; the Twilight Star shed no ray of any kind upon my path.'[69]

The 'strange things' alluded to by Machen seem to have occurred in the months directly following Amy's death. 'And then a process suggested itself to me,' he recalls, 'as having the possibility of relief

CHAPTER 3

… And what I received was not a mere dull lack of pain sensation, but a peace of the spirit that was quite ineffable, a knowledge that all hurts and doles and wounds were healed, that that which was broken was reunited.' He then reported an extraordinary episode in which the pictures on his sitting-room wall began to shake: Machen may have employed a technique from Waite's new *Book of Black Magic and of Pacts* (1898), or he may have taken a measure of the laudanum Amy had presumably used for her pain. Whatever the cause, his grief seemed to vanish and he experienced a transcendent 'rapture of life'. The world appeared to him anew, the sounds of the Holborn streets 'filling the air, filling the soul' as he strode out from Gray's Inn. He claimed to have met and interacted with characters from his books – the man in spectacles and Miss Lally, both from *The Three Impostors*, although this time the man may actually have been Yeats himself, who explained that he was being pursued by a 'fiend in human form, a man who was well known to be an expert in Black Magic' (almost certainly Aleister Crowley).[70] The real Miss Lally was a friend, unconnected with the Order. No wonder he hoped the GD could explain these events to him.

Very few records have come to light regarding Machen's time in the Golden Dawn, but by May 1900 he had advanced to the level of Practicus (3° = 8°). This grade, associated with the element of Water, required candidates to learn geomantic symbols and magic squares. Also included in the Practicus knowledge lecture were Mathers's notes on the Major Arcana, derived in part from his tarot pamphlet. Machen may have been in the middle of the required three-month waiting period known as the 'Regimen of the Elements' that followed the Practicus ceremony, or he may have already completed it, thereby making him eligible for taking the 4° = 7° examination.[71] But by the end of the year he had had enough, and his leaving marked the end of any serious interest in the occult. His opinion of the GD was divided. He was overwhelmingly critical of what he considered its lack of substance, spiritual or otherwise: 'But as for anything vital in the secret order, for anything that mattered two straws to any reasonable being, there was nothing of it, and less than nothing.'[72] What also emerges from his account in the autobiographical *Things Near and Far* (1923) is the genuine glamour he found in the Order's operations. His description of one of the ceremonies is perhaps more evocative than any other account of the time:

> To stand waiting at a closed door in a breathless expectation, to see it open suddenly and disclose two figures clothed in a habit that I never thought to see worn by the living, to catch for a moment the vision of a cloud of incense smoke and certain dim lights glimmering in it before the bandage was put over the eyes and the arm felt a firm grasp upon it that led the hesitating footsteps into the unknown darkness: all this was strange and admirable indeed; and strange it was to think that within a foot or two of those closely curtained windows the common life of London moved on the common pavement, as supremely unaware of what was being done within an arm's length as if our works had been the works of the other side of the moon.[73]

'Strange and admirable', earlier 'glorious and elaborate'; but Machen's repeated dismissals of the GD's 'impotent and imbecile Abracadabras' make it clear that the Order had nothing spiritual to offer him. Though he swore off magic after 1900 and ritual occultism played no part in his later fiction, evidently his experiences still made an impression. Writing to Waite in 1905, it seems that part of the reason Machen did not stick with Isis-Urania related to his dislike of the superiority inherent in the grade structure '& the fashion in which they are taken'. The initiator of the 'average secret society' professes to know more than the initiated, who stands 'without' the occult circle and is brought 'within'. Machen's ideal society would make no such pretence, and rather bid its members 'look within, & uncover, & remove, & Behold, & Make the Great Interior Entrance – from Within to Within'.[74] The students he encountered were too concerned with status, and Florence Farr and M. W. Blackden 'about as complete a pair of "rotters"' as he had ever seen, despite all their Egyptian 'wisdom'.[75] Neither was he convinced of the Order's claim to ancient pedigree, and deduced, with help from Waite, that the Cipher Manuscripts were merely 'a forgery of the early eighties'.[76]

One fortunate result of Machen's time in Isis-Urania was that he met a fellow writer of supernatural tales, Algernon Blackwood, whom he remembered as 'a most interesting and amiable man'.[77] Blackwood, an eager theosophist since the mid-1880s, had returned to London in 1899 after a long spell in North America as a journalist, during which he had begun to write 'weird stories'.[78] He applied immediately to the Theosophical Society's London Lodge, which he entered on 5 May, and the following year was persuaded by Yeats to apply for membership of Isis-Urania. His recollections of the Order members are slight, but reveal the kinds of circles he moved in. 'Machen was a member and I got to know him,' he wrote to a friend in the 1940s, 'and Yeats and Maud Gonne were stimulating people to know.'[79] Gonne, in like appreciation, considered Blackwood to have lent a 'certain literary distinction' to the GD, although she had ceased her attendance by the time he joined.[80] His first collection, *The Empty House and other Ghost Stories*, appeared in 1906, and he continued publishing in a steady fashion until the late 1920s. Blackwood studied with the GD and later offshoots until around 1915, and unlike Machen, used some of what he learned for fictional purposes. 'If not an entirely new world to my searching mind,' he reflected in 1948, 'the use of sound and names at least provided material years later for a book, *The Human Chord* [1910], and the search for the mysterious Name of God, kept hidden by leaving out all the vowels.'[81]

Until 1903, Waite had taken little interest in the Golden Dawn's various political crises, writing in December 1902 that 'I did not go yesterday to the House of the Hidden Stairs [his name for the GD, so-called because of the side entrance members used at Mark Masons' Hall]. I had no wish to hear the final part of the Triad on the "groups question".' I cannot dance to these children however much they dance and sing.'⁸² The triad in question was made up of Percy Bullock, Robert Felkin and John Brodie-Innes, who had been elected as Chiefs in May 1902 for a period of a single year. Yeats ('Brother Devil, well known poet') wrote in January 1903 asking whether Waite would help him petition the triad to reform the Ritual Sub-Committee, 'more especially as regards the 2 = 9 Ritual on which he and I worked together', to which Waite agreed.⁸³ But his attention over the past few years had been directed elsewhere. In 1899 he had accepted a job as Manager of the London Office of Horlick's, purveyors of malted milk, a position that involved sending out promotional material, some of which employed Waite's talent for rhyme: 'On Malted Milk the babies thrive, / By Malted Milk the sick survive.' In 1900 he was promoted to become James Horlick's private Business Manager.⁸⁴

From 1901, his evenings were spent scandalously: first as part of Machen's 'Rabelaisian Order of Tosspots', a Bohemian social club that met to drink and discuss literature in taverns and had its own set of GD-style rules, and later, also with Machen, in the more exclusive 'Sodality of Shadows'.⁸⁵ Its dozen or so members convened regularly in a Queen Street wine cellar, and new 'initiates' were subjected to an alcoholic parody of a ritual ceremony conceived by Waite, involving an 'elaborate, grotesquely solemn' rite of twenty-two stages.⁸⁶ The Sodality also allowed women ('the Daughters of Night'). Waite and Machen's experiences are recorded in a series of thirty-five veiled letters, which Waite eventually edited and published privately in 1904 as *The House of the Hidden Light*.

Only three copies of *The House of the Hidden Light* were printed, none of them bound, and the book was never referred to publicly by either author. When Gerald Yorke discovered a copy in the early 1940s, belonging to its publisher Philip Wellby, he quite plausibly thought that it had been issued as part of the GD curriculum, an opinion that Aleister Crowley seems to have shared when Yorke brought it to his attention.⁸⁷ It is easy to see why: the authors gave Latin mottos as their pseudonyms – 'Filius Aquarum' ('Son of the waters') for Machen and 'Elias Artista' ('Elias the artist') for Waite – and their letters were 'from a Lodge of the Adepts', written in the symbolic, allegorical language of the alchemists. *The House of the Hidden Light* is the ultimate in-joke, an affectionate send-up of the GD and the kind of occult literature in which both men held a deep interest, but it is also a record of something more serious. Machen was still trying to get over Amy's death, and Waite had begun seeing his former love Dora again (although only briefly). Both men were trying to make sense of their lives through drink and new romantic attachments:

> Thus, in the *Annus Mirabilis*, was the hall of the Neophytes opened and the two poor brothers were admitted in solemn form. At this time also there were given unto them two sisters, daughters of the House of Life, for high priestesses and ministers. Into the hands of these sisters were put wands of enchantment, wands of sorcery, wands of power, with liturgies and rituals written in sibylline books, from which they sang and celebrated throughout the wonderful year.[88]

Quick on the heels of the *Annus Mirabilis* came Machen's acquaintance with Dorothy Purefoy Huddleston (known as Purefoy; she, in turn, called him 'Uncle Mac' with affection). They were married in June 1903. 'She drinks absinthe, smokes when she dares, has no conventions & requires none,' Waite recorded in his diary: 'takes no exception to the qualification of Bohemian language, is something of an actress, and with us a gentlewoman'.[89] Machen was also experiencing a revitalization in his creative work, and had turned resolutely to exploring his interest in the Holy Grail legend. Waite, too, had embarked on a literary project: leveraging his influence at Horlick's Malted Milk Company, he began to edit *Horlick's Magazine and Home Journal for Australia, India and the Colonies*, or what he called his 'note-book at large'.[90] Blackden provided this venture with an entertaining account of his time in Egypt in the 1890s, and Waite himself supplied essays on the occult and poetry under various pseudonyms (including 'S. R.', his Order motto). Some of Machen's most important stories were debuted in its early issues, including 'The White People', 'A Fragment of Life' and the first chapters of *The Garden of Avallaunius* (an early title for the novel *The Hill of Dreams*). 'I do not know that the sale of Malted Milk was unfavourably affected,' Machen recalled, but after fifteen instalments the periodical suffered a similar fate to the *Unknown World* a decade before, sputtering out due to 'not selling as it should'.[91]

Now that the original GD was a shadow of its former self, its members struggling to rekindle the society's lost spark, Waite was experimenting with new orders and collecting masonic rites whose copyrights had expired. In 1901 he finally became a freemason, initiated into a Buckinghamshire lodge, and in April the following year he and Blackden joined the SRIA (on the recommendation of Palmer Thomas and Westcott). Along with Palmer Thomas and Blackden, Waite then formed his own 'Secret Council of Rites' in December 1902. He hoped that the Council would function as his own semi-masonic order, formed out of old or disused pre-existing rites, and seemed to think that the GD might in some way benefit from this by restoring its original connections to masonry.[92] Waite had heard rumours through Percy Bullock that the Order was in disarray with respect to its future, and he confided in Blackden that another '*coup d'état*' might be on the cards, though he was ultimately wary of beginning anything himself.[93] He also attended several meetings of a mysterious society known only in his diary as 'S∴O∴S∴', but chose not to continue with it.

At the Second Order's general meeting on 2 May 1903, an opportunity to take charge of the GD arose. The membership quickly became split into two factions, a slight majority supporting Brodie-Innes ('the poor small pope of Edinburgh') versus a resolute minority led by Waite, 'who completely blocked everything'.[94] Brodie-Innes proceeded to read aloud the clauses of a draft constitution, all of which Waite summarily objected to. 'I proposed therefore the rejection of the second draft constitution *in toto*,' Waite recalled, 'with the result that this also lapsed for want of the requisite majority. It being resolved otherwise that the triumvirate as such should not be elected for a third year, I proposed also that those who regarded the Golden Dawn as capable of a mystical instead of an occult construction should and had indeed resolved to work independently, going their own way.' The meeting ended with Brodie-Innes 'in a state of white rage'.[95]

CHAPTER 3

The main dispute between the two sides was the question of whether the Order should revert, as Brodie-Innes proposed in his draft constitution, to a version of the GD as it had been before 1890, but this time with elected Chiefs. Waite's faction agreed that a reversion was necessary, but objected to the Mathers-style system governed by a notional Third Order. The origin of the Cipher Manuscripts had been brought into doubt, thereby invalidating the assertion (now voiced by Brodie-Innes, who claimed to be in contact with the Adepts) that the GD had been founded with supernatural permission. On a more practical level, Waite wanted to modernize the Order's archaic-sounding rituals 'in accordance with good English' and dispense with magic altogether, becoming instead a 'mystical' school of hermetic philosophy.[96] Eventually, Waite's group issued a manifesto for the split: among its demands were that the division 'should be so effected as to secure absolute recognition of the independence and legitimacy of both bodies' and that all property should be distributed fairly, with 'the followers of SACRAMENTUM REGIS [Waite] taking those of the Outer Order and those of SUB SPE [Brodie-Innes] the Inner, the books to be divided equally'. Finally, the First Order members 'should fall to those who introduced them', a curious decision which presumed that those students in low grades must share the views regarding the GD's fate of those who had first brought them into the Order.[97] Throughout the rest of 1903 Waite and Brodie-Innes hashed out the terms of the pact in minute detail, and at last the inaugural meeting of Waite's 'Order of the Independent and Rectified Rite' (also known as the Independent and Rectified R.R. et A.C.) took place on 7 November. Its three Chiefs were Blackden, the Rev. Ayton and Waite himself. Among the First Order students who came with him were Algernon Blackwood, the artist Pamela Colman Smith and Machen.

Machen joined Waite's group in April 1904, Purefoy following in September, but neither were very active members. The Machens appear to have relied on order meetings as opportunities for socializing with their friend. 'We hope to turn up to Tea & Equinox next Saturday,' Machen wrote to Waite in 1907.[98] Another friend who joined the Rectified Rite was the young writer Evelyn Underhill, who had entered the Order in June 1904. She and Machen had known each other since the late 1890s, and he may have encouraged her to join. Waite had commissioned Underhill to write half a dozen stories for *Horlick's*, and she was working on her first novel, *The Grey World*, about the reincarnation of a dying child and his pursuit of the mystical life. The writer, theologian and occultist Charles Williams later wrote about Underhill's friendship with Machen in an introduction to her collected letters, noting that Machen's interests were 'in some respects, very like her own, though in the expression of them she turned rather to actuality and he to myth'.[99] Her third novel, *The Column of Dust*, recounts the finding of the Holy Grail in the form of a glass cup. Dedicated to Arthur and Purefoy ('Friendship's offering'), the book is the first instance of a GD student describing the Order's rituals in a fictional setting.

> There was a piece of cardboard, on which the Pentagram, the Tetragrammaton, and the Caduceus had been traced in coloured inks according to the recipe of Éliphas Lévi. Symbols in outline are seldom impressive, and I am afraid that this talisman had failed to affect her imagination as it should. She hung it across her breast with a piece of string; and, noting the effect, wondered whether this were or were not the ancestor of the scapular. There was also a forked hazel twig, its tips covered with little hazels of steel: the magician's wand.[100]

Underhill later considered her time in the GD to have been a youthful 'moment of puberty'.[101] In every period of 'true mystical activity', she wrote in her study of mysticism in 1912, 'we find an outbreak of occultism, illuminism, or other perverted spirituality'. In a chapter titled 'Mysticism and Magic', she quotes the *Occult Review* in order to dispute Waite's claim that magic is transcendental ('a promise which it cannot fulfil').[102] Having entered the GD and come out the other side, she now saw ritual magic as simply an extension of reality, a distorted form of mystical thinking that 'does not lead anywhere', but she retained a deep respect for its traditions and an affection for occult writers such as Waite and Lévi.[103] It is unclear whether Underhill's friendship with Machen continued after both had left Waite's order: Machen interviewed her for the *Evening News* in 1913 to promote her book *The Mystic Way*, after which he sent her 'a rather harrowing letter' suggesting that he no longer considered her a Christian.[104]

Now that Waite was the head of an order, he was able to begin shaping it towards his own impenetrable mysticism. Machen, like Underhill, let his membership fall into abeyance. The two men nonetheless remained friends for the rest of their lives, corresponding on points of grail scholarship and religion and collaborating on the verse drama 'The Hidden Sacrament of the Holy Graal', published in Waite's *Strange Houses of Sleep* in 1906.[105] The preface describes the work as a 'Mystery Play', for which Machen, referred to only as the author's 'friend and fellow-worker in the mysteries', supplied the initial concept and the play's exhaustive stage directions, as well as the lyrics to several drinking songs.[106] In 1909 Machen also provided research for *The Hidden Church of the Holy Grail*, a 700-page book partly constructed from Waite's early columns for the *Occult Review*. Machen reviewed it for *T. P.'s Weekly*, calling his friend's theory 'entrancing but very subtle'.[107] His own views on the grail tradition are to be found in his novel *The Secret Glory*, early chapters of which first appeared in Lord Alfred Douglas's *The Academy* from 1906.

Though Machen had left the occult behind, he achieved unlikely recognition in 1914 with a short story for the *Evening News*, in which a line of ghostly Agincourt archers appears in the sky to save the British troops at the Battle of Mons. 'The Bowmen' was treated as a factual account by many readers, dissected in parish magazines as well as the *Occult Review* and *Light*, and gave rise to the Angel of Mons legend.[108] Machen's star would rise again in the 1920s, with the discovery of his work by an American readership. Writers such as Vincent Starrett dedicated themselves to publishing new editions of Machen's fiction and essays. Years later, Machen would return to the GD in his autobiography. In a reminiscence printed privately in 1923, he affectionately recalls an adventure with Waite which might explain why he left the Order while Waite continued in it:

> The fact was that both of us had many interests, which led us astray. Waite, perhaps, thought that he might find the Holy Grail, disguised, disgraced and dishonoured in some back shop of a back-street; while I have always had the great and absorbing desire of going the other way. The other way? That is the secret.[109]

4
Babe of the Abyss
Aleister Crowley

> I, Perdurabo, as the Temporary Envoy Plenipotentiary of Deo Duce Comite Ferro & thus the Third from the Secret Chiefs of the Order of the Rose of Ruby and the Cross of Gold, do deliberately invoke all laws, all powers Divine, demanding that I, even I, be chosen to do such a work as he has done, at all costs to myself.[1]

The entry in Aleister Crowley's diary for 12 April 1900 conveys the sacrificial mentality he assumed as he crossed the English Channel as Mathers's representative. He was twenty-four; only two years earlier he had been at Trinity College, Cambridge, discovering the sinful allure of decadent poetry. Now here he was, on his way to wrest control of the Isis-Urania Temple from its dissident members. Resistance would mean expulsion from the Order.

When Crowley arrived in London he first met with his accomplice Elaine Simpson, and together they managed to break into the Second Order rooms at Blythe Road. They changed the locks, and a childish Crowley, annoyed at having previously been denied entry into the Second Order, added his name to the official roll call. Two days later, it was all over. Crowley had yoked himself to Mathers because he had recognized the Imperator's 'extraordinary attainment' in magic and ignored the ethical claims made against him ('Ordinary morality is only for ordinary people').[2] More importantly, he believed that Mathers possessed the only genuine link to the Secret Chiefs. If the GD had acted as a university for Yeats in the early 1890s, then for Crowley the Order was a gateway to higher powers. His initiation as a Neophyte in

1898 was his first step on a path that would quickly transcend the Order. For the time being, however, the Battle of Blythe Road had brought his formal association with the GD to an embarrassing and decisive end. Crowley was cast out at the same time that Mathers was deposed.

Crowley's reputation preceded him, and he fostered it eagerly. Born Edward Alexander Crowley and known to his family as Alec, he eventually favoured 'Aleister' because of a theory that those whose names comprise a dactyl (one stressed syllable, then two unstressed) and a spondee (two stressed syllables), as in 'Jeremy Taylor', are most likely to become famous. 'Alastor' was also the name of a poem by Shelley. Throughout his life he would cultivate a list of other grandiose titles: the Beast 666, Lord Boleskine, the Spirit of Solitude, the Wanderer in the Waste, Perdurabo and, in 1923, 'the wickedest man in the world' (courtesy of the newspaper *John Bull*). Reality provided a more nuanced picture. When the novelist Anthony Powell, then an editorial assistant at the publisher Duckworth, lunched with Crowley sometime in the early 1930s, he half-expected to be met by a thaumaturge in ritual dress. Powell was surprised to be greeted instead by a shabby figure whose Homburg hat disguised the 'unusual formation of his bald and shaven skull', and whose rasping, 'near-cockney' accent and music-hall style of humour offset his reputation for wickedness. 'There was much that was absurd about him,' Powell remembered; 'at the same time it seems false to assert – as some did – that his absurdity transcended all sense of being sinister. If the word has any meaning, Crowley was sinister, intensely sinister, both in exterior and manner.'[3] Other writers who encountered Crowley during his later years arrived at similar conclusions. The journalist Maurice Richardson, while admitting to being charmed by the Beast 666, characterized Crowley as a 'manic paranoid charlatan and mystic mountebank' rumoured to have a 'nasty streak of cruelty'.[4]

Born in 1875 in Leamington Spa, Warwickshire, into a wealthy family of Plymouth Brethren – a Christian nonconformist movement that began in 1830s Dublin – Crowley's early years were constrained by biblical literalism, and he found himself drawn to the prophetic imagery of the Book of Revelation. He was remarkably gifted at free climbing and chess, and spent carefree summers scaling mountains and fishing. After the death of his father in 1888, the family moved in with his religiously dogmatic uncle in London and Crowley began 'sinning' with young women.[5] He went up to Trinity College, Cambridge in 1895, where he did hardly any work and left after coming into an inheritance of £40,000 (several million pounds in today's currency).[6] In 1897, hoping to make contact with the Devil, Crowley entered the Cambridge bookshop Deighton Bell and came away with A. E. Waite's *Book of Black Magic and of Pacts*, which he was disappointed to find was simply a compilation of medieval grimoires. He was put off by Waite's irreverent and pompous style and his unwillingness to treat Satan with the grandeur that he had come to expect from reading Milton and the decadent novels of J. K. Huysmans. In Waite's introduction, however, he detected hints of something far more tantalizing: an inner circle of Adepts who studied the 'science of the old sanctuaries'.[7] He wrote to Waite, asking for information, and Waite responded by recommending *The Cloud upon the Sanctuary*, an eighteenth-century mystical text by Karl von Eckartshausen recently translated by Waite's friend, the artist Isabelle de Steiger. The book confirmed for Crowley the existence of what he called the 'Hidden Church'.[8]

Almost immediately, he found what he was looking for. In 1898, while on a climbing expedition in Zermatt, Switzerland, Crowley met an English chemist and (self-proclaimed) alchemist named Julian Baker.[9] In October, Baker introduced Crowley to George Cecil Jones, a GD student who sensed Crowley's magical potential and advised him to make contact with a spiritual 'Master' using a ritual working described in *The Book of the Sacred Magic of Abra-Melin the Mage*.[10] This was another of Mathers's recent grimoire translations, begun after he had discovered the seventeenth-century manuscript in a Parisian library and, after a falling-out with George Redway, finally published in 1898 by Frederick Leigh Gardner. The book, which Mathers claimed Bulwer-Lytton and Lévi had known about, supposedly contained the revealed teachings of the Egyptian magician Abra-Melin. At the same time as Crowley prepared to work this six-month-long ritual, he was recommended by Jones as a candidate for the GD, and

Moina Mathers, design for *The Book of the Sacred Magic of Abra-Melin the Mage*, translated by Samuel Liddell MacGregor Mathers, 1898.

CHAPTER 4

he entered Isis-Urania on 18 November 1898.[11] He took the motto 'Perdurabo' ('I will endure'), and by May of the next year had reached the Philosophus grade (4° = 7°). The Order already harboured several published poets within its ranks (Yeats, A. E. Waite, Charles Rosher and L. Florence Wynne Ffoulkes), but with the addition of Crowley it gained a prolific, if not commercially successful, new writer.

Crowley had published poems while at Cambridge in the university periodicals *Cambridge Magazine*, *Cantab*, *Granta* (in its first, student-edited incarnation) and *Silver Crescent*. These were mostly ballads sending up college life and a miscellany of what he called 'mixed biscuits'. Shelley was an early influence (as he was to Yeats and Florence Farr) and a ripe source for titles and sobriquets ('the Spirit of Solitude').

Crowley's link with decadent London culture was through his friend and lover Herbert Pollitt, who was ten years older and a patron of Aubrey Beardsley.[12] Pollitt was Crowley's first intimate relationship, and an archetype of avant-garde culture in the style of J. K. Huysmans's Des Esseintes or Maurice Maeterlinck's Tintagiles: he collected fashionable art, performed in drag under the name Diane de Rougy and in 1896 had been fictionalized in E. F. Benson's Cambridge novel *The Babe, B. A.* as an aesthete who subscribed to *The Yellow Book*.[13] It might have been Pollitt who introduced Crowley to Beardsley; Crowley commissioned the ailing artist to design a personal bookplate and a cover illustration for a future poetry collection, but Beardsley died of tuberculosis before he could complete them. Crowley's portrait of a virgin Beardsley, who made physical love only in dreams, featured in his first book *Aceldama: A Place to Bury Strangers In* (1898):

> Aubrey attained in sleep when he dreamt this
> Wonderful dream of women, tender child
> And harlot, naked all, in thousands piled

> On one hot writhing heap, his shameful kiss
>   To shudder through them, with lithe limbs defiled
>   To wade, to dip
> Down through the mass, caressed by every purple lip.[14]

Throughout *Aceldama*, to 'attain' is to reach orgasm, to 'lose ourselves, together, far above / the highest heaven, in one sweet lover's / kiss'.[15] The collection was dedicated to Pollitt and marked Crowley's first foray into the erotic, avant-garde literary currents of the *fin de siècle*. Alongside influences from Shelley, Milton and Blake, Pollitt had introduced him to Algernon Swinburne, Charles Baudelaire and the world of modern French and English verse. Crowley admired these poets because they succeeded in 'celebrating the victory of the human soul over its adversaries'. To an undergraduate suddenly having a lot of sex – with both women and men at this point – the 'victory' was the physical act of love, and the 'adversary' any institution that stood in the way of its consummation. 'Love,' wrote Crowley, in full rebellion against his Plymouth Brethren upbringing, 'was a challenge to Christianity.'[16] The sentiment was fundamental to the early work of Swinburne, the English poet whose *Poems and Ballads*, published in 1866, had been decried as immoral for its themes of lesbianism and defiance of religious dogma. Crowley latched onto Swinburne as a model for conveying radical ideas, and hoped to surpass him in poetic mastery.

From 1898 to 1899, Crowley wrote an enormous amount of verse, publishing half a dozen collections in very limited formats. After *Aceldama* (by 'A Gentleman of the University of Cambridge', in imitation of Shelley) came the ornate and sexually explicit *White Stains*, presented as the 'literary remains of George Archibald Bishop: a neuropath of the second empire'.[17] 'Bishop' was a puckish reference to Crowley's uncle, the austere Tom Bond Bishop, and 'neuropath' a term employed in the 1880s by the German psychiatrist Richard von Krafft-Ebing to suggest that a strong sexual instinct was the result of a diseased and nervous mind. *White Stains* is presented as a rebuke to this theory (with tongue firmly in cheek, though Crowley liked to say he wrote it as a 'testimony of my praeterhuman innocence'), and was issued in a run of only 100 copies by Leonard Smithers.[18] The almost-bankrupt Smithers, then notable as a publisher of *fin-de-siècle* literature including the work of Arthur Symons and Ernest Dowson and *The Savoy* magazine, had to arrange for typesetting to be carried out by a Dutch firm to avoid English censorship laws. The manuscript of Crowley's next collection, *Green Alps*, was destroyed by a fire at the printers in the summer of 1898 and never appeared (the same fire also destroyed Waite's *Doctrine and Literature of the Kabbalah*), only hastening Smithers's eventual bankruptcy.[19] Unfazed, and apparently unwilling to spend any time editing, the prolific Crowley followed up with *The Tale of Archais* (1898), *Songs of the Spirit* (1898), *Jephthah and Other Mysteries* (1899) and *Jezebel and Other Tragic Poems* (1899).

Crowley's discovery of the 'Hidden Church' and his induction into the GD were already shaping his poetic output. *Songs of the Spirit* was dedicated to Baker for his part in leading Crowley to the GD, their spiritual quest rendered into metaphors of climbing and exploration ('Thine was the hand that guided me / By moor and mountain, vale and lea'). While some of these poems were written before 1898, there are many in which Crowley experiments with basic ideas from his reading in the occult. 'The Philosopher's Progress', with an epigram from Hermes Trismegistus, charts the narrator's realization of the unity of the world; that 'The Depth is one with That Above' and therefore the sin of lust is equated with 'clean' love.[20] 'The Initiation' was an attempt at writing Blakean apocalypse, in which Crowley's 'neophyte' battles the elements:

> Darkness, a dragon, now devours
> The vision of those deadly powers,
> The legions of the lords of sin.
> It is an hour ere dawn begin.

The play *Jephthah: A Tragedy* was written in the month of his initiation into Isis-Urania, and begins with a preliminary 'invocation' to Swinburne. His continuing debt to Swinburne and possibly to Beardsley's *Under the Hill* (partly serialized in *The Savoy* in 1896) was also reflected in a verse retelling of the Tannhäuser legend, about a medieval knight who discovers the goddess Venus in an underground land and falls in love with her. Crowley's own view of his poems was characteristically vain; he considered them complex and multifaceted, with the 'slightest phrase' requiring individual interpretation.[21] He had begun to think of them as in some sense occult, containing both exoteric and esoteric meanings.

Crowley's books were lavish, expensive objects that became increasingly talismanic following his GD initiation and the commencement of his magical studies in earnest. The consecration of talismans (wands, pentacles, the Rosy Cross lamen) was a key part of GD ceremonies, and the 'Z' documents outlining the symbolism of the Neophyte degree stressed the care candidates must take in their design in order to attract the desired 'Universal Forces'.[22] Astrological calculations were essential to many GD magical practices, and as the 1900s progressed Crowley began to record the exact time and planetary position on the title pages of a selection of his books. Each volume of his magazine *The Equinox*, first published in 1909, gives the date as '☉ in ♈' (Sun in Aries) or '☉ in ♎' (Sun in Libra) on the cover, title page and spine, depending on whether they were published at the spring or autumn equinox. Colour was also rich in occult symbolism, and for the GD its combinations at various points in their rituals could represent or even act as potent moments of transformation. Florence Farr's notebooks from the 1890s contain painted examples of how students were taught to think about colour when designing talismans or ceremonial robes. Crowley's books often adopt this scheme of symbolism, as in *The Blue Equinox* (1919) or the six *Holy Books* (1909), which were printed within gold borders and bound in gold-blocked vellum (gold corresponding with *tiphareth*, beauty, on the Kabbalistic Tree of Life).[23]

Crowley valued assertiveness, genius and virility above all other traits, and expected to find these qualities in the leading magicians of the day.

Aleister Crowley, cover of *Konx Om Pax*, 1907.

Instead, he was introduced to a group he later described as 'nonentities ... as vulgar and commonplace as any other set of average people'. He considered Yeats the GD's sole accomplished writer, though when Crowley approached the 'lank, dishevelled demonologist' with proof pages of *Jephthah and Other Mysteries*, he was apparently given no encouragement beyond 'a few polite conventionalities'.[24] Several years later, Yeats described Crowley as a madman who had written 'six lines, amid much bad rhetoric, of real poetry'.[25] Among the other GD members, Crowley confessed an admiration for Florence Farr, 'for whom I always felt an affectionate respect tempered by a feeling of compassion that her abilities were so inferior to her aspirations', but the rest he found frankly disappointing. He only met Westcott once, when sent on an errand by Mathers 'to tell him he had incurred a traitor's doom', and later wrote to him to demand that the Cipher Manuscripts be deposited in the British Museum.[26] Despite this brief contact, he would become the butt of many of Crowley's literary satires.

In the grand tradition of magical tutelage, Crowley's relationship with the young GD Adept Allan Bennett proved to be one of the most enduring influences on his life, beyond even Mathers. Astonished to find that Bennett was penniless and living in lodgings with another GD member, Charles Rosher, Crowley insisted that his friend come to live with him in his expansive Chancery Lane rooms (in a bid to cut himself off from his family, he had signed the lease under his pen name, Vladimir Svareff). Bennett was an asthmatic who maintained seasonal addictions to opium and cocaine, and his experience in the GD, particularly the elaborate rituals he had created for his work with Farr and Rosher, made him an apt teacher. Crowley was willing to absorb anything that Bennett had to impart. 'He showed me where to get knowledge, how to criticize it and how to apply it,' Crowley recalled. 'We also worked together at ceremonial Magick; evoking spirits, consecrating talismans, and so on.'

> During this time, magical phenomena were of constant occurrence. I had two temples in my flat; one white, the walls being lined with six huge mirrors, each six feet by eight; the other

black, a mere cupboard, in which stood an altar supported by the figure of a Negro [sic] standing on his hands. The presiding genius of this place was a human skeleton, which I fed from time to time with blood, small birds and the like. The idea was to give it life, but I never got further than causing the bones to become covered with a viscous slime.[27]

One of Crowley's magical adventures of the period was recorded in 'At the Fork of the Roads', a short story published in 1909. Count Swanoff's flat, blood-stained skeleton and all, forms an outpost against the forces of the White Brothers, a rival magical society. A 'long lank melancholy unwashed poet' named Will Bute (Yeats) has sent Hypatia Gay (based on Althea Gyles, an Irish poet and illustrator of Yeats's books with whom Crowley had an affair) to pick up a magical link through which Swanoff can be destroyed.[28] Hypatia manages to extract a drop of his blood using her brooch pin, and during the night the Count is attacked by a succubus. Only by remembering the words of his 'master' (Bennett) does he succeed in banishing her. The story is an early example of Crowley's tendency to distort episodes from his life for playful, sensational fiction.

Crowley continued to prepare for his Abra-Melin ritual, and at great expense purchased Boleskine House, a one-storey manor built on the shores of Loch Ness. Boleskine was to be the secluded temple required by the conjuration, the eventual goal being to invoke and converse with his Holy Guardian Angel (a magician's ideal self, or 'Genius' in GD parlance).[29] Postponing what was to be an exhausting and possibly dangerous feat, in 1900 he travelled to Mexico, where he met up with the climber Oscar Eckenstein and practised the Enochian scrying system of the Renaissance occultists John Dee and Edward Kelly. He also worked on the GD's invisibility technique, which involved summoning an aura around one's person. Crowley was satisfied with the result and appeared 'invisibly' on many future occasions.[30]

Having decided to consult Bennett about his misgivings about Mathers, Crowley then sailed west from Hawai'i via Japan, eventually arriving in Ceylon (now Sri Lanka), where Bennett, by this time a converted Buddhist, was employed as a tutor. On his trip he purchased vellum-bound editions of Chaucer, Shakespeare and Browning. He also carried with him poetry by Shelley, Keats, Swinburne and, significantly, a copy of Mathers's *Kabbalah Unveiled*, which he had been reading since before his introduction to the GD.[31] 'I carried these volumes everywhere, and even when my alleged waterproof rucksack was soaked through, my masterpieces remained intact.'[32] These authors (perhaps excepting Mathers) were Crowley's connection to 'the great men of the past'.[33] What Crowley and Bennett talked about is not known, but evidently Crowley was satisfied with Bennett's advice: 'Mathers thus disposed of, to business!'[34]

After 1900, Crowley was no longer an official student of the GD, but was instead seeking magical advancement on his own. He had concluded that the Secret Chiefs were no longer in communication with Mathers: 'We [Crowley and Bennett] simply dismissed from our minds the whole question of the G∴D∴ and restated the problem on first principles.'[35] In 1903, he married Rose Edith Kelly, the widowed sister of the British painter Gerald Kelly, and the newlyweds honeymooned in Europe and with Bennett in Ceylon. Crowley and Rose then travelled to Egypt, and it was in Cairo in March 1904 that Crowley claimed that the text of *The Book of the Law* had been revealed to him. The event has become part of his personal mythology, retold by Crowley in several publications. He had desired to conjure the sylphs to impress Rose, by then pregnant, but she instead went into an involuntary trance state and started to repeat the words 'They are waiting for you'.[36] During a later invocation, Rose, who knew nothing about ancient Egyptian religion, declared that it was the god Horus who was waiting, and gave Crowley instructions on how to invoke him. She then led her disbelieving husband to a funerary stele in Cairo's Boulak museum, on which was depicted Ra-Hoor-Khuit with his son Horus. The exhibit's catalogue number was 666. Crowley was slowly convinced that the Secret Chiefs had sent a messenger 'to confer upon me the position which Mathers had forfeited'.[37] The messenger's name was Aiwass (or Aiwaz), Crowley's Holy Guardian Angel of the grade Ipsissimus ($10° = 1°$). Over three hour-long sessions Aiwass dictated to Crowley

CHAPTER 4

over his left shoulder what would become *The Book of the Law*, the central text of Thelema.

Thelema was Crowley's system of magick (the 'k' was added to distinguish it from stage magic), an expansion of his theory of will. 'Do what thou wilt shall be the whole of the law' is its oft-repeated mantra, from which springs Thelema's entire body of teachings. The 'will' is an individual's driving force or purpose, and needs to be performed to be realized. 'Do what thou wilt' is the command to discover this purpose. Crowley also considered will to be a kind of love, an idea that produced Thelema's answering refrain 'Love is the law, love under will'. Though at first sceptical, Crowley began to see Aiwass's revelations as a sign that he was a prophet of a new age, and in 1907 he founded Thelema's first organization, based on the same ritual structure as the GD. The 'Argenteum Astrum' (the Silver Star, or A∴A∴) was to be his successor to Mathers's Order.

Of the triad of Secret Chiefs required to establish a ritual order of this kind, only Crowley had been a GD student. For the other two, J. F. C. Fuller and Victor Neuburg, the A∴A∴ was their first taste of ceremonial magic. Captain Fuller was serving in the First Oxfordshire Light Infantry when in 1905 he entered a contest (advertised by Crowley) to write an essay on Crowley's poetic oeuvre. His submission, in fact the sole entry, was later published in 1907 as *The Star in the West*, and Fuller became devoted to Crowley. Like Mathers, Fuller combined occultism with an interest in warfare, though unlike him he would go on to have a decorated career as a military strategist and historian. He later praised Oswald Mosley and expressed Nazi sympathies. The 'faunlike' Victor Neuburg, on the other hand, was a young English poet and Trinity College graduate whom Crowley met in 1906. Together the two men developed and performed sex-based rituals, some under gruelling conditions in the Algerian desert, during which Crowley advanced to his Second Order grade of 'Babe of the Abyss'.[38] Neuburg also organized meetings of the Pan Society, a

Cambridge-based poetry discussion group that doubled as a place to enlist A∴A∴ students.[39] Crowley was brought in to lecture in 1907, and met promising young acolytes such as Kenneth Martin Ward and the mathematician Norman Mudd (though they would not join officially until several years later). Another early recruit was the young artist Austin Osman Spare, who became a Probationer (a preparatory grade before Neophyte) in July 1909. Spare, whose distinctive, fantastic black-and-white drawings were full of hermetic imagery, did not last long in the A∴A∴: he had his own sigil-based magic system, which he much preferred.

The A∴A∴ entered the public eye in March 1909 with the first issue of *The Equinox*, published from the 'offices' of Crowley's Victoria Street flat. The magazine's ostensible purpose was to spread the teachings of Crowley's order and to attract new students. It styled itself as 'The Review of Scientific Illuminism: "The Method of Science – The Aim of Religion"' and was to be published twice a year in hardcover. Crowley was adamant that *The Equinox* could not make money, otherwise he would lay himself open to aspersions of profiteering (printing costs were high, but the magazine sold enough subscriptions to break even).[40] It was also an outlet for fiction, poetry, essays and illustration, with issues often supplemented by book-length appendices. Spare provided drawings for the second issue, and Neuburg gladly supplied poems. There were also articles on pharmacology by the chemist Edward Whinery, from whom Crowley purchased his ritual perfumes and incenses, and the Irish American writer Frank Harris sent in a few short stories. Another regular contributor was the young poet Ethel Archer; her early poems for *The Equinox* formed the basis for her debut collection *The Whirlpool* in 1911, and her occult novel *The Hieroglyph* (1932) would become an important source for the history of the A∴A∴.

But just as A. E. Waite had done when editing the *Unknown World* and *Horlick's Magazine*, Crowley had to provide the majority of the contents himself. He had been experimenting with fiction since 1902, but the pieces that appeared in *Sword of Song* (1904) were undeveloped, more like prose poems than conventional short stories. Crowley's first tale to feature in a literary publication was 'The Drug', printed in the

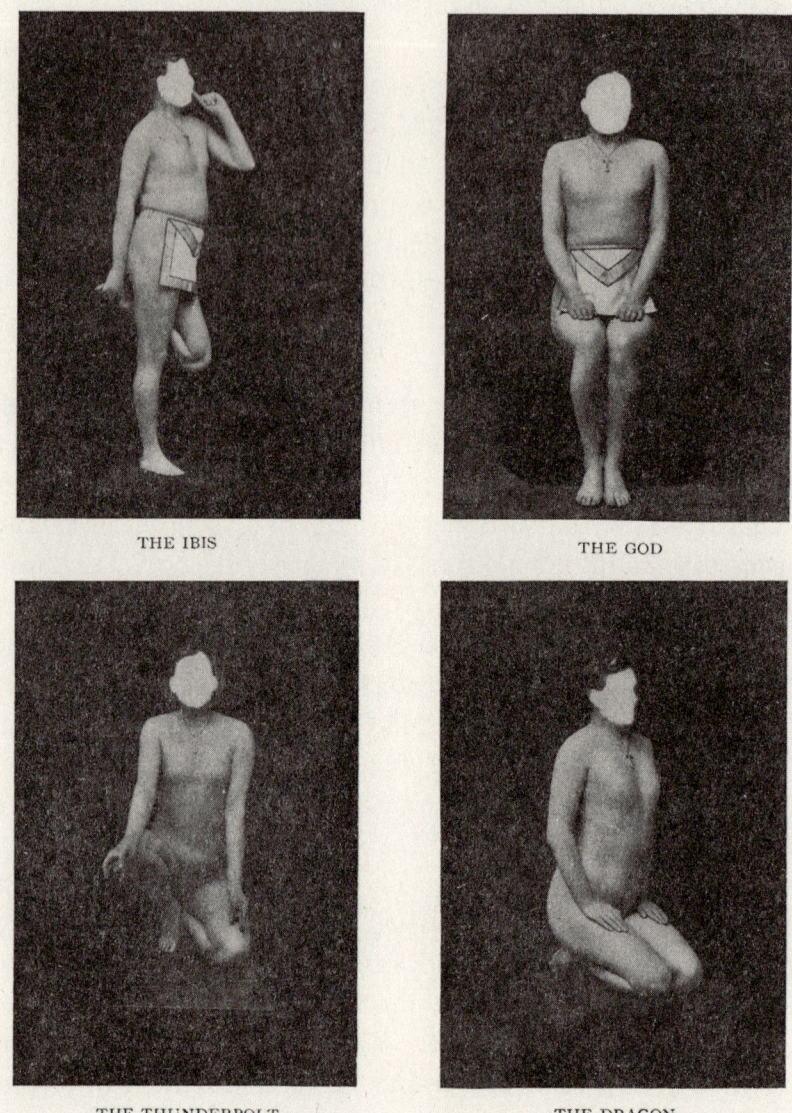

Yoga poses, from *The Equinox*, vol. 1, no. 1, 21 March 1909.

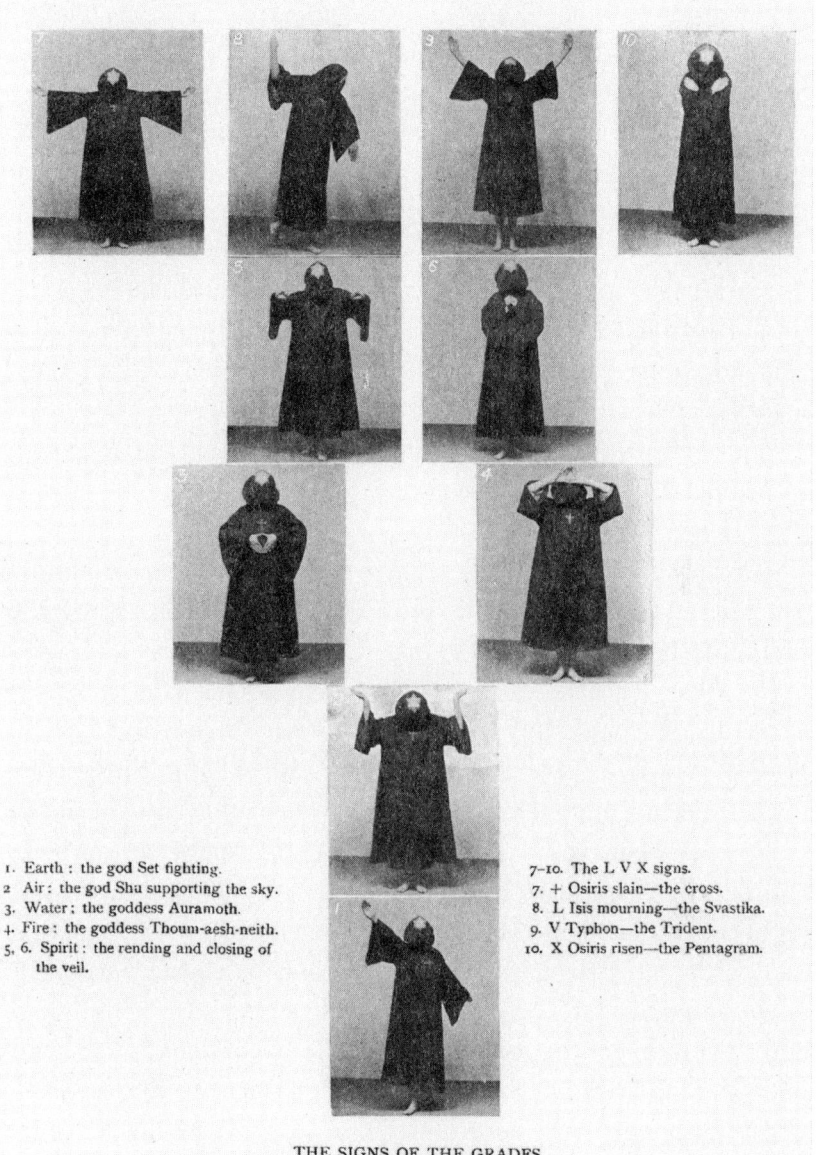

1. Earth: the god Set fighting.
2. Air: the god Shu supporting the sky.
3. Water: the goddess Auramoth.
4. Fire: the goddess Thoum-aesh-neith.
5, 6. Spirit: the rending and closing of the veil.

7–10. The L V X signs.
7. + Osiris slain—the cross.
8. L Isis mourning—the Svastika.
9. V Typhon—the Trident.
10. X Osiris risen—the Pentagram.

THE SIGNS OF THE GRADES

'The Signs of the Grades', from *The Equinox*, vol. 1, no. 2, 24 September 1909.

January 1909 edition of *The Idler*. Over the next four years he filled *The Equinox* with short stories, often autobiographical in nature. He began to develop a clearer, more restrained style, and after the first *Equinox* run finished was able to sell his work to paying outlets. Crowley considered this newfound short form a way to express emotion with precision: 'I take fits of it,' he wrote,

> I go for a month without thinking of the subject at all, and then all of a sudden I find myself with ideas and writing them down. I entirely agree that the short story is one of the most delicate and powerful forms of expression. It forms a link with poetry because one can work up to ecstasy of one kind or another in a more lyric manner than is possible in a novel.[41]

Crowley also used his periodical to champion writers he admired. The second issue featured the prose poem 'The Sphinx at Gaza' by the Anglo-Irish writer Lord Dunsany, a friend of Yeats and patron of the Abbey Theatre who was already making his name as a fantasist with collections such as *The Gods of Pegāna* (1905) and *Time and the Gods* (1906). Crowley became a great supporter of Dunsany during this period, and maintained that his tales of invented lands and strange pantheons conveyed authentic magical experiences – whether Dunsany himself knew it or not.[42] He held Arthur Machen in the same high regard, and though Machen never contributed to *The Equinox*, his name cropped up regularly in its reviews and in Crowley's articles for *Vanity Fair* and later *The International*. 'The distinction of his thought and style is one of the most unmistakable of contemporary literary phenomena,' Crowley wrote in a review of Machen's 1917 novel *The Terror* (although in the same review Crowley calls for Machen's execution for his openly 'pro-German' tendencies).[43] This had nothing to do with Machen having been in Isis-Urania: other GD students such as W. T. Horton and Algernon Blackwood were consistently reviewed poorly. Blackwood especially was considered a plagiarist, 'suffering from indigestion brought on by a surfeit of ill-cooked Theosophy'.[44] Crowley was kinder to John Brodie-Innes, whose novels *Morag the Seal*

(1908) and *For the Soul of a Witch* (1910) he considered works of passable refinement and imagination. Brodie-Innes, having published mostly on legal procedure, was then embarking on a serious career as a writer of self-consciously historical romances set around the Scottish witchcraft trials. *The Devil's Mistress*, published in 1915 and dedicated to the memory of his friend Bram Stoker, would prove a huge success.

As the chief organ and recruiting arm of Crowley's new order, *The Equinox* also acted as a useful venue for insulting rival magicians. Waite regularly came under fire in the column 'My Crapulous Contemporaries': its fourth instalment, 'Wisdom While You Waite', was a review (under the name 'I. Biss') of *The Book of Ceremonial Magic* (1911), a repackaged edition of Waite's *Book of Black Magic and of Pacts* with an updated preface. Crowley owed his introduction to the GD partly to the book, but he nevertheless took the opportunity to mock Waite's prose style and point out his hypocrisy in failing to treat the Catholic mass as ritual magic: 'The ceremonies which might be practised by, say, a neophyte of the A∴A∴ would be as sublime as, and less tainted than, the services of the Church,' he noted.[45] The review ends with a lengthy accusation of plagiarism, tabulated for the reader's judgment over three pages.[46] Yeats, or 'Weary Willy', is neatly sent up in 'The Shadowy Dill-Waters' as a poet whose work is dully inoffensive and lacking in any real magical insight: 'The fact is that you are both myopic and tone-deaf,' Crowley wrote. 'You peer into the darkly splendid world, the abyss of light – for it is light, to the seer – and you see but "unintelligible images, unluminous, formless, and void".' Then you return and pose as one who has trodden the eternal snows.'[47]

Several apocryphal stories about Mathers, which have stuck to him ever since, also originated in the pages of *The Equinox*. These include an incident in which he supposedly threatened to shoot Bennett with a revolver for repeating the mantra 'Shiva, Shiva, Shiva' in the Matherses' sitting room.[48] In the short story 'The Dream Circean', set in Montmartre, one character asks after the 'Scotch Count', in reference to Mathers's Jacobean fantasies, 'who always spoke like a hanging judge': 'Went to Scotland – he could get no more whisky here on credit,' comes the answer.[49]

Oversize and totally obscure to uninitiated readers, *The Equinox* was Crowley's most ambitious literary venture to date, and in many ways his legacy. It contains most of his A∴A∴ teachings (or '*libri*') from that period, including a facsimile of *The Book of the Law*, accompanied by extracts from his 1903–4 diary. Reviewers were baffled by its magical content: 'It is the sort of thing no fellow can understand,' admitted the *Morning Leader*. 'One gathers vaguely out of the confusion that it deals with such things as Magic, wizardry, mysticism and so on.'[50] The *Review of Reviews* called it a 'strange, weird, incomprehensible magazine ... a curious sign of the times'.[51] There was obvious trouble with publishing material relating to a secret society, especially in a magazine accessible to any subscribing member of the public.

Fuller was writing a serialized biography of Crowley for the magazine under the title *The Temple of Solomon the King*, the second instalment of which summarized Crowley's time in the GD. Consequently, this meant that many of the Order's teachings and fabled origins were laid out for all to see, beginning with Westcott's 'Historical Lecture' on its founding. This was followed by an alternative version of the GD's history, presumably written by Crowley himself, which exposed Mathers's 'unhappy juggleries' and his 'verbose and pretentious' rituals, which, according to Crowley, were never of any real worth. The entire workings of the First Order rituals were printed verbatim, including the GD's diagram of correspondences (linking the *sefirot*, the zodiac, the elements and the Major Arcana). All of this, the authors claimed, had been lifted from the 'actual MSS. in our possession relating to the G∴D∴', occupying twelve hundred pages and containing 'over a quarter of a million words'. Fuller was critical of the grades, judging that they were so packed with symbolism and the names of angels and deities that the initiate is left bewildered, 'rolled in a heap of tinselled draperies'.[52] Only Crowley was able to see past these 'pyrotechnics', he continued, and take what was useful to him. Fuller made it plain that the next part of Crowley's GD story would be told in future issues – this would mean outlines of the Second Order rituals.

With the September 1909 issue, the GD's secrets had been dragged into the blinding light of public scrutiny. Crowley considered his

Neophyte pledge of secrecy to have been invalidated by his becoming a Secret Chief of a new order, and was of the view that by printing the GD teachings he would be able to start afresh. As a character in one of his later novels explains, magical societies are secret only to avoid their activities being interrupted; the actual teachings should be free to all, because only the serious student will be able or willing to use them: 'We guard our magick just as much and as little as our other branches of physics.'[53] Mathers, however, thought otherwise. He had seen the second instalment of *Solomon* and got wind of Crowley's plan to expose the Second Order material before the third issue's publication in early March 1910, going so far as to file an interim injunction calling upon Crowley to desist due to copyright infringement and the breaking of the GD secrecy oath. He had also written to Brodie-Innes alerting him to 'the exceptional circumstances of the shameful publication of the M.S.S. of our Order by that scoundrel Aleister Crowley', appearing not to know whether or not Brodie-Innes was still involved with the GD (he was – possibly as Praemonstrator in the newly formed Stella Matutina).[54] Brodie-Innes wrote back, distancing himself from the affair by suggesting that they should give Crowley their blessing '& stand by to see what he does'.[55] When the injunction was granted by a judge on 18 March, Crowley immediately filed an appeal. The case was heard on 21 March 1910. Both parties were in attendance, the white-haired Mathers now diminished with age (though he was only fifty-six) but still capable of answering the solicitors' questions with self-assurance. He was introduced as the 'chief of the Rosicrucian Order' and subjected to an examination that prompted laughter from delighted spectators.[56] The exchanges by the legal teams were reported in sensational detail in the press:

> Sir F. Low: Our complaint is that wherever our ritual was got from, it was a gross breach of faith for the defendant, after being admitted and allowed to attend the meetings, and then being expelled from the Order, to start publishing this matter.
> Lord Justice Moulton: He has as much right to publish what is in the old books about the Rosicrucians as anybody else.

> Sir F. Low: He is not entitled to publish a ritual ceremony which he had pledged himself to secrecy about, even if it was got from the Bible.⁵⁷

In the end, Crowley won. Mathers had apparently left it too long before filing an injunction, and there was no evidence that the revelations in issue two had caused him any harm. Interest in Crowley's A∴A∴ rose sharply in the immediate aftermath of the ruling, and the number of candidates seeking initiation almost doubled from that of the previous year. Members of other orders, masonic and otherwise, sought Crowley out to bestow upon him the high ranks of their societies. One of these callers was Theodore Reuss, head of the Ordo Templi Orientis, or the O. T. O., a German-speaking group founded along esoteric masonic lines in the 1890s. Their central teaching was sexual magic, a kind of illumination through sex acts that explained, according to the O. T. O.'s originator Karl Kellner, 'all the secrets of Nature, all the symbolism of Freemasonry and all systems of religion'. Crowley was naturally interested, and accepted Reuss's request to induct him into the first three degrees of the Order. Shortly afterwards Crowley agreed to make *The Equinox* a voice for the O. T. O. as well as his A∴A∴, and in 1912 he was made head of the Order in Britain, known, in a further addition to his tangle of acronyms, as the M. M. M. (the 'Mysteria Mystica Maxima').⁵⁸

The second occasion on which Crowley and Mathers appeared in court together stemmed from a series of seven performances in late 1910, written and choreographed by Crowley himself: the Rites of Eleusis. Following in the footsteps of the Matherses' Egyptian theatrics in Paris, the rites were designed as a spectacle. For a costly £5 5s a ticket, audiences could witness Crowley and half a dozen A∴A∴ initiates take the stage at a candlelit Caxton Hall in Westminster. Crowley's muse at the time, the Australian musician Leila Waddell, accompanied them on the violin. H. G. Wells was invited but apparently declined to attend.⁵⁹ Reviewers fretted about blasphemy and the implications of 'sex worship', but legal trouble only began following several articles in the *Looking Glass* newspaper investigating Crowley

'Ceremonial Magic as the Gateway to Ecstasy', from *The Sketch*, 24 August 1910. Photograph of Leila Waddell.

and his old associates, namely Bennett and the chemist George Cecil Jones. Jones was mentioned in the same paragraph as an aspersion that Crowley and Bennett had engaged in 'unmentionable immoralities', and he decided to sue for libel.[60] In April 1911, Crowley watched in the courtroom as his character was taken apart as proof of moral indecency. Mathers and Edward Berridge were called as surprise witnesses, providing testimony on Crowley's time in the GD. The *Looking Glass* won the case, and Crowley's name (not for the last time) was dragged through the mud.

Crowley issued a pamphlet later that year titled 'The "Rosicrucian" Scandal', ostensibly to 'make clear' the facts of the case on the grounds that GD members had been attacking him. It was less a defence of Crowley's actions and more an opportunity to cast Mathers in an unflattering light and to promote his own poetry; the recollections showed Mathers as an astute reader of Crowley's work:

> Scorpio, K.C.: And that is all there is against Mr Crowley?
> Mathers: There is *The Sword of Song*.
> Scorpio, K.C.: What is that?
> Mathers: Out of some hundreds of marginal notes, there are two (some say four) the initials of whose words make other most improper words. [For an example of what this kind of criticism may lead to, see Appendix.]
> Scorpio, K.C.: Did anyone discover this before you did?
> Mathers: Not to my knowledge.
> Scorpio, K.C.: Did Captain Fuller in his three years' laborious study of Mr Crowley's works discover it?
> Mathers: No.
> Scorpio, K.C.: Is there any point in these — do you call them jokes?
> Mathers: No point at all.
> Scorpio, K.C.: Are Mr Crowley's jokes usually pointless?
> Mathers: Alas, no!
> Scorpio, K.C.: And did not the reviewers discover this?
> Mathers: Unfortunately, no. On the contrary, Mr G. K. Chesterton wrote a column in the *Daily News*, in which the book is treated as a serious contribution to Philosophy.

Scorpio, K.C.: Is there anything else?

Mathers: There's *The Mother's Tragedy*.

Scorpio, K.C.: What is that?

Mathers: A book of poems, one of which deals with a subject which I blush to mention.⁶¹

Crowley's marriage to Rose, whom he had long mistreated and who was by then suffering from alcoholism, ended in 1909. Despite having by then developed a reputation for ritual dramatics, magical pedagogy and deviant sexual practices, Crowley had not abandoned his literary ambitions. He appears to have achieved, if only for a short time, the kind of balance between the occult and the respectable outer life of a jobbing writer that only Yeats had so far been able to match. Both men filtered esoteric and mystical subject matter into their professional work. Crowley found himself able to exist in the world as both a Secret Chief and as a poet whose verse might be printed in the *English Review* and the London edition of *Vanity Fair*, his articles in the *Occult Review*. A dozen of his poems featured in the anthology *Cambridge Poets, 1900–1913*, among them 'The Rosicrucian' and 'Perdurabo', both inspired by his time in the GD. Literary connections multiplied. He came to know the writer John Middleton Murray, and through him met the New Zealand-born Modernist Katherine Mansfield in 1913. Crowley apparently fed her the hallucinogen anhalonium (derived from peyote) at a party hosted by the socialite Gwendoline Otter, after which Mansfield nibbled biscuits and talked to the buttons on her nightdress.⁶² He had also befriended the author Louis Wilkinson, first in 1907 and again in 1915 after Crowley moved to America. Wilkinson remembered Crowley as a generous and impressive man, easy to ridicule and sincere in his identity as a prophet of a new aeon.⁶³

Crowley was also getting used to being cast in other writers' work. While living in Paris in the early 1900s, the novelist W. Somerset

Maugham had befriended Gerald Kelly, Rose's brother. Maugham dined regularly at the restaurant Le Chat Blanc with Kelly's circle of friends, including the novelist Arnold Bennett, Clive Bell and Roger Fry of the Bloomsbury set and the sculptor Auguste Rodin. It was there that he came across Crowley. 'He was a great talker and he talked uncommonly well. In early youth, I was told, he was extremely handsome, but when I knew him he had put on weight, and his hair was thinning.'[64] Maugham subsequently wrote *The Magician*, with its striking villain, Oliver Haddo, who is rumoured to be a practitioner of the black arts. Crowley was surprised and not offended by the apparent likeness: 'He attributed to me certain characteristics which he meant to represent as abominable, but were actually superb.'[65] He was less impressed by the author's explication of magic, and retaliated with an article for *Vanity Fair* in December 1908 titled 'How to Write a Novel! After W. S. Maugham', accusing Maugham of simply ripping off others' work.

> The first essential is to choose a vague subject – one on which everybody is curious and almost nobody well-informed. For example, we might take 'magic' and 'art'. It will thus be rather difficult to catch us out. Anyway, we can ensure correctness by making a photographically-accurate portrait of someone great with whom we have scraped acquaintance.[66]

The occult content of Haddo's dialogue was a blend of *The Kabbalah Unveiled*, Waite's editions of Éliphas Lévi and Franz Hartmann's *The Life of Paracelsus*. Crowley's examples do indeed show passages reproduced almost word for word. Less convincing, however, was his assertion that Maugham had borrowed scenes from novels by H. G. Wells and Mabel Collins, whose *The Blossom and the Fruit: A True Story of a Black Magician* Crowley had included on a reading list for his A∴A∴ students. Crowley met Maugham again a few weeks after the article appeared; 'I almost wish,' Crowley remarked, 'that you were an important writer.'[67]

Crowley spent the First World War in America, and turned increasingly to ritual to ensure his literary success. Meticulously recorded in his diaries covering the period 1914 to 1920 are his experiments in sex magick as part of his work for the O. T. O. Entries were comprised of the date, the name and description of the willing partner (many of whom were sex workers; others married women), the 'Object' (the desired outcome), the Operation (a brief summary of how it went) and the result (if there was one). Objects ranged from money and 'Perfect physical health' to wisdom and successful relationships. Also included among the Objects was literary success, and many of his experiments were related to a series of detective stories he was in the middle of writing, about a figure named Simon Iff. 'Object: Success to Simon Iff stories', 'Object: Dramatic power, especially to finish Simon Iff stories' and 'Object: New Simon Iff series', for which the result is recorded as 'Immediate'.[68] In summer 1916 he visited Adams Cottage, near Bristol, New Hampshire, which belonged to the astrologer Evangeline Smith Adams, and it was there that he penned a series of eight short stories based on his reading of Frazer's *The Golden Bough*, and later that year he followed them up by writing six Simon Iff stories in a flurry of activity while in New Orleans.[69]

> I wrote day and night continuously – poems, essays and short stories. My principal invention was the detective Simon Iff, whose method of discovering the solution of a problem was calculation of the mental and moral energies of the people concerned.[70]

Iff was a perfect version of Crowley as he wanted to be, and to his mind offered a promising avenue for supporting himself financially. Also in 1916, he sold his story 'The Strategy' to H. L. Mencken, then editor of *The Smart Set*, whose contributors included the notable American writers Ambrose Bierce, O. Henry and Jack London. A year later Crowley accepted the editorship of a small pro-German magazine called *The International*, still grappling with the fact that since he had squandered his inheritance, he now had to write for money. Its pages provided a convenient outlet for his *Golden Bough* and Simon Iff stories.

Crowley's interest in Simon Iff continued, and he now became part of his next project, Crowley's 'first serious attempt at a long novel', then called *The Butterfly Net* or simply *The Net*.⁷¹ He had also begun a second novel during his fertile 1916–17 period, described as a 'Novelissim' and titled *Not the Life and Adventure of Sir Roger Bloxam*, though this remained unfinished. Chapter headings such as 'How Sir Roger Comported Himself With the C.U.N.T.S.' and 'Contains What I Meant to Write in Chapter Twenty. Or Nearly' convey the intended tone. *Moonchild*, as *The Butterfly Net* became on its eventual publication, was also a fool's gallery of GD magicians, the kind of send-ups that had peppered issues of *The Equinox* half a decade before, this time made to play dramatic roles in a battle between White and Black magical Lodges. Mathers appeared as Douglas (or 'S.R.M.D.', Mathers's First Order motto), the whisky-drinking mage who prostitutes his wife for money; Waite was cast as the bumbling and unintelligible Arthwaite; and William Westcott was Dr Victor Vesquit, 'the most famous necromancer of his age' (a reference to Westcott's profession as a coroner).⁷² Yeats features as the harmless 'Gates', a Protestant Irishman 'with the scholar's stoop' who is only in the Black Lodge to live out his fantasy as a 'terribly wicked fellow'.⁷³ Allan Bennett, the American dancer and choreographer Isadora Duncan, Crowley's magical partner Mary d'Este Sturges and Edward Berridge also make appearances. Crowley cast himself in two starring roles, as both the familiar Simon Iff and a young magician named Cyril Grey. Grey is a handsome bohemian of noble birth who, like Crowley, joined Douglas's order at the age of twenty, only to discover 'the trick' and scheme to become Douglas's right-hand man.

The plot centres around an attempt by the White Lodge (who broadly follow A∴A∴ teachings) to create a perfect spiritual being, a homunculus to be conceived by impregnating a woman named Lisa la Giuffria in conjunction with the power of the moon. The 'Butterfly Net' is the house where she is kept in preparation for this operation, though the task is almost thwarted by a group known as the Black Lodge, a once-great occult order headed by Douglas. The fictionalized GD magicians meet various sticky ends: Gates is sacrificed to the cause, his body used in gruesome rites which involve Vesquit conjuring a demon into the body of a goat and, at the moment of possession, slaying the animal on top of Gates's corpse 'in a kind of hideous marriage'.[74] The birth of the 'moonchild', however, is ultimately a smokescreen to distract from Simon Iff's true machination: the triggering of the First World War as a spiritual rebirth for humanity.

Set in 1914, *Moonchild* was written against a backdrop of international conflict, its frantic occult rituals charging the war with apocalyptic, transformational potential. More importantly for Crowley, it is an explication of his personal 'magickal' system communicated in the form of a fictional thriller. The real-life Crowley is also present within the book's world, as the unnamed publisher of *The Equinox*. His pivotal role in history is related as part of a discourse on the occult characteristics of the moon: 'The wise men gathered together, discovered a student who was trustworthy and possessed of the requisite literary ability; and by him the old knowledge was revised and made secure; it was finally published in a sort of periodical encyclopædia.'[75] The novel is at its most engaging when Crowley uses his alter egos to explain his system of magic, far more lucidly than do any of the GD's Flying Rolls or even his own *libri*. 'I have given an elaborate description of modern magical theories and practices,' he wrote of the novel in 1929. Iff, asked by Lisa why his order never performs magick under test conditions, responds:

> Unfortunately, my child, creative magick, which is the thaumaturgic side of the business, depends on a peculiar excitation which objects to 'test conditions' very strongly... Another difficulty about true magick is that it is so perfectly a natural process that its phenomena never excite surprise except by their timeliness – so that one has to record hundreds of experiments to set up a case which will even begin to exclude coincidence. For instance, I want a certain book. I use my book-producing talisman. The following day, a bookseller offers me the volume. One experiment proves nothing. My ability to do it every time is the proof. And I can't even do that under 'test conditions'; for it is necessary that I should really want the book, in my subconsciousness, whose will works with miracles.[76]

In this sense, *Moonchild* is an important part of Crowley's instruction, and the novel is considered *Liber LXXXI* – or 81, the magical number derived from the Roman numerals in its title – by followers of Thelema.

Moonchild was left unpublished for a time after its completion. Other events were keeping Crowley preoccupied. In 1916 he conducted a brief affair with the musician Ratan Devī, who became pregnant and miscarried (Crowley was unsympathetic). While staying at Adams Cottage, he had invented a new variation of bridge that he called 'pirate bridge', and he achieved minor celebrity explaining its rules in articles in *Vanity Fair*; the game remained popular for years afterwards.[77] Significantly, he had also decided to turn his attention to fine art. He became what he termed in an interview a 'subconscious impressionist' and a painter of 'dead souls'.[78] 'I have been under the misapprehension that I was a great poet,' he boasted to a friend. 'Paint is my real medium, and I am destined to become one of the outstanding artists of my age.'[79] His paintings, monstrous, morbid and blindingly colourful, were exhibited at Greenwich Village's Liberal Club in February 1919. One of his artworks featured in the resurrected *Equinox* (vol. III, no. 1), portraying the birth of the Children of the New Æon alongside a lynched figure representing Christianity.

But true infamy was not achieved until Crowley, seeking utopia, abandoned America in 1921 to establish his Abbey of Thelema in Cefalù, Sicily, a location now associated with lurid headlines and satanic worship. The Abbey was a remote coastal farmhouse without electricity and running water, surrounded by olive groves and plenty of rocks for Crowley to scale.[80] A great pentagram was painted on the floor of the central chamber, known as the Sanctum Sanctorum of the Thelemic Mysteries. Crowley and his lover Leah Hirsig (one of his 'Scarlet Women'), their newborn daughter Poupée, and a French woman named Ninette Shumway and her two young sons were the first to arrive, in early 1921. Assuming the role of cult leader that fitted him all too well, Crowley organized daily magickal workings according to the Thelemic laws, and sent out cryptic letters encouraging more followers to join him ('COMME CEFALU' was the message wired to the silent film star Jane Wolfe).[81] Drugs were made freely available, supposedly to remove temptation.[82] Due to the unsanitary conditions Leah contracted dysentery, and in October Poupée, weak since birth, died in a Palermo hospital.

Crowley was deeply affected, but the tragedy did little to curtail his Abbey activities. More willing initiates arrived, among them the writer Mary Butts ('Soror Rhodon'), who spent most of the time revising her first novel *Ashe of Rings*. Butts's literary and magickal aspirations coincided: 'I want to study and enjoy, and to enter if I can into the fairy world, the mythological world, and the world of the good ghost story,' she recorded in her journal before arriving in Cefalù, 'I want to make this world into material for the art of writing.' She hoped also to write a book 'to show the relation of art to magic, and show the artist as the true, because the oblique, adept'. No wonder she had been pulled into Crowley's orbit. She was only resident at the Abbey for twelve weeks; discomfited by the liberal drugs and sex, she decided that she would rather be 'the writer I am capable of becoming' than an Adept of the Crowleyan variety.[83]

In 1922 Crowley dedicated his next (and first published) novel, *The Diary of a Drug Fiend*, to Leah and their second child, Astarte Lulu Panthea, whom he named Thelema's 'youngest member'.[84] Across the book's three acts, Paradiso, Inferno and Purgatorio, Sir Peter Pendragon and his wife Lou experiment with taking extraordinary quantities of heroin and cocaine. They are eventually guided by a figure known as King Lamus to the Abbey of Thelema at Telepylus (the city of the Laestrygonians in Homer's *Odyssey*). This is Crowley's ideal, sanitized version of the Abbey, which acts as a kind of drug rehabilitation retreat for Peter and Lou as they acclimatize themselves to the rules of Thelema and eventually discover their true 'will' (Peter's is engineering; Lou's is to aid her husband).

> The beauty of the place beat hard upon our brains. It was unbelievable. Patches of cancer like London or Paris were cut ruthlessly out of [Lou's] consciousness. We had come from the ephemeral pretentiousness of cities to a land of eternal actuality.

CHAPTER 4

We were re-born into a world whose every condition was on a totally different scale to anything in our experience.⁸⁵

As King Lamus, Crowley figures himself a 'pioneer', persecuted by society for his ideas much like Shelley or Galileo.⁸⁶

'Black Record of Aleister Crowley,' ran the *Sunday Express* front-page headline on 26 November 1922: 'Preying on the Debased … Profligacy and Vice in Sicily'. Three days earlier the paper had singled out *The Diary of a Drug Fiend* as a 'Book for Burning' for its 'ecstatic eulogy' to cocaine, and now Crowley's Abbey was exposed to the world. Crowley was accused of sending women onto the streets of Palermo to earn him money, of conducting 'unspeakable orgies' and ritually slaughtering a goat while the animal copulated with his 'Scarlet Woman'. It was Mary Butts who had provided these exaggerated details (in reality, the goat had refused to go near Hirsig), having recognized herself and her partner Cecil Maitland as Lou and Peter in *Drug Fiend*.⁸⁷ The Abbey project ended in further tragedy. Raoul Loveday, a young undergraduate from St John's College, Oxford, had caught typhoid from drinking untreated spring water there. 'Raoul developed paralysis of the heart and died at once without fear or pain,' Crowley remembered: 'It was as if a man, tired of staying indoors, had gone out for a walk.'⁸⁸

Mussolini's government deported Crowley from Cefalù in April 1923, and he and Hirsig left for Tunisia to escape the explosion of negative press. The sensational headlines stalled Crowley's professional career as a man of letters: no English publisher would go near him for six years. In the intervening period, he dictated his self-mythologizing autobiography to Hirsig and wrote a celebrated occult textbook, *Magick in Theory and Practice*, managing to get it printed in Paris in 1929. *Moonchild* was finally published by Mandrake Press almost simultaneously. The Australian writer and activist P. R. Stephensen had taken over the press that year – its inaugural publication was *The Paintings of*

D. H. Lawrence, which prompted a police raid on Lawrence's art show.[89] Stephensen and Crowley shared a disregard for women as intellectuals and an anarchic, later fascist spirit derived from reading Nietzsche.[90] In the face of draconian censorship laws in Britain, Stephensen looked to Crowley as a new and unorthodox focus for his press, and alongside *Moonchild* he also published the first three volumes of Crowley's autobiography, the text of a lecture on Gilles de Rais that Cambridge University had banned him from giving in February 1930, and a volume of Crowley's short fiction, *The Stratagem and Other Stories*, as part of the Mandrake Booklets series. The press folded not long after, due, according to Stephensen, to Crowley putting 'the Basilisk Eye on my unfortunate co-director … and [frightening] the hell out of him through sheer devilry'.[91] *Magick in Theory and Practice* and the Mandrake publications marked the final flurry of real literary activity during Crowley's lifetime. They are the works for which he is now best known.

The GD and Mathers's brief mentorship had been his chaotic entry into the world of ritual magic, formative stepping stones that led to the establishment of the Argenteum Astrum and ultimately Thelema, which remains a basis of practice to this day for certain occult groups. Appropriately for a man who was constantly reinventing himself, Crowley has been enshrined in various novels as a practitioner of black magic, both before and after his death in 1947. Other than Haddo in Maugham's *The Magician*, he was a model for John Buchan, Christopher Isherwood, Anthony Powell (as Dr Trelawney in *A Dance to the Music of Time*) and perhaps most famously the writer of occult thrillers Dennis Wheatley, in *The Devil Rides Out* (1934). Wheatley had bought Crowley dinner the same year the book was published, and in repayment Crowley sent an inscribed copy of *Magick in Theory and Practice*. Ever one to play the part, and perhaps hoping that Wheatley would feature him in his new novel, Crowley accompanied the gift with instructions to 'Read "Hymn to Pan" aloud at midnight when alone with INTENTION to get HIM'.[92]

5
'The Spell of Sound'
W. B. Yeats, Florence Farr & Pamela Colman Smith

As the new century began, the future of the Golden Dawn's network of temples was looking uncertain. Mathers was deposed, Aleister Crowley was communing with his own Secret Chiefs in the desert and a wave of resignations was shrinking membership numbers. Adepts transferred allegiances, names were changed and after a period of further discord there emerged four main groups – some clinging to memories of the original Order, others eager to adapt and expand. In 1900 magicians loyal to Mathers (including Edward Berridge, William Westcott, George Cecil Jones and Crowley) had broken away from the main GD and formed a rival Isis temple, later to be called Alpha et Omega (A∴O∴). The remaining students, known for a while as the Hermetic Society of the Morgenröthe, split in July 1903, with A. E. Waite, M. W. Blackden and the Rev. W. A. Ayton forming the Independent and Rectified Rite, and Robert Felkin, W. B. Yeats, John Brodie-Innes and others continuing the Morgenröthe under a new name, the Order of the Stella Matutina (the Morning Star). Crowley established his Argenteum Astrum (A∴A∴) in 1907. These groups all operated with differing, even opposing, ideas of how the hermetic tradition should be studied. Waite's order, for example, no longer taught practical occultism and was now wholly mystical, whereas the Stella Matutina kept strictly to the original GD curriculum. 'The Hermetic Order of the Golden Dawn' might have been dead in name, but its structural grade system, ceremonial rituals and teachings continued into the twentieth century.

Having been integral to the 1901 crisis, Yeats chose to remain on the sidelines of the Stella Matutina. He had failed in his attempt to reform the Order according to his own ideas about magical hierarchy, but at least the new group stuck to the GD's Kabbalistic grounding and maintained a serious commitment to the practical magic once so formative to his early poetry. Now, however, three of his intimate friends, Florence Farr and Dorothea and Edmund Hunter, had resigned. Mathers, his mentor and confidant, could no longer be trusted. Yeats loathed the 'bitter & violent & absurd' Crowley, but remained on civil terms with Mathers: 'We have barbed our arrows with compliments and regrets and to do him justice he has done little else,' he wrote to Lady Gregory.[1] These sudden changes were hard to bear, but did not stop Yeats from nurturing the artists with whom he maintained occult ties. The illustrator W. T. Horton, who had lasted as a GD student for only a month in 1896, remained an important figure in Yeats's life. In 1898 Yeats had written the introduction to Horton's *A Book of Images*, a collection of black-and-white drawings depicting the artist's 'waking dreams'.[2] But it was through Yeats's creative relationships with two women that he became exposed to new currents in literature and art. Farr, once an integral player in the world of magic, struck out on her own in theosophical theatre and journalism for the *New Age* magazine, while the American-born Pamela Colman Smith, who had joined the GD in its final months in 1901 and followed Waite into his Independent and Rectified Rite, rubbed shoulders with the avant-garde and embraced esoteric forms of Modernism.

In 1901, soon to be free from ceremonial responsibilities at Isis-Urania, Farr was initially at a loss as to where to direct her energies. Her magical papers from the early 1900s contain a whirl of disparate topics that reflect the restlessness she was no doubt feeling. There are notes for a study of the Major Arcana of the tarot deck, animal archetypes and their correspondences, and what appears to be an attempt to teach herself pharmacology, including notes on 'convulsives' and depressants.[3] Though her Sphere group was now using the grail as its main symbol, ancient Egypt also remained a crucial element in her imagination. In collaboration with the novelist Olivia Shakespear, who had

W. T. Horton and W. B. Yeats, *A Book of Images*, 1898.

been Yeats's lover in the mid-1890s, Farr wrote two one-act plays that retold stories from Egypt. 'What plot could I have for 5th Dynasty play involving 2 women & a man,' she asked herself sometime in mid-1901.[4]

The Beloved of Hathor was first staged in November 1901, followed by a performance of both plays at Victoria Hall in January 1902, hosted by the Egyptian Society. Promoting wisdom as a spiritual ideal, *The Beloved of Hathor* was set in 1500 BCE and told of how the chieftain Aahmes was tempted away from his impending marriage to the Priestess of Hathor by the sorceress Nouferou. *The Shrine of the Golden Hawk* developed this theme, advocating for a mystical union with divine power over the earthly rites and talismans of ceremonial magic, a firm indication of Farr's thinking about the efficacy of the GD. The stage design was to be straightforward and cost-effective, 'with a simple white background or pale sienna hangings, so arranged that the figures of the actors, moving across the stage, may reproduce the effect of the ancient frescoes or illuminated papyri'.[5] The plays' reception made it obvious that Farr and Shakespear had produced something thoroughly unusual. Yeats thought the pieces amateurish, and wrote that neither 'stirred in me a strictly dramatic interest', but was impressed by their otherworldliness: 'One understood that something interesting was being done – not very well done, indeed – but something one had never seen before, and might never see again.'[6]

Yeats's interest in the avant-garde and its possibilities for staging was already set by April 1901, when he was sent to Stratford by *The Speaker* for an article on the Shakespeare season put on by the Frank Benson Company (he might also have glimpsed Arthur Machen, who had been assigned small parts in *King John* and *Richard II*, onstage). His review rails against 'naturalistic' scene painting and the continued use of the Elizabethan 'half-round' stage, recommending instead the narrower theatres once used by Wagner that would centre the 'idealistic art of the poet'.[7] By this time, he and Farr were also working together on a new form that would foreground the poet's art, but through a medium other than theatre: music and rhythm.

Considering the animosity of their attacks on one another during the GD's political struggles, it seems a wonder that Yeats and Farr's relationship survived, but the spirit of collaboration that had first drawn them together in Bedford Park remained intact. In the early 1890s, they had begun experimenting with speaking verse to music. A lack of ability had stalled his and Farr's efforts until Yeats witnessed her perform with a psaltery, an ancient stringed instrument, in *The Beloved of Hathor*.[8] Farr's 'half psaltery, half lyre' was designed to harmonize with the spoken or chanted word. With tuition from Arnold Dolmetsch, a French musician living in Dulwich who specialized in recreating early instruments, Yeats and Farr became captivated by what they saw as a new form of art.[9] Yeats first aired his vision for a new kind of theatre incorporating spoken verse at meetings of the Fellowship of the Three Kings, a 'crazy Irish' literary society, in the words of Pamela Colman Smith, which met to discuss mysticism and may also have acted as the venue for brainstorming sessions for Yeats's Celtic Order.[10]

The enthusiasm with which Yeats related his 'discovery' for the *Monthly Review* in March 1902 made it seem as if he had begun the article just moments after Farr had left the room:

> I have just heard a poem spoken with so delicate a sense of its rhythm, with so perfect a respect for its meaning, that if I were a wise man and could persuade a few people to learn the art I would never open a book of verses again. A friend, who was here a few minutes ago, has sat with a beautiful stringed instrument upon her knee, her fingers passing over the strings, and she has spoken to me some verses from Shelley's *Skylark* and Sir Ector's lamentations over the dead Launcelot out of the *Morte d'Arthur* and some of my own poems.[11]

The revelation of this 'new art' and the possibilities it opened up to Yeats for the recitation of his verse provoked a new creative phase in his and Farr's relationship. Throughout 1902 the pair gave demonstrations, first in Yeats's rooms near Euston Station and later to the Irish Literary Society, Yeats delivering an explanatory lecture before Farr's performance. While the art was 'new', the tradition, as Yeats saw

Florence Farr with her commissioned psaltery harp, n.d.

it, was not: he imagined himself to be resurrecting the oral practices of the Celtic bards in modernity, and, by extension, recreating a specifically Irish form of magic. It was a project he had already started in his retellings of Irish legends and his introductions to Lady Gregory's translations of folktales, but here it took on a different quality. 'A poem and an incantation were almost the same,' Yeats wrote of the early Irish storytellers in 'Bardic Ireland', stressing their role as a 'brotherhood' who communicated the dreams and imagination of the Irish people through song.[12] Bardic investigations into the music of speech through Farr's psaltery performances represented an extra strand in Yeats's order-based, mystical project. It also became foundational to his ideas for the theatre. In the same letter to Farr in which he chastised her for her unconstitutional groups in the GD, he made her a wholly different proposition: 'The G.D. is only part of a much greater movement … We can make a great movement & in more than magical things.'[13]

At the same time as he was working 'at the chanting' with Farr and Dolmetsch in December 1901, Yeats continued to experiment with 'magical things' at his lodgings, with a group that included the Rev. Ayton.[14] In a letter to Lady Gregory lamenting the reception of his collaborator Edward Martyn's plays and the fate of the Irish theatre, his postscript mentions 'my Alchemist', who is anxious to consult Robert Gregory's valuable 'Magic book', and describes the singular instance of occult vivisection: 'Could you bring it when you come? He has just made what he hopes is the Elexer [sic] of Life. If the rabbits on whom he is trying it survive we are all to drink a noggin full – at least all of us whose longevity he feels he could honestly encourage.'[15]

As A. E. Waite described it, Pamela Colman Smith 'drifted into' Isis-Urania in 1901.[16] Born in 1878 to American parents in London, her family connections with Swedenborgians and spiritualists (her maternal grandfather Samuel Colman had published early editions of Swedenborg and Blake) meant that she grew up in a world in which the afterlife and angelic communication were real possibilities. In 1888 she moved to Boston with her parents, and the year after to Kingston, Jamaica, where she spent her teenage years drawing, writing and producing plays for her miniature theatre, accompanied by sound effects and a musical score. At the age of fifteen she began studying at the Pratt Institute, New York, where she improved in printmaking and painting, despite not graduating. She also continued to put on plays she had written herself, including the pirate adventure *Henry Morgan* (inspired by a passion for Walter Scott, Robert Louis Stevenson and the stories of the writer and illustrator Howard Pyle).[17]

Living between New York and Kingston, Smith identified strongly with Jamaican culture. While there is no clear evidence that she had Jamaican heritage, she presented herself and was perceived by others as biracial, an identity accentuated by her early interest in Caribbean folktales. John Butler Yeats and the English actor Ellen Terry both thought that she might be Japanese, others that she was mixed race or from the West Indies. Her originality and 'naiveté' were frequently commented on in ways that have clear racialized overtones, and these impressions became a source of professional frustration for Smith, whose work was often dismissed as rudimentary or primitive.[18] She was an unusual member of the GD: a transnational, possibly biracial, most likely queer artist who embraced bohemianism, underground communities and the promotion of women's art and rights.

In 1896 two of Smith's folk retellings were published in the *Journal of American Folklore* under the titles 'Annancy and the Yam Hills' and 'De Story of de Man and Six Poached Eggs'.[19] The short tales, along the lines of the Br'er Rabbit stories, adopted the same creole dialect that she would use for her first full-length collection, *Annancy Stories*, in 1899. These were tales about the Akan spider god (commonly spelled 'Anansi'), a popular trickster figure in West African, Caribbean and African American folktales whose stories had mostly been printed in versions by white authors. Smith's unusual decision to employ dialect may have resulted in the collection's less than positive reception, although its full-page illustrations and blend of motifs from European fairy tales made it stand out. Her other early commissions included

CHAPTER 5

drawings for a collection of Yeats's verse, Seumas MacManus's *In Chimney Corners: Merry Tales of Irish Folklore* and two English ballads adapted from earlier retellings by the clergyman and folklorist Sabine Baring-Gould. It was also at this point that she began a professional relationship with the Lyceum Theatre. While in England with her father, Smith met the actor Henry Irving and the theatre's business manager Bram Stoker, who was already gaining notoriety for his gothic novel *Dracula* (its titular character based on Irving), published in 1897. She also befriended Ellen Terry, who gave her the nickname 'Pixie'. Based on several sample drawings, Smith was commissioned to illustrate Stoker's promotional booklet on Irving, which was to be distributed as part of the theatre's American tour. A decade later, she would illustrate Stoker's novel *The Lair of the White Worm*.

On her return to England, Smith quickly came to know Yeats and his family, furthering her interest in Irish folklore and legend. Her first impression of Yeats in 1901 was anything but deferential:

> W.B.Y. was there and he is a rummy critter! Seemed most stupid and had on a tea party air and posed about and looked bored –. And when all the ladies with ermine collars had gone, who all told him how very much they liked his bloomin poetry, which probably they had never read or heard of ... then W.B. began to talk! Folklore – songs, plays, Irish language, and lots more – reciting a sort of folksong which was splendid, and not stopping for interruptions by Mrs. E. pig – who made silly remarks; it was fun and we all liked it very much![20]

In June 1901 she stayed with Yeats's brother Jack and his wife Mary in their Devon cottage, enchanting the painters with performances of her Jamaican folktales, complete with cardboard cut-outs. She travelled to Ireland in the autumn, and spent time with Yeats, Jack and their sisters, Elizabeth ('Lolly') and Lily. Yeats soon became her mentor. *The Land of Heart's Desire* had been one of the first plays Smith had staged for her miniature theatre, and now she was preparing *The Countess Cathleen*, which Yeats urged her to perform at a meeting of

Edith Craig, photograph of Pamela Colman Smith, Ellen Terry, Lindsay Jardine and Christabel Marshall, 1902.

The Green Sheaf

THE world of imagination is the world of eternity. It is the divine bosom into which we shall go after the death of the vegetated body.

The world of imagination is infinite and eternal, whereas the world of generation or vegetation is finite and temporal.

There exist in that eternal world the eternal realities of everything which we see reflected in this vegetable glass of nature.

William Blake.

The Green Sheaf

It seemed to Constans that the sun shone from the *heart* of the mountain, and Constans laughed and danced for joy.

Therewith he drew nearer to the *Hill*, and now he felt himself hurt that he had not known at once that Sun to be the *hair* of his lady . . . Nor did it trouble him that she was not clad in the princely *robes* of his dreams, but wore a mean *beggar's* garment.

"Mercy on me, my lady," cried Constans. "Since we have loved so long in *dream* . . . I pray you tell me how to reach you."

"Then should you taste of death Master Constans," said the lady, and Constans saw that she was whiter than snow.

"Yet I will come nearer," said Constans. And he walked into the icy side of the mountain, and his faith like flame melted the *ice*, and he came to her.

Pages from *The Green Sheaf*, vol. 2, 1903. Illustrations by W. T. Horton (top) and Pamela Colman Smith (left).

the Fellowship of the Three Kings (though this probably never happened).[21] Smith was also present for a private reading of Yeats's *The Shadowy Waters*, an experience which caused her much amusement:

> Florence Farr and W.B.Y. and a chorus of <u>such</u> funnily picked men for sailors a small meek one, then a larger poppieeyed [sic] frightened one and then a <u>huge</u> fat man with a voice out his boots ... I had sat opposite the sailors and had to laugh in my hankie most of the time![22]

It might have been Yeats who recommended her for the GD. Assuming the motto 'Quid tibi id aliis' ('Do to others as you would to yourself'), Smith was initiated into Isis-Urania in November 1901, accompanied by her friend and roommate Ethel Fryer-Fortescue.[23] When the Morgenröthe divided in 1903, Smith followed Waite to his Independent and Rectified Rite along with Machen and Blackwood, and although she only ever reached the Zelator grade ($1° = 10°$) during her time in both orders, she took advantage of the social and artistic connections it opened up to her. It was also the point at which her art took on a more mystical bent.

Smith began to make her mark in the London arts scene as the editor of two small journals. With Jack Yeats, she made plans for an experimental magazine to be called *A Broad Sheet*, based on the large single-sheet 'broadsides' common as a form of publication in the seventeenth and eighteenth centuries. Its content was mostly Irish Revival poetry, with work from W. B. Yeats ('A Spinning Song' and an excerpt from his play *Diarmuid and Grania* in the first issue), George Russell, Lady Gregory and George Moore. The pair provided hand-coloured drawings for each issue, but this exhausting task strained their relationship and eventually led to Smith leaving the project in 1903. She was not, however, disheartened: almost immediately she brought *The Green Sheaf*, a magazine printed in colour on handmade paper, into the world. Published by Elkin Mathews (who had now split from John Lane at the Bodley Head), Smith was keen to use *The Green Sheaf* to promote work by women just starting out in their careers, but she also leaned on her Lyceum Theatre and other literary contacts to fill the pages each month with poems, drawings and songs. Only a handful of GD members supplied work, among them John Todhunter, Yeats and W. T. Horton, whose illustrations of Blake and Keats fragments added a Beardsley-ish air to the venture. In fact, *The Green Sheaf*, described as 'quite unlike gloomy magazines like the *Yellow Book* and the *Savoy*', quickly became a venue for playful esotericism.²⁴ Smith's own drawings, clear in outline and heavy in symbolism, might suggest the kinds of experiments being carried out in GD meetings; some seem quite clearly to have been inspired by the tarot arcana. The second volume was devoted to dreams, and featured oneiric accounts by Yeats ('Dream of the World's End'), J. M. Synge and a young John Masefield. Smith's own contribution recalls the image-laden visions experienced by Farr in the previous decade: 'Suddenly on the left there was the sound of solemn music – and many spirits floated by. Mild faces had they; and every one carried a red heart from which dropped a pearl – hung by a golden chain'²⁵

Yeats brought a flavour of the psaltery lectures to an American audience in 1903 and 1904, speaking mainly on Irish literature and tradition. Meanwhile, Farr's formal separation from the GD (although not from its membership) had led her back to the drawing rooms and lecture halls of the Theosophical Society, now headed by Annie Besant and G. R. S. Mead. Since the 1880s, men and women with feminist ideals had been increasingly attracted to theosophy's promotion of individual spiritual realization.²⁶ For activists such as Besant, its founder Madame Blavatsky's emphasis on using ancient wisdom to prepare for a new spiritual era charged their radical politics with a mystical importance; Farr's own blend of feminism and the occult made the society a natural home for her, and it also became a useful platform for her experiments in the avant-garde. The *Theosophical Review* published her allegorical masque *The Mystery of Time*, which was first performed in early 1905 at the Royal Albert Hall, using the same austere staging as her Egyptian plays. *The Shrine of the Golden Hawk* had become a favourite among theosophists for its 'strong and simple language' and use of Egyptian lore, and in July that same year Farr staged it alongside Yeats's *Shadowy Waters* for the Theosophical Society's European Federation annual congress in London, with the young actress Italia Conti in the role of the princess. During this period Farr also directed the first private performances in England of *Salome*, Oscar Wilde's 1893 one-act play condemned by censors as 'half-Biblical, half-pornographic'.[27] She continued to perfect her psaltery lectures, and in January 1907 embarked on a solo American tour (with five performances in Boston, arranged by Dolmetsch). On arrival in New York she met up with Smith, who was staying at the Martha Washington hotel. To Farr's delight, her lectures on the music of speech drew enthusiastic audiences, and one evening in Brooklyn she performed to a group whose number included the novelist Mark Twain.

Back in England, Farr began to find a readership for her political and mystical views in the *Occult Review* and the *New Age*. Started in 1894 as an organ for Christian socialism, the *New Age* magazine had been reinvigorated and relaunched in May 1907 under the editorship of the theosophist Alfred Richard Orage. Orage had been a teacher and the founder of the Leeds Arts Club, and in the late 1900s he was lecturing to the Theosophical Society on his own concoction of Plato, Nietzsche and Marx. He also championed the Craft Guild movement and women's suffrage. Funding for the magazine came from George Bernard Shaw and his fellow Fabians, and so naturally much of its content reflected the socialist and radical views of many of its contributors, who included H. G. Wells, Arnold Bennett, Katherine Mansfield and Shaw himself. Shaw recommended Farr as a regular columnist after her return from America, and she used this new platform to develop the ideas first gestured to in *The Dancing Faun*.[28] Didactic essays on marriage, child-rearing and sex work (one, titled 'The Rites of Astaroth', argues for the 'Daughters of Joy' to be allowed to carry out their business from 'well-regulated' houses) provoked flurries of correspondence.[29] The fact that Farr signed her articles meant that she was open to attack, but she continued to defend her positions, often with the help of the more tactful Shaw. 'Countless wives no doubt endure the horrors of a loveless marriage,' she declared in an article assessing the novels of the hugely popular Marie Corelli, 'but no man will ever understand the disgust a woman feels in contact with a man she does not love, because nearly every woman is too polite to tell a husband or patron in brutal words the real state of the case.'[30] In 1908, along with unpaid theatre criticism for the middle-class *Mint* magazine, Farr was also writing for the *Occult Review* on subjects equally familiar to her: the Kabbalah, Egyptian symbols and Rosicrucian alchemy.[31] Memories of the Blythe Road battle were reawakened when Orage, who had become friends with Crowley after meeting him at the Society for Psychical Research in 1906, gave Farr the task of reviewing J. F. C. Fuller's *The Star in the West*, a book-length essay on Crowley's poetry. Her even-handed assessment of 'the Beast 666' in the face of the 'hydra-headed monster, this London Opinion', suggests that she had gone some way towards forgiving him. Crowley remembered being 'enormously encouraged' by the article.[32]

With the exception of *The Dancing Faun*, her books in the 1890s had been on esoteric themes and largely unread, but now, approaching her fiftieth year, Farr was achieving unforeseen success in journalism. Through Olivia Shakespear, she met the young Ezra Pound. She decided to try once more to find a publisher for *Modern Woman*, a manuscript put aside after its rejection by *The Realm* magazine. But when it was finally published by Frank Palmer in 1910, the book's ideas about marriage and economic independence appeared dated and overfamiliar.[33] In 1912 she published a second novel, *The Solemnization of Jacklin: Some Adventures on the Search for Reality*, again exploring the strictures of the marriage institution through an autobiographical lens. To pay for the printing costs, she sold her original ink drawing of Beardsley's Avenue Theatre poster to Shaw for around £60. Reviewers found *Jacklin* convincingly naturalistic, yet at the same time reminiscent of 'the wildest of Futurist landscapes';[34] the suffragette weekly *The Freewoman* compared it to the experience of 'straying into the chapel of some vast cathedral'.[35] None of this was enough, however, to give Farr the reputation she longed for. She could no longer find acting work, and her musical recitals had become infrequent. In the end, she took a teaching position at a girls' college run by Sir Ponnambalam Ramanathan (a prominent lawyer, Tamil political leader and one-time yoga instructor to Allan Bennett) in Ceylon (now Sri Lanka). Farr was never clear about why she chose this new occupation. Dorothy Paget guessed that her aunt did not want to be seen to grow old: 'The withering of the leaf before an audience was not for her.'[36] The same year that *Jacklin* appeared, Farr packed up her belongings and sold her library for £15, full of books inscribed to her by her now-famous friends. She left her psaltery to Yeats.[37]

Smith experienced her first 'music picture', a synaesthetic vision initiated by music, on Christmas Day 1900, while listening to Ellen Terry's son, Gordon Craig, playing Bach.[38] She remembered a scene of 'bluish mist' behind tree trunks, and suddenly, from left to right, a troupe of 'dancing and frolicking little elfin people with the wind blowing through their hair and billowing their dresses'.[39] These musical visions, which would become the subject of her paintings over the next decade, became more frequent around 1903. It is possible that Smith had learned techniques in the GD to control or intensify her visions, either under Yeats's tutelage or as part of her general occult studies; coupled with her new nickname, 'Pixie', she was now beginning to embrace a Celtic-occult identity. Also around this time, she and the poet Lady Alix Egerton travelled to a healing well in County Kildare, Ireland, where they claimed to have heard 'harps, violins, reed-pipes, strike of cymbals, beat of drums, with much singing' followed by seeing riders galloping on white horses from the river, their colourful cloaks streaming in the wind.[40] Occult symbolism and a kind of mystic Celticism gradually replaced Smith's use of Jamaican tradition in her art.

Although *The Green Sheaf* did not provide Smith with a steady income, she could also advertise her storytelling services, and in 1904 she established The Green Sheaf Press with Ethel Fryer-Fortescue.

They published at least ten books, mostly by women.[41] While her publishing adventures were taking shape, Yeats was forming the 'Masquers' for the production of 'plays, masques, ballets and ceremonies, which convey a sentiment of beauty'.[42] Smith was present at their first meeting and began to appear alongside Farr in her psaltery performances. She was one of the women who, as the artist William Rothenstein remembered, 'sat on the floor and chanted stories, or crooned poems to the accompaniment of a one-stringed instrument'.[43]

Far more significant for her professional life was a series of exhibitions of her work between 1902 and 1908, at least three in London and a further four in America. In 1907 a total of seventy-two of her watercolours were shown in the photographer Alfred Stieglitz's gallery. Smith explained that they had been painted 'automatically'.[44] They are 'just what I see when I hear music,' she wrote to him. 'Thoughts loosened and set free by the spell of sound. I put them down with haste. Sometimes they are so strange that they almost shock me as they come.'[45] Stieglitz would become an influential promoter of modern and avant-garde art, noted especially for his relationship with Georgia O'Keeffe. Smith's exhibition marked his gallery's first non-photographic show, and despite his friends' misgivings, it quickly sold out. Reviewers compared Smith's work to that of symbolist and mystic artists, her titles alone causing James Huneker of the *New York Sun* to 'dream of Blake, of Fantin-Latour, of the Japanese ... of James Ensor, or Beardsley, of Edvard Munch, of Maeterlinck'.[46] Her unconventional, otherworldly style was viewed as revolutionary, and Smith as a fantasist whose hermetic imagery had the potential to revitalize the conservative art world: 'How many American artists ... are drifting out into dreamland and seeing visions and speaking as prophets in strange symbols?', another critic asked.

> At last the veil of tradition [is] being lifted from art ... It has been given this woman to see far and speak eloquently; for these tiny canvasses [fill] one with a sense of living among vast mountains, at the edge of shoreless oceans in the heart of wild cadences, and close to the profound sorrow and pain and madness of all ages.[47]

Pamela Colman Smith, *Sea Creatures*, n.d.

Marius de Zayas, *Pamela Colman Smith*, c. 1910.

Although Stieglitz later disavowed his patronage of Smith as an error in judgment, critics now consider this exhibition the photographer's first step towards his eventual embrace of Modernism.[48]

Smith also found a final opportunity for collaboration within the former GD membership. A. E. Waite had noticed her attraction to the ceremonial aspect of his Order, 'without pretending or indeed attempting to understand their sub-surface consequence', and believed that under proper guidance she could produce a tarot deck 'with an appeal in the world of art and a suggestion of significance behind the Symbols which would put them on another construction than had ever been dreamed'.[49] Aware that there was no accepted or 'canonical' form of the tarot then in circulation, Waite felt that the time was ripe for a new deck designed to his specifications, with Smith as his 'draughtswoman'.[50] The tarot had been plundered for its rich symbolism ever since Éliphas Lévi declared it as 'strong and simple as the architecture of the pyramids'.[51] Others before him had linked the cards with Egyptian magic, but Lévi was the first to map them onto the *sefirot* of the Kabbalah and the first to popularize them as an occult device.[52] The GD used tarot as a fundamental pool of symbolism, its Major Arcana slotting neatly into the Order's system of occult correspondence. A lecture to his students titled 'The Tarot and the Rosy Cross' shows that these correspondences remained an important part of Waite's curriculum. In his explanatory text, *The Key to the Tarot*, published alongside the tarot deck in 1909, he outlines the view that tarot was part of the Secret Tradition, which alongside freemasonry and the grail represented a surviving strand of hidden knowledge:

> The true Tarot is symbolism; it speaks no other language and offers no other signs. Given the inward meaning of its emblems, they do become a kind of alphabet which is capable of indefinite combinations and makes true sense in all. On the highest plane it offers a key to the Mysteries, in a manner which is not arbitrary and has not been read in.[53]

What the process of collaboration was actually like, and whether Smith, as Waite recalled, had to be 'spoon-fed' the symbolism of some of the more important arcana (according to Waite's system, the Priestess, the Fool and the Hanged Man) or was able to assert her own vision, is hard to say.[54] His instructions to Smith were precise, according to his research, and the 'spoon-feeding' is explained by the fact that, being a Zelator, Smith had not previously been exposed to the GD's full tarot interpretations. She was clearly not paid well for the project, which must have taken her months to complete: 'I've just finished a big job for very little cash!', she was writing to Stieglitz in November 1909.[55] Smith used a similar style of clear figures and block colours as in *A Broad Sheet* and *The Green Sheaf*, and the tarot pack, consisting of eighty separate designs, was to be 'printed in colour by lithography – probably very badly'.[56] Waite acknowledged Smith's contribution in an article for the *Occult Review*, but her name was omitted from what has commonly been referred to as the 'Rider-Waite' tarot after its publisher William Rider. It was released in a limited run by December 1909, supplemented by Waite's explanatory booklet. An advertising article, 'The Tarot: a Wheel of Fortune', was also written for the *Occult Review* in the same month, with the editor noting their 'far higher quality in respect of artistic merit than any pack that has hitherto been published'.[57] The booklet was updated as *The Pictorial Key to the Tarot* the following March, when Rider decided to publish an expanded version. The backs of the cards were also changed from the initial rose and lily design to one of cracked earth. Smith was very pleased with the end result, promising to send Stieglitz a deck to be exhibited in his gallery; neither she nor Waite could have foreseen the now-ubiquitous presence of the Rider-Waite designs in modern tarot packs.

Smith's miniature theatre, her Jamaican folktales, art magazines, Modernist-mystical paintings and finally the Rider-Waite tarot reflect the work of an uncategorizable artist. Like Farr, she moved in diverse social and professional circles, using the GD both for occult study and as a resource for creative work. Smith also displayed her more explicitly political side when in 1911 she contributed stencils to Laurence

Housman's satirical handprinted *Anti-Suffrage Alphabet* ('W's the Washing / which women must do / Day in & day out, / & on polling day too') and made campaign posters for his activist group, the Suffrage Atelier.[58] She must have left the Rectified Rite shortly after designing the tarot deck, for when Lily Yeats visited her in 1913 she found that Smith had exchanged the occult for Catholicism. 'She now has the dullest of friends,' Lily reported, 'selected entirely because they are R.C., converts most of them, half educated people, who want to see both eyes in a profile drawing.'[59] Not long afterwards, an inheritance from an uncle allowed Smith to purchase land on Lizard's Point. She spent the rest of her life in Cornwall.

Since its founding in 1903, the Stella Matutina had flourished under the missionary, anthropologist and medical doctor Robert Felkin's leadership. As Imperator, he conducted Amoun Temple meetings from his home in North Kensington. Felkin had been assembling rituals for the higher grades, supposedly communicated through a group of Adepts he called the 'Sun Masters', and the Temple now had a Second Order.[60] Yeats was thus able to enter the Theoricus Adeptus Minor ($5° = 6°$) grade in 1912 and the Adeptus Major ($6° = 5°$) two years later. But by 1914 membership had begun to wane, and only twenty students remained. Felkin was increasingly away in Europe, seeking Rosicrucian contacts and material for Third Order grades (which did not exist, as Mathers had never written them), and so Yeats briefly stepped up as Imperator. According to one source, he seems to have attained Adeptus Exemptus ($7° = 4°$), the highest grade of the Second Order, sometime in 1915.[61] An unpublished manuscript contains a draft of a poem titled 'For initiation of 7 = 4', written in the same year:

> We are weighed down by the blood & the heavy weight of
>   the bones
> We are bound by flowers, & our feet are entangled in the green

> And there is deceit in the singing of birds.
> It is time to be done with it all
> The stars call & all the planets
> And the purging fire of the moon
> And yonder is the cold silence of cleansing night
> May the dawn break, & gates of day be set wide open.⁶²

Now that he stood on the edge of the Third Order, Yeats was longing for a world beyond the 'heavy weight' and 'deceit' of material existence. By the mid-1910s he was turning once more to psychic investigation, although with a more serious intent than the seances of his Dublin student days. In 1915 two of his close friends died – Lady Gregory's nephew Sir Hugh Lane in May, and Horton's partner Audrey Locke in June – and Yeats began looking to the spiritualist Elizabeth Radcliffe and various other mediums for seances and sessions in automatic writing.⁶³ For several years, he had been claiming to have made contact with a secondary personality or 'daimon' called Leo Africanus, seemingly based on the historical Johannes Leo Africanus, the sixteenth-century Andalusian writer of *The History and Description of Africa*, although he suspected the daimon of impersonation. 'I think he is masquerading and gets himself out of an encyclopaedia,' he wrote to a friend in 1915.⁶⁴ But a 'cross correspondence' of two messages, one channelled by the automatic writing of the spiritualist Lady Edith Lyttelton and another noted on a 'scrap of paper' by Horton, gave Yeats pause. Both referred to the 'double harness' of Phaethon (in Greek myth, the son of Helios, who drove the sun chariot too close to Earth), and Horton cautioned Yeats to 'give the dark horse wings & subordinate it to the white winged horse' lest the white horse break away '& leave you to the dark horse who will lead your chariot into the enemies camp'.⁶⁵ This was enough to convince Yeats that something greater was being communicated to him and was in need of explication, but for the time being he did not act on it.

In October 1917, shortly after being rejected by Iseult Gonne, his former beloved Maud's daughter, he married Georgina 'Georgie' Hyde-Lees. Yeats called her George. She was twenty-seven years his junior, and they had met through her aunt and his former lover, Olivia Shakespear. She had been a member of the Amoun Temple since 1914, probably under Yeats's guidance, and was already versed in mediumship and astrological charts.[66] Within a week of their marriage she began to experiment with automatic writing, initially to divert her husband's paralysing feelings of guilt and inadequacy, but increasingly as a tool for transmitting what would become *A Vision*, Yeats's occult schema of human personality types and historical gyres.[67] Over a total of 450 sittings across the next three years, with George as the medium and Yeats the questioner, more than 3,600 sheets 'in disjointed sentences, in almost illegible writing' were preserved.[68] Their partnership recalls that of the fourteenth-century alchemist Nicolas Flamel and his wife Perenelle or, in more recent memory, Mathers receiving Third Order instructions through Moina.

How exactly these writings became *A Vision* is obscured by the sheer amount of material, but evidently Yeats began to use the spectral messages for literary purposes almost as soon as the sessions commenced. 'I am writing it all out,' he wrote to Lady Gregory in January 1918, 'in a series of dialogues about a supposed medieval book the "Speculum Angelorum et Hominum" by Gyraldous & a sect of Arabs called the Judwalis (diagrametists). Ross helped me with the Arabic. I live with a strange sense of revelation & never know what the day will bring.'[69] In an extension of the correspondence system learned in the GD, Yeats sorted his data alphabetically into an index of around 750 cards, using headings such as 'Images', 'Freewill', 'Myth', 'Christ, Judas, etc', 'Ugliness' and 'Joy'.[70] Even his and George's two children, Anne and Michael, who were born during this period, had their own entries. 'I have moments of exaltation,' he wrote, but 'I doubt if I can make another share my excitement.' Much of Book I is built up around the core duality of Sun and Moon, representing the 'primary' (or 'objective') and the 'antithetical' (or 'subjective') in man. Based on a diagram from the *Speculum Angelorum et Hominum*, a chart called the 'Great Wheel' shows the twenty-eight phases of the lunar cycle, which Yeats uses to map out 'all possible human types'. The four human 'faculties' or 'tinctures' (an occult term borrowed from Jakob Böhme) – the *Will*, the *Creative Mind*, the *Body of Fate*, and the *Mask* – are superimposed onto the wheel in order 'to show when and in what proportions' they influence one another.[71] Book 2 developed this system, tabulating the combinations of types into further divisions based on the zodiac. In Book 3 Yeats outlined the theory of history communicated to him by George's instructors, in which the past is divided into 2,000-year spans or 'eras'. These, too, are 'wheels' or 'gyres' with their own four historical faculties and their own preordained courses. Two 'eras' make a 4,000-year 'cycle', and encompassing them all is the 'Great Year', lasting 26,000 years.[72] 'A millennium is the symbolic measure of a being that attains its flexible maturity and then sinks into rigid age'.[73] This is also the idea behind Yeats's 'The Second Coming', a poem written in 1919 that opens with the famous lines:

> Turning and turning in the widening gyre
> The falcon cannot hear the falconer;
> Things fall apart; the centre cannot hold.

In Yeats's eyes, the current cycle of history was coming to an end and a new one was in the throes of being born: violent events such as the First World War and the Irish Easter Rising were proof of this.

There is little in *A Vision* that links it explicitly to the GD curriculum, or to Yeats's occult experiments with fellow students. Its mystic philosophy comes from readings in Blake, Swedenborg and Jakob Böhme, the gyre and cone imagery from the Kabbalah. Critics have long grappled with the book, which was printed privately in 1925, either treating it as a guide to Yeats's poetry or else as something more profound in scope that ultimately misses its mark.[74] Northrup Frye viewed it in the same apocalyptic tradition as Blake's prophecies, and judged it a failure.[75] Later in the twentieth century the idea surfaced that the book demonstrates an ironic distance from its subject, with Yeats himself a dramatic character. In fact, his own fictional creations (Michael Robartes and Owen Aherne, who first appear in his occult short stories in the 1890s) are assigned narratorial roles.[76] Yeats gestured to this possible literary interpretation in his introduction to the 1938 revised *Vision*, in which he recalls asking the spirit instructor whether he should spend the rest of his life 'piecing together those scattered sentences'. 'No,' the answer came, 'we have come to give you metaphors for poetry.'[77] This second version was smoothed of its harsh occult edges and made more palatable to a general audience by over a decade of revisions. Yeats ended by conceding that his system of Sun and Moon was in fact all symbolic, his divisions of history into equal periods 'stylistic arrangements of experience comparable to the cubes in the drawing of Wyndham Lewis'.[78]

Whether or not *A Vision* was intellectually reliant on GD ideas, its writing clearly caused Yeats to dwell on his time in Mathers's Order: the first edition opened with a dedication to Moina Mathers as 'Vestigia'. 'Perhaps this book has been written because a number of young men and women, you and I among the number, met nearly forty years ago in London and Paris to discuss mystical philosophy', Yeats mused.[79] He had seen Moina at least twice since her husband's death in 1918. She had written to him in 1924, angered by his characterization of Mathers in *The Trembling of the Veil* (1922) as a man of 'learning but no scholarship' whose mind had later become 'unhinged', and demanded that Yeats correct it.[80] 'With this awful book of yours between us I can never meet you again or be connected with you in any way save you make such reparation as may lie in your power.'[81] Yeats conceded the point, although in the end he changed very little. He may have felt that dedicating *A Vision* to Moina would serve as an apology.[82]

The dedication continued its resurrections, with Yeats referring to those GD members who had since become 'dead or estranged': Florence Farr, who had died from breast cancer in 1917; Allan Bennett, who had lived as a Buddhist monk in Burma (now Myanmar) under a new name and died in London in 1923; W. T. Horton, who swore himself to celibacy, only to fall in love and live platonically with a 'young fellow-student' until her death.[83] Then there is the 'learned brassfounder in the North of England', who might have been the watchmaker Thomas Henry Pattinson, a very early Isis-Urania recruit.[84] A previous draft also mentioned Maud Gonne, Dorothea

Hunter and Mathers himself. Only Farr is named, perhaps because she was the only figure that a public readership would have recognized.

An epilogue, again dedicated to 'Vestigia', was written and discarded. Instead, *A Vision* ends with 'All Souls' Night', a poem written in Oxford in August 1920, in Yeats's rooms on Broad Street. Opening at midnight, as the 'great Christ Church bell' sounds through the room, the poet calls up his departed fellow occultists to appear before him. 'I have mummy truths to tell / Whereat the living mock.'

> And I call up MacGregor Mathers from the grave,
> For in my first hard spring-time we were friends,
> Although of late estranged.
> I thought him half a lunatic, half knave,
> And told him so; but friendship never ends,
> And what if mind seem changed,
> And it seemed changed with the mind,
> When thoughts rise up unbid
> On generous things that he did
> And I grow half contented to be blind.
> He had much industry at setting out,
> Much boisterous courage, before loneliness
> Had driven him crazed;
> For meditations upon unknown thought
> Make human intercourse grow less and less;
> They are neither paid nor praised.
> But he'd object to the host,
> The glass because my glass;
> A ghost-lover he was
> And may have grown more arrogant being a ghost.[85]

The poetic eulogies are not rose-tinted portraits of his former friends: Farr left England for vanity's sake ('knowing that the future would be vexed / With 'minished beauty'), and Horton's experiment was a 'sweet extremity of pride'.[86] The poem is nevertheless haunted by a heartfelt sense of loss, and a sense that as spirits (or memories) his friends have taken on a new dignity. Perhaps Yeats hoped that 'All Soul's Night' would rehabilitate these figures in his mind, or perhaps he wished to show them what he had accomplished. The conjuring of ghosts at midnight and the imagery of the Egyptian mummy-cloth end *A Vision* on a lingering, haunting note. Yeats alone, the surviving magician of the old Golden Dawn, continuing to practise his occult art: poetry.

It is not clear when exactly Yeats severed his ties with the Stella Matutina, or if he ever did. With new responsibilities to his family and an increasingly active role in Irish politics, he could no longer commit the same amount of time and effort to his magical studies. He and George remained with the Amoun Temple until its closure in 1920 (though it would be revived later in the decade), and after this point his interest in the ceremonial side of the occult began to wane, at least for a time. 'My connection with the "Hermetic Students" ended amid quarrels caused by men, otherwise worthy, who claimed a Rosicrucian sanction for their own fantasies,' Yeats wrote in 1926, three years after accepting the Nobel Prize for Literature, 'and I add to prevent needless correspondence that I am not now a member of a Cabbalistic Society.'[87] But the GD was never far from his mind. In October 1929 he was trying to trace GD documents connected with the Order's dubious origins, and travelled to Bristol to the Stella Matutina's Hermes Temple, 'a most able group'.[88] In London he met with Dr Carnegie Dickson, a student of the Stella Matutina, to go through his papers: 'He has Westcott's diary', Yeats reported to his wife, arriving at the implausible conclusion that 'Fräulein Sprengel was authentic' and adding: 'I also have the name of another Third Order person'.[89] This late obsession with GD history shows that while he was distancing himself publicly from Rosicrucian brotherhoods, even into his sixties Yeats remained enthralled by the mythology and legitimacy of the group that had so powerfully shaped him.

6

Metaphysical Thrillers
Charles Williams & Dion Fortune

In the summer of 1915, in the London office of Oxford University Press (OUP), a young editorial assistant had been given the unenviable task of seeking permission from every author (or literary estate) whose work was scheduled to appear in the forthcoming *Oxford Book of English Mystical Verse*. The book's editors, D. H. S. Nicholson and the Rev. A. H. E. Lee, declared in their introduction that the 'forces of mysticism', which had lain dormant for so long, were in the process of being mended. 'It has emerged from the morass of apathy which characterized the eighteenth and the greater part of the nineteenth century', they wrote; 'it is reawakening to the value of its own peculiar treasure of thought and word.'[1] The editorial assistant, Charles Williams, went diligently through the list of contributors, sending out letters and checking off their replies. He did not know it at the time, but he had just corresponded with four students of the Golden Dawn: W. B. Yeats, Aleister Crowley, Evelyn Underhill and A. E. Waite. Williams was already an admirer of Yeats and had used a quotation from *The Shadowy Waters* as an epigraph for his first poetry collection, *The Silver Stair*, published in 1912. He had also begun to plan an epic poem based on the Arthurian legend, inspired by Malory and Tennyson, and for research had read Waite's *The Hidden Church of the Holy Graal*. Discovering that Waite was a gifted poet as well as an expounder of grail theories, Williams sent him a copy of *The Silver Stair*, and Waite responded by inviting Williams to his house in South

XVI The Great Seal of the Rosea Rubeae et Aureae Crucis, the Second, or Inner, Order of the Golden Dawn, *c.* 1892. On the reverse, William Wynn Westcott has written 'drawn by Mathers'.

XVII J. F. C. Fuller, *The Portal of the Outer Order*
(A∴A∴ temple painting), 1909.

XVIII J. F. C. Fuller, *The Portal of the Abyss* (A∴A∴ temple painting), 1909.

XIX Aleister Crowley, *The Sun* (*Auto Portrait*), 1920.

xx William Alexander Ayton, Telesmatic angelic figure, *c.* 1892.

XXI Pamela Colman Smith, illustration from Bram Stoker, *The Lair of the White Worm*, 1911.

XXII Pamela Colman Smith, *The Wave*, 1903.

XXIII Pamela Colman Smith, tarot cards, 1909.

Ealing, where he dropped tantalizing hints about a new order he had founded that very July: The Fellowship of the Rosy Cross.[2] Williams was intrigued, and asked to be involved.

When Williams made contact with Waite in the summer of 1915, the Independent and Rectified Rite was no longer in operation. For a number of years Waite had been trying unsuccessfully to purge the Order of its magical vestiges (such as astral travelling, visions and Egyptian-based rituals), but many students would not be persuaded.[3] Others shared his mystical views but preferred to implement them using their own methods. Unlike members such as M. W. Blackden, Waite also still doubted the provenance of the Cipher Manuscripts, and in 1914, finding that this 'infighting' impeded the Order's smooth functioning, the Independent and Rectified Rite was dissolved and with it the name of Isis-Urania. 'A few persons attempted to carry on by themselves,' Waite recalled, 'but it proved a failure.' Almost immediately, Waite and a dozen loyalists had made plans for his new Fellowship, to be grounded in a Christian interpretation of Kabbalah. Its symbolism, declared the constitution, 'is concerned only with the quest and attainment of the human soul on its return to the Divine Centre'.[4] Its rites were intended as a sacrament, and 'those who can receive into their hearts the life and grace of the symbolism may attain both knowledge and experience thereby and therein'. This was Waite's chance to continue the Rosicrucian-masonic tradition and to shape a mystical path for his students using his own esoteric theories. There were no Secret Chiefs or supernatural Adepts, only the priestly Waite, who remained Hierophant of the Fellowship until his death in 1942. In the 1930s, years after Williams had ceased attending meetings, his friend Anne Ridler remembered him speaking of having 'belonged to the Golden Dawn'.[5] Williams would have been well aware of the Fellowship's descent from Mathers's GD, but Waite's new order was decidedly different. For one thing, it did not teach its students the practical side of magic.

Williams had been at the press for seven years when *The Oxford Book of English Mystical Verse* was commissioned. Born in north London in 1886 to 'straightforward Anglican' parents, his father was a foreign correspondence clerk who had read widely and published moralizing poems and short fiction in magazines.[6] When they moved to St Albans, the young Charles won a place at the local grammar school and learned to love Jules Verne and Nathaniel Hawthorne; he acted in plays and wrote stories of his own. With a friend, he created 'Silvania', a detailed imaginary world complete with an invented political system and military history inspired by *The Prisoner of Zenda*. In 1902 Williams entered University College London on a scholarship, but lack of family money to supplement his studies meant that he was forced to withdraw without completing the BA course. Doubting his once-golden future, he found a job in the Methodist Book Room in Holborn and discovered friendship at a church debate group called the Theological Smokers. It was during this time that he began to develop his poetic voice; he had also started to think deeply about romantic love and its place in a spiritual life, and in 1908 had fallen in love with a young teacher named Florence Conway, whom he would marry in 1917. Based on a reading of the Victorian poet Coventry Patmore, increasingly Williams came to the heterodox idea that love was in some sense a religious state, even 'the same thing' as Christianity.[7]

Also in 1908, a contact at Amen Corner, then the London headquarters of OUP, just west of St Paul's Cathedral, got Williams a job proofreading a new edition of Thackeray. He would remain at OUP for several decades, and it quickly became, as his colleague Gerard Hopkins remembered, 'the moving force of his life'.[8] It was where most of his early work was published, under the auspices of the imperious Humphrey 'Caesar' Milford, and where he conducted a nineteen-year (though unconsummated) affair with the young librarian Phyllis Jones. The patronage of the writer Alice Meynell funded the publication of his first book of poems, eighty sonnets on the theme of an 'ideal' celibate love that would lead a couple closer to God. The Arthurian legends were also forefront in his mind, forming another part of his nascent spiritual system and guiding him ever nearer to occult territory. He read recent scholarship in comparative myth, the grand fertility cult theories of Frazer's *The Golden Bough* and Jessie Weston's *From Ritual to Romance*, and the grail legend as it appears in Malory,

Tennyson and the Welsh *Mabinogion*. It was at this stage that Williams found Waite's *The Hidden Church*. In his notebook he even references Machen's *The Great God Pan* to substantiate a theory that Pan is 'the terrifying father of Merlin, by his desire to become incarnate'.[9] Fiona Macleod and Yeats were also early influences, and fed into the Celtic revivalism of what was shaping up to be an extremely eclectic and unusual project.

Williams was rejected from military service due to his nerves and poor eyesight, and by 1915, with Arthurian Britain still a chief preoccupation, he was hungering after a more structured and esoteric mysticism. It was fortunate, therefore, that his work on the *Oxford Book of English Mystical Verse* brought him unknowingly into the fringes of one of the GD's creative networks. Both of its compilers had until very recently been active students of Waite's Independent and Rectified Rite, and were themselves literary men. D. H. S. Nicholson had been initiated in August 1910, and in the intervening years had translated two books on mystical theology published by the Theosophical Society and the occult bookseller J. M. Watkins; Waite had provided an introduction for one of them.[10] A. H. E. Lee, who had entered the Rectified Rite in March 1908, was an Anglican chaplain and theosophist, a founding member of the Leeds Arts Club and a contributor to Alfred Orage's *New Age* along with Florence Farr, who had lectured to the Arts Club in 1906. Nicholson and Lee's anthology represented another public collaboration of GD members. By this time the Order could be seen in the broad light of day; its existence was already public knowledge, following the heavily publicized Horos scandal. Of the three poems included by Crowley, 'The Neophyte' actually gives a name to the GD: 'This poem,' reads Crowley's footnote, 'describes the Initiation of the *true* "Hermetic Order of the Golden Dawn" in its spiritual aspect.'[11] Yeats's 'The Rose of Battle' and 'To the Secret Rose' also featured, as did six of Waite's poems, and Evelyn Underhill was represented with five poems taken mostly from her 1912 collection *Immanence*, published after she had left the occult behind. Also represented were poets from the wider GD network, including Edwin Ellis, whose Blake books were co-edited with Yeats.[12]

CHAPTER 6

Nicholson and Lee may have had some influence on Williams's application to the Fellowship of the Rosy Cross, though neither of them joined themselves. A letter from Waite confirms that Williams had requested to join the new fraternity: 'And that leads me to that Order, about which I once spoke to you and which you now ask to join. It is concerned with the mystery of Divine Love unfolded in ritual and symbolism.'[13] Williams requested a Form of Profession, which he signed on 18 July 1917, and after his initiation in September as 'Qui Sitit Veniat' ('Let he who thirsts come') he went to Spencer & Co. to purchase the costly masonic-style uniform.[14] During the first few years, meetings of the Salvator Mundi Temple were held in a series of hotel rooms, but in 1919 the Fellowship settled more permanently at a flat in Earl's Court. As per the rules, Williams kept his Fellowship activities secret while he was a member, discussing them only with his wife. For Florence Williams, the society was merely another excuse for her husband's absence from the family home. Their son Michael was born in 1922 and Williams clearly saw the child's arrival as an obstruction to his literary pursuits. 'I am sure a baby brings a sword, to slay all the happy little innocent busynesses of one's life,' he complained to his friend John Pellow after Michael's birth. 'But he is a nuisance: does one write verse? Never. A hundred unfinished poems lie about the flat.'[15]

Williams's literary career, his unorthodox Christianity and his links to a Golden Dawn offshoot during the first half of the twentieth century parallel the trajectory of another writer of this period, Dion Fortune. Born Violet Mary Firth in December 1890, she occupied a wholly different world, socially, geographically and metaphysically, to Williams. The Firths were upper-middle-class, proud of their Yorkshire roots, and owed their substantial wealth to the nineteenth-century Sheffield steel industry and the provision of weapons to the British government. By 1890 they were living in Llandudno, a North Wales seaside resort where her parents operated a 'Hydropathic' bathing centre. Wales did not shape Fortune's identity in the same way it did Arthur Machen's (the Celticness to which she was drawn later in life was of a more general sort), but she may have liked the myth later circulated among her followers that she had been born an orphan, and was in fact a fairy changeling swapped in the cradle.[16] She would also later claim to have experienced 'unbidden' visions of an Atlantean world, full of prehistoric jellyfish and porpoises under a 'copper-coloured' sun, at the age of four.[17] Perhaps the watery environments of the Welsh coast and her family's baths had imprinted themselves on her imagination after all.

In around 1902 the Firth family moved south, to Somerset, and Fortune was sent to a school in Weston-super-Mare (where the GD's Osiris Temple had long since disbanded). There she wrote two books of verse, their printing costs paid for by relatives. From a poem titled 'Myself', it is apparent that she was a precocious child, still comfortable in her family's Christianity: 'The wild desire is past, and now I know / That in the sphere God placed me I am best'.[18] She had a scientific eye for the natural world, though it could quickly become coloured by romanticism, as in her essay on Autumn: 'there is a feeling sadness, of mystery about her, as if she stood at the portal of the Great Unknown, and was about to pass through to the land of shade beyond'.[19] In 1906 the family decamped to London, and it was around this time that Fortune's parents converted to Christian Science, a New England religious movement, barely thirty years old, that advocated for prayer in place of modern medicine. 'Angels', a poem printed in the *Christian Science Journal*, suggests its early, but ultimately fleeting, influence on Fortune's thinking.

In 1911 Fortune began to attend the Studley Horticultural College for Women in Warwickshire, run by the tyrannical warden Lillias Hamilton, whose unusual punishments sent girls into hysterics. 'It was her custom to control her staff by means of her knowledge of mind-power,' Fortune later recalled in her book *Psychic Self Defence*. She felt convinced that Hamilton had displayed occult powers picked up during her time in India. Fortune collaborated in writing annual plays with students and after graduating became a member of staff, but a final, drawn-out confrontation with the warden sent her into a semi-conscious 'stupor' and left her psychologically wounded for the next three years.[20] What she remembered as a psychic battle of wills convinced her that Hamilton's powers were real, and required investigation.

The interrelation between psychology and the occult has a long history. In the early twentieth century, new fields of psychical research and parapsychology were allowing psychologists to examine occultism from a scientific standpoint. The theosophist Annie Besant wrote books on multiple personality and trance states and followed the work of Jean Piaget, the renowned psychologist of early childhood, while the Swiss psychologist C. G. Jung famously studied esoteric traditions such as alchemy, astrology and Kabbalah to inform his own theories of archetypes and the collective unconscious. When she had recovered from her battle with Hamilton, Fortune left the horticultural college and enrolled as a student at a psychological clinic on London's Brunswick Square, where as a 'lay psychoanalyst' she encountered the theories of Freud, Jung and Alfred Adler. After growing discouraged by her inability to help her patients, she dropped her formal studies. By then, she had read Besant's *The Ancient Wisdom* at the Theosophical Society's library in Tavistock Square, where she had been going to eat lunch:

> I had felt as if I stood in the centre of a small circle of illumination cast by scientific knowledge, and the darkness of the unknown pressed in upon every side. A number of threads were placed in my hands, and I was bidden to unravel them, but the ends thereof disappeared into the darkness, and those threads were human lives. I had come to the point where I felt I could no longer carry on my work as a medical analyst owing to the poor percentage of success that attended our efforts, when the doctrines of occultism were brought to my notice.[21]

Fortune had first been drawn to psychology by occult experience, and here she was turning once more to the occult. But this time she brought her study with her: occultism, as Fortune saw it, was the

Dion Fortune in ritual dress, n.d.

knowledge of the powers of the mind, and became for her the 'real key' to psychology.[22] 'We can define occultism as an extension of psychology, for it studies certain little-known aspects of the human mind,' she wrote in *Sane Occultism*, one of her practical manuals first published in 1930. 'Its findings, rightly formulated and understood, fit in with what is already established in psychology and natural science. This mutual corroboration must be the test of occult science.'[23]

Fortune was probably introduced to London occult society by a woman named Maiya Tranchell-Hayes, a family friend of the Firths who lived in a house in Kensington Square and may have been the widow of a psychologist, which could explain why the two women reconnected. Her first encounter with an occult order was with the Alpha et Omega, part of the group that Mathers had founded in Paris from the ashes of his GD. John Brodie-Innes presided over its two British temples, founded first in Edinburgh, then London.[24] It would later take hold in America, with temples active in New York, Chicago and Philadelphia. Fortune was initiated into the London temple in 1919, taking the name 'Deo Non Fortuna' (the Firth family motto, 'By God not by luck'), but was unimpressed by what the GD had become since its early days. 'The glory had departed,' she recalled in an article for the *Occult Gazette* in 1933, 'for most of its original members were dead or withdrawn; it had suffered severely during the war, and was manned mainly by widows and grey-bearded ancients.'[25] The following year she transferred allegiance to another Alpha et Omega temple, also operating in London and also run by a widow, Moina Mathers, who had returned from Paris after her husband's death in 1918 and was concerned with guarding his memory and preserving his GD teachings. It was during this period that Fortune began to contract 'Deo Non Fortuna' into the pen name 'Dion Fortune'. The new pseudonym signified a number of things for her: a cultivation of her emerging magical persona through Alpha et Omega rituals, an attachment to her family upbringing and a belief that her life was taking shape through faith in God. As she began to write as Dion Fortune during the mid-1920s, the name Violet M. Firth and its ties to her books of Edwardian nature poetry were steadily left behind.

METAPHYSICAL THRILLERS

At the same time as Fortune was beginning her studies in the Alpha et Omega temple, Williams was rising up the grades of the Fellowship of the Rosy Cross. But its Kabbalah-inflected Christian mysticism was not the only school of esoteric thought that Williams found himself exposed to. Having chosen not to join Waite's society, Nicholson and Lee had instead started a fortnightly discussion group at Lee's vicarage in St John's Wood, and in 1919 Williams was invited to attend. Topics may have included alchemy, astrology, Kabbalah and a kind of spiritual yoga with Christian overtones.[26] Lee had also managed to borrow the GD's Flying Roll VII from Dr Carnegie Dickson, a consultant pathologist and student of the Stella Matutina, and was taking notes on Westcott's alchemical lectures.[27] Not much can be gleaned about the contents of the group's discussions during the 1920s, but Williams's commonplace book reveals that he was reading in the *Collectanea Hermetica* series – *Numbers: Their Occult Powers and Mystic Virtues* (vol. IX) and *Sepher Yetzirah* (vol. X), Westcott's translation of the famous Jewish mystical text – and keeping up with the various theosophical books by G. R. S. Mead (secretary to Madame Blavatsky before her death, and founder of the influential Quest Society).[28] He was also enthralled by Waite's *The Secret Doctrine in Israel* (1913), a study of the Kabbalistic text known as the Zohar, which may have stimulated ideas about the symbolic correspondence between Kabbalah and the female body.[29] The book's frontispiece depicted an Adamic figure with arms outstretched, enmeshed in the paths and *sefirot* of the Tree of Life. Through this combination of the works of Westcott, Waite and the mystical duo of Nicholson and Lee, Williams was absorbing a good chunk of the GD curriculum, filtered through an explicitly Christian framing.

Within two years Williams had reached the Fellowship's Adeptus Minor ($5° = 6°$) grade. Like the GD before it, initiation into the Second Order required the candidate to enter the seven-sided vault and witness the resurrection of Christian Rosenkreutz. Prior to this, Williams

CHAPTER 6

would have endured a symbolic crucifixion, strapped to the 'Cross of Christhood'.[30] To complicate matters, Waite had divided the F∴R∴C∴ into four orders according to the four Kabbalistic realms (Action, Formation, Creation and the World of the Supernals).[31] As an Adept, Williams was given new responsibilities and ceremonial roles, and in 1921 was made the 'Master of the Temple'. While other students preferred to read their lines from a script, Williams made a point of reciting from memory, so that he could 'celebrate with dignity'.[32] According to a previous lecture delivered by Waite to the Rectified Rite, students were required to remain an Adeptus Minor for a period of six years (a number Waite had derived from the 'theosophic addition' of the thirty-three years that Jesus lived on Earth), but he must have decided to shorten this, as it only took Williams until June 1923 to reach Adeptus Major ($6° = 5°$).[33] The rituals became more demanding and erotically charged, which must have appealed to Williams, who was in the midst of writing *Romantic Theology*, which argued that sexual love was akin to religious sacrament. A repeated image in Waite's ceremonies was the metaphor of the soul in intercourse with the divine lover; the candidate was impelled to kiss a ceremonial dagger offered to them by a priestess.

Hints of the F∴R∴C∴ rituals and the magic discussed at the St John's Wood meetings overspilled their boundaries and began to colour Williams's outer life. In 1924 the OUP office moved from Amen Corner to the impressive Amen House, and his affair with Phyllis Jones was in full swing when he wrote a Christmas 'masque' for the office's Dramatic Society. Full of inside jokes and members of staff playing heightened versions of themselves (including an enthroned Humphrey Milford as 'Caesar'), the play was titled *The Masque of the Manuscript* and was actually performed in April 1927.[34] As she asked ritual questions to the Manuscript, Phyllis's character had to make 'the sign of the magical pentagram'; in preparation for this, Williams sent her a diagram with accompanying instructions: 'This is the Banishing Pentagram of Magic, for the expulsion of demons, ghosts, and such like intruders ... The whole of this, and indeed of the opening dialogue, should be acted and spoken in the seriousness of high fantasy. It is a shadow of the Mysteries.'35 The pentagram ritual had been the only magical instruction taught to GD students outside the Second Order, and Williams must have learned of it from Nicholson and Lee (unless he had been reading Crowley's *Equinox*). Waite had himself written conjurations to be performed by Arthur Machen in a 1901 production of *Henry VI Part II*, though his Latin spells were 'much wickeder than the Grimoires'.36 Machen probably did not end up speaking them, but Williams succeeded in inserting genuine GD ritual into *The Masque of the Manuscript*. Why had he done it? The masque is concerned with the creation of the perfect book, and the Manuscript first appears in ragged costume: no doubt the idea that the OUP staff were unwittingly involved in a spiritual-alchemical process was a thrill to Williams. In fact, a second masque (*The Masque of Perusal*) would be performed in 1929, although a planned third never materialized to complete what Williams saw as the three stages of the 'Mystical Way'.37

After reading a thriller by the pulp writer Sax Rohmer (author of the *Fu Manchu* books, and falsely rumoured to have been connected with the GD), Williams became convinced that he should begin writing occult novels, or 'metaphysical thrillers', primarily as a quick method to pay for Michael's schooling. His first attempt was titled *Adepts in Africa*, and concerned an Englishman's attainment of immortality through an occult 'transmutation of energy' and his attempts to take over the world by inciting a revolution in South Africa.38 It was rejected by Faber & Faber in 1926 and consigned to the manuscript box in Williams's office. His next attempt was *The Corpse*, which imagined the discovery of the grail in the modern-day English village of Fardles, and the struggles of the bookish Archdeacon Julian Davenant to prevent Sir Giles Tumulty, black magician and antiquarian, from obtaining it. The book was published by an enthusiastic Victor Gollancz in 1930, its name changed to *War in Heaven*, a quote from Book I of *Paradise Lost*.

This unexpected partnership with Gollancz led to a sequence of four more novels over the next half-decade: *Many Dimensions* (1930), *The Place of the Lion* (1931), *The Greater Trumps* (1932) and *Shadows of Ecstasy* (1933), a re-edited version of the earlier *Adepts*. Williams's thrillers are short and pacy, each exploring an ambitious concept to its logical and often very satisfying conclusion. They follow a similar structure: an artefact is stolen or a power unleashed; a romantic pairing reflects the spiritual symbolism with which Williams viewed his relationship with Phyllis; there is a clash of good with evil, after which the protagonist must make a crucial decision. In *The Place of the Lion*, for example, Platonic archetypes begin to bleed into the material world and become larger, more powerful and more 'real' than their real-world counterparts. *The Greater Trumps* plays with the idea that an ancient set of tarot cards can be used to control the elements. The novels improve on the plot of Crowley's muddled but entertaining *Moonchild*, which was published just a year before *War in Heaven*, though it is unlikely that Williams would have read it. The poet John Heath-Stubbs described them as entertainments in which magic is seen 'not as something which may provide a fanciful escape from a dull reality, but, at least, as the image of something which is part of the world as we know it'.[39] The Christian-mystical teachings of the Fellowship of the Rosy Cross are surely responsible for this feeling, although the occult devices of tarot arcana, the Tetragrammaton and the archetypes are usually nothing more than decorative in the novels. One early fan of Williams's thrillers was T. S. Eliot, then an editor at Faber & Faber, who had been encouraged by the socialite Lady Ottoline Morrell to read *War in Heaven*.[40] The two poets were instantly at ease with one another when they met at one of Morrell's Gower Street soirées, and Williams promptly sent Eliot *The Place of the Lion*. 'I have found these two books so exciting that I am incapacitated from making any purely literary judgement of them,' Eliot wrote back. 'It is surprising how few people seem to have any awareness of other than material realities, or of Good and Evil as having anything to do with the nature of things – as anything more than codes of conduct.'[41] Faber & Faber would publish Williams's two final novels, *Descent into Hell* (1937) and *All Hallows' Eve* (1945).

Fortune was also turning her experiences of the occult into fiction. Far more influential than the GD was her apprenticeship to the Irish freemason Theodore Moriarty (again, Tranchell-Hayes may have brought them together). Moriarty, who had worked in South Africa as a civil servant and become a mason in 1903 – though not, as far as is known, a member of any GD temple – was a decade older than Fortune and had published two works on masonic etiquette. When Fortune knew him, he had already attracted a small community of mostly women to his Science, Arts and Crafts Society in Bishop's Stortford, where he worked psychic experiments and taught a system of masonic-tinged 'Universal Theosophy'.[42] This translated into a kind of occult school along the lines of the GD (though unaffiliated with its temples), with initiatory ceremonies and practical and written assignments.

Fortune began to use her experiences with Moriarty for a series of short stories, fictionalizing him as Dr John Taverner, a charismatic medical practitioner, occultist and amateur Egyptologist who runs a nursing home on Harley Street. The stories, which appeared between February and July 1922 in the *Royal Magazine* and were eventually collected in 1926 as *The Secrets of Dr Taverner*, were a dramatized casebook of Moriarty and Fortune's experiments. Taverner's 'cases' are nearly always exposed as instances of unusual psychological phenomena, although as a student of an occult brotherhood he is also aware of the 'profound effect' ritual magic can have on the mind.[43] Like Algernon Blackwood's *Dr Silence* stories, several of which Blackwood claimed were based on genuine situations, Fortune's Taverner belonged to the well-established occult detective sub-genre, whose protagonists were sleuthing Adepts such as Crowley's Simon Iff and William Hope Hodgson's Carnacki the Ghost Finder. Fortune cast herself as Taverner's sidekick, the ex-army medic Dr Rhodes, who recounts the incidents in a similar manner to Conan Doyle's Dr Watson. The story 'Blood-lust' was, according to Fortune, 'literally true', relating the case of a dying German soldier who has attached himself subconsciously to an Englishman in an act of psychological 'vampirism'.[44] In 'The Return of the Sign' she uses ceremonial magic to the same dramatic effect that Crowley had just achieved in *Moonchild*: fearing that a ritual manuscript belonging to his own brotherhood has been stolen by one of the Chelsea Black Lodges, Taverner hypnotizes himself to access the Akashic Records, a theosophical concept in which every human thought and deed is stored 'in the mind of Nature'.[45] He is then able to trace the manuscript. The Taverner stories betray the influences of Sherlock Holmes and Bram Stoker's *Dracula*, but also more contemporary writers of supernatural fiction: 'A Daughter of Pan', the story of a wild girl content to dance in the woods with the spirits of nature, reproduces Algernon Blackwood's 'A Touch of Pan', first published in 1917.

At the same time, Fortune was starting to develop an aptitude for trance mediumship. On a moonlit night in 1922, while visiting Chalice Well in Glastonbury, she met a man named Charles Loveday. In the following months the pair made contact with a group who called themselves the Company of Avalon. The Company spoke of Glastonbury as a centre of the old faith, which would one day be restored. 'We are met here for the down pouring of the power,' came one proclamation (in Fortune's voice): 'The Chalice is above the Tor. This is the hour of the power of the Chalice.'[46] Loveday and Fortune, accompanied by a third participant known as 'E. P.' or Edie, held further trance sessions and in time established that they were speaking with three separate personalities. One voice belonged to a chatty Coventry-born man named David Carstairs, another to Thomas Erskine, an eighteenth-century lawyer. The third was Socrates. Erskine and Socrates gave lectures on an occult system of seven planes (Fortune was a '4th plane medium', and could talk to Carstairs, while the other two occupied higher planes and had to be called down). Fortune claimed to have used the knowledge received from the Company to write her later book *The Cosmic Doctrine*, though it in fact bears a strong resemblance to Moriarty's teachings. Erskine also gave a strange piece of advice to the assembled group: 'The Masters, as they are supposed to be in popular would-be esoteric thought, are pure fiction,' he declared. 'Learn to write novels on the astral because it is by creating a true-to-type thought form that you get in touch with that which transcends thought.'[47] Erskine's comment foreshadowed the kind of fiction

Fortune would end up writing. Her books, particularly her novels, were aimed at initiating readers into the magical life.

Williams considered his long-planned Arthurian poetry cycle to be his finest work, even his life's true purpose. Armed with two decades' worth of research and Phyllis as his muse (mythologized as 'Celia'), he produced the collection *Heroes and Kings* in 1930, its poems mapping the constituent parts of Celia's body onto Arthur's Dark Age Britain. The hermeticism he had learned from Waite's Fellowship and the gatherings at St John's Wood was baked into this central imagery. But this book only represented Williams's first attempt at his grail vision; it was followed by *Taliessin through Logres* (1938) and *The Region of the Summer Stars* (1944), two books of verse that use the Arthurian legend as a pattern by which to explain humanity's relationship with God.[48] Williams had employed the Holy Grail as a device in *War in Heaven*, but now he considered it the most important symbol of all: 'No invention can come near it; no fabulous imagination excel it.'[49] In its legendary origins the cup is connected with the inauguration of the eucharist and the death of Jesus, and in turn it represented Williams's ideas about exchange and substitution: in dying, Jesus took on the sins of humankind, and before he died he offered his body to his disciples. Williams's entire design is 'submerged in occult argument', a fact noted by reviewers, who saw the poems as communicating a glory 'hidden in a darkness more impenetrable than that which obscures Blake's Prophetic books'.[50] The poem 'The Vision of the Empire', from *Taliessin through Logres*, imagines the wizard Merlin as a mythic figure embodying 'time's metre', climbing 'through prisms and lines / over near Camelot and far Carbonek, / over the Perilous Sell, the See of union', while the young bard in 'Taliessin's Return to Logres' arrives in Wales at nightfall and sees the stars as 'a diagram played in the night', with a mathematical significance that requires interpretation.[51] Williams's friend C. S. Lewis feared that the view of these poems as obscure would become consensus unless the cycle was given a commentary.

Williams reached his highest level in the F∴R∴C∴ in June 1927, when he participated in the first ritual of the Fourth Order, which Waite had named 'The Hidden Life of the Rosy Cross'.[52] After this, his activities ceased. Waite turned up at OUP the following year, apparently to convince Williams to resume his Adeptship, but Williams was no longer interested. He may have felt that he had experienced all that he could in reaching the Fourth Order, or he may have decided to focus exclusively on literary endeavours. But while he was no longer affiliated with Waite's society, he was not averse to becoming professionally acquainted with several other ex-Order members. Yeats's work was a continual presence in Williams's life. Though he had found his edition of *Blake* unedifying, in the 1910s he had seen a performance of *The Countess Cathleen* at which Yeats was present, and by 1923 he was beginning to include Yeats in his public lectures. Yeats's poems are also discussed in Williams's survey of modern verse, *Poetry at Present* (1930), in which his lyricism is rapturously compared to the Elizabethans, regarded as a bulwark against the materialism of the early twentieth century: 'Mr. Yeats, exploring the nature of the world, has come down heavily on the side of the elementals, and of all else that may be implied by a theory of the universe which has a place for such beings.'[53] In 1938 Williams reviewed the revised edition of *A Vision* for *Time & Tide*, and found similarities with his own *Taliessin* poems. The two men first met properly at another of Ottoline Morrell's gatherings, where Williams found Yeats 'vivid and entertaining'. Morrell was clearly eager to hear the two men exchange intellectual blows: '*Please* do when you come – draw him out,' she implored Williams in 1933. 'He is interesting on the topic of genius. Whether it is the glorifying and impersonality of the *inner* man only, or whether it has to do with observation of the outer world as well.'[54] In 1940 he also befriended Evelyn Underhill, who had by then thoroughly shed her occult dispositions, when she asked him to give a lecture at the Chelmsford Diocese Retreat House. On her death in June the next year, it fell to Williams to edit a selection of her letters. His critical and lengthy introduction mentions that she had joined 'an occult companionship known as the Order of the G.D., and belonged to it for some years', and in surveying her early work he considered the description of the magical ritual in *The Column of Dust* to have been accurate.⁵⁵

In 1925, while Williams was still progressing through the grades of Waite's Fellowship, Fortune and Loveday's medium group was advised by their astral contacts to seek a connection with the Theosophical Society. They applied to become members of the Society's Christian Mystical Lodge, formed earlier in the decade to study the Christian element in theosophy. Fortune rose rapidly to become the lodge's president, but by 1928 she had resigned her position to focus more exclusively on the Fraternity of the Inner Light, a GD-related group she had founded in 1922. It was all part of the plan. At this stage, the groups connected to the Theosophical Society probably had very little to do with GD teachings. Fortune was also still a student of Alpha et Omega, though not for much longer. Ever protective of GD secrets, Moina Mathers took against her for publishing a series of manuals in practical occultism intended for a general audience throughout the 1920s:

> She nearly turned me out for writing *The Esoteric Philosophy of Love and Marriage*, on the grounds that I was betraying the inner teaching of the Order, but it was pointed out to her that I had not got the degree in which that teaching was given, and I was pardoned. She suspended me for some months for writing *Sane Occultism* and finally turned me out because certain symbols had not appeared in my aura – a perfectly unanswerable charge.⁵⁶

Another story goes that Fortune and Loveday showed Moina drafts of *The Cosmic Doctrine* and were given the option either to give up their extra-curricular pursuits or else leave the Alpha et Omega altogether.⁵⁷

Whether or not she left of her own accord, Fortune seems eventually to have transferred her membership to the Hermes Temple of the Stella Matutina, founded by Robert Felkin, where she encountered students more sympathetic to trance mediumship.[58]

For most of her life, Fortune was a Christian mystic, though of a slightly different variety to A. E. Waite and Evelyn Underhill. At the centre of her developing view of the world was the idea that humankind occupied an intermediate rung on the evolutionary ladder, and that as a species we are being guided towards a perfect state of consciousness by hidden 'Masters'. The goal of occultism, and the dissemination of occult knowledge through initiation into secret orders, was a 'speeding-up' of this process, a raising of consciousness to the level of the Abstract Mind.[59] At this point an individual is able to receive the wisdom of the Masters, with the Adept as intermediary. These theories were broadly theosophical, worked through the Jungian lens of archetypes and the collective unconscious. As theosophy had used contemporary science and scientific language to carve out a religion fit for modernity, Fortune looked to psychology to make the occult palatable to a new readership. At the same time, she derided theosophy for its over-reliance on Eastern traditions (in Fortune's novel *The Sea Priestess* (1938), Wilfred Maxwell reads 'a lot of Theosophical stuff' and develops 'spiritual scurvy'[60]). She remained convinced that the closely guarded knowledge of occult orders should be made open to the public, and thus became a great exposer and communicator of GD ritual information, most explicitly in *The Esoteric Orders and their Work*, published in 1928. 'There is no legitimate reason that I have ever been able to see for keeping these things secret,' she explained in an article for *The Occult Gazette*. 'If they have any value as an aid to spiritual development, and I for one believe that they have the highest value, there can be no justification for withholding them from the world.'[61]

According to Fortune, the Fraternity of the Inner Light was first conceived of as an 'outer court' of the Order of the Golden Dawn, approved by Moina Mathers in 1922.[62] Possibly this meant that it would act as a formal sub-group, but operating outside the GD's main ceremonies and hermetic teachings. The Fraternity began advertising for its correspondence course in the *Occult Review* and other esoteric magazines. Its facilities included a Lecture Centre and Library in Bayswater, London, and a square of land at the foot of Glastonbury Tor. It also began publishing *Inner Light*, a periodical 'devoted to Esoteric Christianity, Occult Science, and the Psychology of Superconsciousness'. The correspondence course soon developed into in-person rituals, and by 1930 candidates were being initiated into a series of three degrees called the 'Lesser Mysteries', before advancing to the 'Greater Mysteries'; these were akin to the Outer and Inner orders within the Alpha et Omega and Stella Matutina, and their initiation ceremonies were identical.[63] Although the GD influences would gradually fall away, it is clear from a 1932 letter to the occultist Israel Regardie that Fortune was still using original GD material to form her ideas about the Kabbalah: 'I judge from the correspondences given in "The Garden of Pomegranates" that you are using the old "Golden Dawn System", which is the one I use myself. I think it is far and away the best. Crowley gives it away in 777, but I have also got the Mathers MSS to check it by.'[64]

The Inner Light used Chalice Well and the Chalice Orchard Guest House in Glastonbury as centres of spiritual and ritual activity throughout the 1920s, but Fortune's interest in Glastonbury, 'our English Jerusalem', took firmer shape in a series of essays for *Inner Light*, later collected as *Glastonbury: Avalon of the Heart* (1930). These convey Fortune's romanticized picture of the town and the terror of the 'primitive', barrow-strewn plain that surrounds it. Glastonbury was the meeting place of two traditions that she valued above all others, Christianity and Celtic paganism: 'The Abbey is holy ground, consecrated by the dust of saints; but up here, at the foot of the Tor, the Old Gods have their part. So we have two Avalons, "the holiest erthe in Englande", down among the water-meadows; and upon the green heights the fiery pagan forces that make the heart leap and burn.'[65] At this point in Fortune's life, she was beginning to feel a greater attraction to British paganism, a shift that no doubt had something to do with the man she married in 1927. Dr Thomas Penry Evans, whom she nicknamed Merlin, or 'Merl', was a Welsh medical doctor who had paused his career to help with Inner Light operations. By the early 1930s he was giving lectures combining Celtic and Christian spirituality.[66] The Inner Light sub-group known as the Guild of the Master Jesus was renamed the Church of the Graal, and Fortune began to stage public performances of rites to Isis and Pan. Conducted in a converted Presbyterian church called the Belfry in West Halkin Street, Belgravia, these were grand events reminiscent of the Matherses' Isis ceremonies in Paris and Crowley's Rites of Eleusis in Caxton Hall. In attendance one evening was the writer Bernard Bromage, who in an article for *Light* described the Rite of Isis as 'one of the best attempts I have ever witnessed to stimulate the subconscious by means of "pantomime" drawn from the more ancient records of the hierophant's art'.[67] Even Crowley showed up to lend his support. For Fortune, Isis was the embodiment of the Great Goddess, a figure that was being rediscovered by academics and folklorists as central to ancient fertility cults. The grail, too, was in Fortune's eyes a palimpsest of pagan and romantic Christian traditions. In her novel *The Winged Bull*, the character Colonel Brangwyn links it to the magical cauldron of Ceridwen, a sorceress in medieval Welsh literature: an indication that Fortune had been reading scholarship on the grail's origins (perhaps, like Williams, Waite's *Hidden Church*).

A series of articles written in 1929 and 1930 for the Inner Light's periodical of the same name provided readers with lists of personal book recommendations from Fortune. Arranged under subheadings ranging from 'Books for Beginners' to 'Books on Atlantis', they give an idea of the kind of material that had inspired her own literary projects, and as with Crowley's booklist for the A∴A∴, include a range of genres and thought (though the two lists rarely overlap).[68] Books on Kabbalah by Mathers and Westcott ensure that some of the core GD teachings are represented, as does Farr's *Egyptian Magic*, albeit mistakenly attributed to Mathers. Waite features heavily – not only his scholarship, but also three volumes of poetry under the heading 'Some Books of Mystical Beauty'. The novels listed convey a familiarity with supernatural tales and 'pulp' adventure fiction, including books by John Buchan, Lord Dunsany, Sax Rohmer and Talbot Mundy.

Novels by GD Adepts such as Brodie-Innes's *The Devil's Mistress* and Crowley's *Moonchild* appear, but there is nothing by Yeats or Machen, which suggests that Fortune had not yet come across *The Great God Pan* or Machen's grail stories. She includes Algernon Blackwood in sections on 'Books for Beginners' and 'Ceremonial Magic', and he is the sole author to feature in 'Some Occult Novels': Fortune clearly recognized the authenticity of his writing and valued his books as teaching aids for her own Inner Light students.

Like Williams, Fortune went on to publish a series of novels on occult themes, mostly in the 1930s: *The Demon Lover* (1927), *The Winged Bull* (1935), *The Goat-Foot God* (1936) and *The Sea Priestess* (1938). A sequel to the latter, *Moon Magic* (1957), appeared posthumously. She also wrote four novels of a more conventionally romantic type under the pseudonym V. M. Steele, with titles such as *Hunters of Humans* (1935) and *Beloved of Ishmael* (1936). She was always adamant that she wrote because she felt compelled to, and she viewed her six magical 'thrillers' as part of her work for the Inner Light, because they were read by people who were unlikely to be interested in her occult textbooks. Importantly, she described them as being 'closely akin to the initiation dramas of the ancient Mysteries'.[69] In an article for the *Inner Light* in 1936, she divides readers of fiction into those who read as an intellectual exercise (selecting, for example, Henry James, Thomas Hardy and Balzac) and those who read adventure stories such as *Tarzan of the Apes* as forms of wish-fulfilment. Fortune hoped to attract both types of readers, by producing 'at the same time an interpretation and a day-dream'.[70] She claimed to write her novels using the same method that she used to compose her Inner Light rituals, expanding the germ of an idea using the correspondences of the GD's hermetic Kabbalah system, then mapping out the plot armed with her readings in current psychoanalysis:

> In each case I have taken a basic idea, attributed it to its appropriate Sephirah in the proper Qabalistic manner, and then proceeded to work it out on the basis, not of Qabalistic symbolism as I should have done if I were writing an

Lanta Spurrier, cover of Dion Fortune, *The Demon Lover*, 1927.

occult treatise on the subject, but of the dream symbolism of psychoanalysis. Consequently, anyone who knows psychoanalysis can take these novels to pieces as if they were dreams, and anyone who knows the Qabalah can 'place them on the Tree'.[71]

Beyond simply telling an immersive story, Fortune's intention was to replicate the ceremonial union of the human soul with cosmic forces, so that her readers would experience the novel as dreamlike. *The Winged Bull*, for example, tells the story of Ted Murchison, demobilized from the army and now adrift in the London fog, being ushered into occult society by the bohemian Colonel Brangwyn (Fortune's use of the Brangwyn name, particularly for the colonel's sister, Ursula Brangwyn, is a strange intertextual nod to D. H. Lawrence's *The Rainbow*, a book she admired).[72] Possibly modelled on Fortune's idea of Mathers, Brangwyn witnesses Murchison's attempt to invoke Pan before the 'winged bull of Babylon' in the British Museum and asks for his assistance in developing certain psychological techniques. Murchison is gradually introduced to magic, or the 'powers of the human mind', and together the two men try to save Brangwyn's sister Ursula from the mental attacks of Fortune's stand-in for Crowley, the 'well known but not well liked' black magician Hugo Astley. Adding an embellishment of recent GD folklore to her narrative, Astley is pushed down the stairs after trying to gain access to Brangwyn's rooms, in a semi-re-enactment of the Battle of Blythe Road.[73] *The Goat-Foot God*, meanwhile, charts a more literal indoctrination into magic by Fortune's own method: pulpy occult thrillers. The protagonist Hugo Paston is recommended Naomi Mitchison's *The Corn King and the Spring King* (a novel set in ancient Sparta, published in 1931) and *The Devil's Mistress* by John Brodie-Innes (whose literary agent, incidentally, now represented Fortune) by a bookseller who insists that there are 'some very curious things if you read between the lines. Writers will put things into a novel that they daren't put into sober prose, where you have to dot the I's and cross the T's'.[74] Through Mitchison and Brodie-Innes, Paston is led to the Neo-Platonist philosopher Iamblichus, who wrote of building up 'god-forms' in imagination, and finally arrives at a plan to recreate the rites of the pagan mystery cults.[75]

Fortune's occult thrillers were part of her wider goal not merely to provide information about magic to a receptive audience, but to stage a revolutionary act of mass initiation into the Mysteries, something no other GD author had yet attempted. The hoped-for result – readers' realization of an interconnectedness with the universe, while at the same time retaining a sense of personal identity and purpose – sits alongside the various literary modernisms of the time, which sought to fashion new forms of selfhood in a changing, fractured world. Fortune hoped that an 'egalitarian' form of initiation (though most of her audience would have been middle-class), made accessible by her straightforward prose style, would lead to a widespread spiritual revival.[76] Her novels were also an expression of her realignment with paganism during the 1930s: *The Sea Priestess* was her paean to the Great Goddess; *The Goat-Foot God* a fictional invocation of Pan.

After Fortune's death from leukaemia in 1946, her novels became fully integrated into her wider system of thought. Throughout 1957 the poet and occult writer Margaret Lumley Brown made regular 'contacts' with Fortune on the astral plane, during which the departed priestess reiterated the esoteric power of her novels and their potential for use in meditation or visualization practices. She also took the opportunity to divide the books into their masculine (*The Goat-Foot God, The Winged Bull*) and feminine (*The Sea Priestess, Moon Magic*) god-forms, presumably to further aid ritual work.[77] During this period, it was suggested by Inner Light members that Lumley Brown, channelling the words of the astral Dion Fortune, write a new piece of fiction to be used for future magical working. The resulting short fragment, 'The Death of Vivien Le Fay Morgan', was considered an epilogue to *Moon Magic*, and was later published in Fortune's *Aspects of Occultism* (1962). 'I am the same being who dominated Dion Fortune when she wrote *The Sea Priestess* and *Moon Magic*,' the story begins. 'I am the figure in the evolutionary background of the authoress through the ages.'[78]

Williams and Fortune spent the Second World War in materially quite different circumstances, but both were leading spiritual groups whose actions, they believed, were a necessary defence in a time of strife. In 1936 Williams had become friends with the novelist and theologian C. S. Lewis when OUP published his *Allegory of Love*, and he began to receive regular invitations to meetings of the Inklings, an Oxford-based Christian literary discussion group that during this period included Lewis, the philosopher Owen Barfield, the Anglo-Saxon scholar C. L. Wrenn, the Shakespeare expert Hugo Dyson and the novelist and philologist J. R. R. Tolkien. In Lewis's rooms in Magdalen College, or at various pubs in the city, members would gather to read aloud from works in progress and engage in lively debate on theological or literary subjects. When in 1939 the staff of Amen House were exiled to Southfield House in Oxford, Williams became a more frequent attendee. He also began lecturing to undergraduates, met the writers Kingsley Amis and Philip Larkin (who respected Williams as a critic, but didn't 'give a fart' for his poetry) and in 1943 received an honorary MA.[79] Maddened by the 'flatulence' of its upper classes, he found Oxford 'friendly, but sterile'.[80] But from his lodgings in South Parks Road, he was free to carry out the work of his new religious order, the Companions of the Co-inherence, formed in 1939. Without formal constitution or rites, and with 'no decision, no vote or admission', the group's chief concern was the practice of 'co-inherence', a kind of orchestrated prayer that channelled an active 'sympathy' towards suffering individuals in the hope of relieving their pain.[81] Throughout the war Williams directed its members, scattered around the country, 'asking each one to help another when he or she heard of trouble'.[82] In one such instance, knowing that his friend Anne Hadfield was about to make a dangerous sea voyage with her son, Williams asked one Companion, Lois Lang-Sims, to 'present yourself shyly to Almighty God in exchange for her'.[83]

In a coordinated and far more dramatic resistance to the horrors of war, Fortune mustered the Inner Light to stage a series of nationwide psychic attacks now referred to as the Magical Battle of Britain. In October 1939, she wrote an open letter to her remaining Adepts

CHAPTER 6

(many of the younger men had gone off to fight), instructing them to meditate *en masse* from 12.15 to 12.30 pm every Sunday: 'face towards London ... Your hands should rest on the weekly letter lying on your lap, for these letters will be consecrated before they are sent out in order that they may form a link'.[84] From her headquarters at Queensborough Terrace near Hyde Park, Fortune ordered her magicians to open their minds 'as a channel for the work of the Masters of Wisdom' by focusing on the Rosy Cross, a familiar GD symbol. By 1940, the group were visualizing angelic hosts in red robes patrolling the British coastline; they gradually expanded their territory to include the North Sea and the fjords of Norway. Fortune was forced to move to new lodgings during the early stages of the Blitz, when Queensborough Terrace was bombed and the roof fell in. The group meditations ceased in 1942, but the work of the Inner Light continued for several years more.

In Oxford, just as the war was ending and life returning to normal, Charles Williams died suddenly from an intestinal obstruction. Fortune followed eight months later, at the beginning of 1946. As Lumley Brown recorded at the close of Fortune's posthumous 'Death of Vivien Le Fay Morgan': *'A strong, deep line now seemed drawn across the paper'*.[85]

A puzzling coda to the development of Fortune's magical worldview is her relationship with Aleister Crowley in his final, ailing years. Rumours that the two worked together in the 1920s have persisted, based on Fortune claiming to have once encountered an Adept 'whom I soon realised to be on the Left-hand Path [i.e. a practitioner of sex magic]', apparently part of a 'Black Lodge', after which she severed her connection.[86] In fact, Crowley and Fortune seem to have mostly operated in isolation, with only superficial notions of what the other was doing. Fortune evidently found Crowley's *777* useful for her Kabbalistic enquiry, and in *Psychic Self Defence* cited an incident in his autobiography as an example of a faulty invocation.[87] She may even have visited Crowley in the 1930s to enquire how to invoke the god Mercury (as Florence Farr and Allan Bennett had planned in 1896); Crowley apparently advised her 'to stop all the clocks in her Fraternity headquarters and to go on a diet of steamed cod and sweet white wine'.[88] They definitely met in 1939, when, according to Crowley's diary entry, he invited Fortune and her husband round for a dinner of 'Chili con', although in the same entry Crowley unkindly calls her 'Public Bat No 1 at the Belfry. Like a hippo with false teeth. Talk – bubbling of tinned tomato soup'.[89] Despite this comment, the two corresponded well into the 1940s (in 1942 Fortune revealed that by then she owned all of Crowley's books), and Kenneth Grant, Crowley's one-time secretary, recalled being present at several in-person meetings between the two where they discussed the possibilities of the prophesied New Aeon.[90]

With Williams's death in 1945, on the heels of his old acquaintances Yeats in 1939 and Waite in 1942, the long afterlife of the GD was almost over. Crowley would die in poverty in a Hastings boarding house in 1947, followed two weeks later by Arthur Machen at the age of eighty-four. Only Pamela Colman Smith held on, living alone in the Cornish town of Bude until 1951. But Crowley and Fortune's friendship during the last few years of their lives represents a final mustering of a magical alliance. The two influential magicians may have felt that they had been mutually responsible for ushering in a new era of the spirit, and now that they were growing old, they were eager to share in their achievement. In 1944 Fortune was one of around fifty subscribers to *The Book of Thoth*, Crowley's essay elucidating his Thoth tarot, a deck designed by the artist and O.T.O. student Lady Frieda Harris. His inscription in Fortune's copy (no. 9) praised her 'attainment in the Science of Wisdom' and 'eminence as an Artist in Words'.[91] Was this an expression of genuine admiration, or just another example of Crowley's natural insincerity? Crowley also sent her two paintings given to him by J. F. C. Fuller, titled 'The Portal of the Outer Order' and the 'Portal of the Second Order'. Fortune kept them.[92]

'An Elaborate Appendix'

The current order of Moon and Serpent Grand Egyptian Theatre of Marvels was inaugurated following a chance event in early 1994. While browsing at a Farringdon Road bookstall, folded in a Look-In annual from the early 1970s, we found a letter from Frau Anna Sprengel. Honestly, I ask you, what are the chances of that? In the letter, Annie (as she insists we call her) states that all her earlier letters were, as she puts it, 'eine vind-up. Who says ve Germans haf no sense of humour?' Revealing that the one true mystic order of the ages is in fact the aforementioned Moon and Serpent Grand Egyptian Theatre of Marvels, she then authorised us to found lodges throughout the western world, to dress up in fancy frocks like girls, and to take everybody's money. We admit that various other occult orders and authorities have cast aspersions on the authenticity of our Frau Sprengel letter, but fuck 'em.[1]

Several months after his fortieth birthday, on which he had declared himself a magician, the Northampton-born comics writer Alan Moore founded the Moon and Serpent Grand Egyptian Theatre of Marvels.[2] Moore had been in high demand following his revitalization of the comics medium with series such as *Watchmen* (1986–7), *V for Vendetta* (1982–9) and his run on *Swamp Thing* (1984–7), but in the early 1990s, disillusioned with the amoralities of the mainstream comics industry, Moore turned to magic. A project based on the Jack the Ripper murders, *From Hell* (1989–98), had led him to research the occult and masonic resonances alive in the streets of central London. His subsequent announcement that he would start practising ritual magic was knowingly eccentric and 'played nicely into the "mid-life crisis" line', but it was also a serious declaration of intent: from here on, magic would be his bread and butter. Concluding that it was purely a 'linguistic phenomenon', based on Aleister Crowley's definition of magic as 'a disease of language', and that 'grimoire' was in fact a derivation of 'grammar', Moore was delighted to find that magic aligned perfectly with his work in comics and fiction. In collaboration with Steve Moore (no relation), also a comics creator, and several other artists and musicians, he thus began his journey with the Moon and Serpent Grand Egyptian Theatre of Marvels. The 'Moon', Selene, was Steve's chosen lunar deity, and the 'Serpent' was Glycon, the Gnostic snake god who had become Alan's personal guide or 'imaginary playmate'.[3]

In a rejection of the standard formalities of ceremonial magic, the Theatre of Marvels had no established teachings or initiation rituals. Its long and colourful history was invented, with heavy reference to the Order of the Golden Dawn's own origin myth, in an article for the journal *KAOS* in 2002. It had no 'pretentious' grade structure or 'self-aggrandizing' titles, all of which demonstrated, the two Moores wrote, that 'despite all appearances to the contrary, we are in fact ordinary common-as-muck people like you and everybody else'. In fact, the pair revealed that the Theatre 'doesn't actually exist in the conventional sense'.[4] It was a product of the writers' anarchic sense of humour and Alan's anarchist politics, and also an excuse to experiment with magic's stagier side.

As a teenager Alan had been involved with an Arts Lab in Northampton, writing music, plays and poetry and combining all three into messy hybrid performances.[5] His early magical encounters in the 1990s, mostly fuelled by magic mushrooms, inspired him to start writing music again. He used his songs to stage the Theatre of Marvels' first public ritual in July 1994, which blended spoken word and dance and was hosted by the writer Iain Sinclair.[6] A later piece titled *Snakes & Ladders* was first performed in 1999 at a symposium at Conway Hall, Holborn, curated by an Oxford-based branch of the

Israel Regardie, 'The Garden of Eden before the Fall', from Regardie, *The Golden Dawn*, vol. I, 1937.

Golden Dawn. Did this mean that Alan Moore had participated in a GD meeting, however tangentially? Conway Hall is a stone's throw from Gray's Inn Fields, where Arthur Machen was living in the late 1890s. Part of the narrative of *Snakes & Ladders* recounts Machen's grief-induced visions from around the time he joined Isis-Urania in 1899, adapted into comic form by *From Hell* artist Eddie Campbell along with some of Alan's other ritual workings. The Theatre's early relationship with the GD was often indirect, but always playful and irreverent. Its conception perhaps owed more to the Arts Lab, but its grand dramatic style recalled the Matherses' public Isis performances and Crowley's Rites of Eleusis. Over a century since the founding of Isis-Urania, the spectre of Mathers's society continued to inspire new art and new ritual.

When the Second World War came to an end in 1945, the Order of the Golden Dawn was barely still in operation, and by 1947 the leaders of its greater factions – Mathers, Robert Felkin, A. E. Waite, Dion Fortune and Aleister Crowley – were all dead. Many smaller British offshoots and 'daughter temples' had come and gone, among them the Cromlech Temple (a Christian order claiming to operate 'within the Church'), the Secret College and the Merlin Temple. Some groups persevered, such as the Fraternity of the Inner Light and the alchemy-focused Hermanubis Temple, though their ties to the GD grew steadily more tenuous. But the GD itself had extended its reach well beyond Britain and Paris. Robert Felkin, founder of the Stella Matutina in 1903, had proceeded to travel around Germany seeking a connection to Fräulein Sprengel or her Rosicrucian fraternity, and in 1912 decided upon Hawke's Bay, Aotearoa New Zealand, as an ideal location to establish a new Stella Matutina temple. This was called Smaragdum Thallasses, and became known by the Māori name Whare Ra ('House of the Sun'). Also around this time, the first American Alpha et Omega temple was founded in New York. It called itself Thoth-Hermes, and its leaders, Charles and E. D. Lockwood, were conferred honorary Adeptus Exemptus (7° = 4°) grades by Mathers. Two further temples took root in Philadelphia and Los Angeles. After a dispute with Moina Mathers, the astrologer Paul Foster Case left Thoth-Hermes in 1922 to found The Builders of the Adytum (B.O.T.A.), which is still in operation. The group's teachings emphasize tarot and Kabbalah, with the goal of expanding initiates' consciousness and improving their memory.

The afterlife of the GD, its ability to survive in various transmutations even up to the present day, was made possible only through the widespread availability of its teachings. Their publication began with Crowley's *Equinox* in 1909 and continued in repackaged form in Dion Fortune's non-fiction, but the first earnest attempt to gather Order material into a complete reference work was the publication of *The Golden Dawn* by the Chicago-based Aries Press. Its four volumes collected the official grade rituals, knowledge lectures and some of the Flying Rolls of the Stella Matutina.[7] Their compiler, Israel Regardie, had come to Paris as a young art student from the US in 1928, and had worked as Crowley's unpaid secretary (becoming Frater Scorpio).[8] In 1932 Regardie wrote two books exploring the Kabbalah, *The Tree of Life* and *A Garden of Pomegranates*, stoking anger in the occult community, who thought that he had revealed too much.[9] He had entered the Stella Matutina's Bristol Temple in 1934, sponsored by Fortune, but became disillusioned by the GD's system after a few years and vowed to publish it in its entirety. 'Disaster and corruption have long been trailing in the wake of the Golden Dawn,' he wrote in his accompanying explication *My Rosicrucian Adventure* (1936), 'shadowing it since the date of its English inception', and it was therefore of 'dire necessity' that the Order's important magic system be published to prevent it from vanishing into obscurity. *The Golden Dawn* was Regardie's rescue mission. He was unimpressed by the GD of the 1890s, and found its posturing, vice and absorption of the general decadence of that period evidenced by the 'superficiality and self-satisfaction' of its theatrical members (probably in reference to Yeats, Farr and Annie Horniman).[10] The gaps in Regardie's work were subsequently filled, as more accurate versions of GD material were discovered in private archives. It was only in 1987, a century after Mathers began devising the Order's curriculum, that the missing thirty-two original Flying Roll manuscripts were finally made public.

The 1970s produced a wave of responses to ceremonial magic, in academic, artistic and magical spheres alike. A renewed interest in the GD and its immediate offshoots was initiated by Ellic Howe's 'documentary history' *The Magicians of the Golden Dawn*, published by Routledge in 1972. Further studies followed by Francis King, George Mills Harper, R. A. Gilbert and others, as privately owned papers came to light and new information was made available. The surrealist painter Ithell Colquhoun wrote the first and only biography of Mathers, *Sword of Wisdom* (1975), after years of occult study. As a young woman she had attended meetings of G. R. S. Mead's theosophical Quest Society, and after her application to join Alpha et Omega was rejected (possibly, she thought, due to her naivety and 'crude attempts at intellectual honesty'), she eventually joined the GD-inspired Order of the Pyramid and Sphinx.[11] Her art was influenced by the GD's colour theory, alchemy and tarot symbolism, and while in her seventies she created an oversize set of seventy-eight tarot cards using enamel paints, exhibited in 1977.

Much of the interplay between art and occultism in the twentieth century can be ascribed to the magnetic pull of Aleister Crowley. Crowley attracted a host of young disciples throughout his life, and responses to his biography and fiction have produced a number of unusual results. In the spring of 1946, the pioneering rocket scientist Jack Parsons and the pulp science fiction author L. Ron Hubbard, who would go on to invent the religious movement Scientology, performed the 'Babalon Working', a series of rituals intended to evoke the Moonchild of Crowley's novel and launch the fabled New Aeon.[12] Parsons and a woman named Marjorie Cameron performed sexual magic while

Hubbard received communications from the Thelemic goddess Babalon. Crowley was evidently confused by Parsons's descriptions of events, and wrote to a friend: 'Apparently he or Ron or somebody is producing a Moonchild. I get fairly frantic when I contemplate the idiocy of these goats.'[13] The operation ended unsuccessfully, and Parsons produced an account in verse titled 'The Book of Babalon'.[14] The American avant-garde filmmaker Kenneth Anger was also a devotee of Crowley, having encountered his writings as a teenager in the 1940s. Over a long career, Anger produced a sequence of short films known as the 'Magick Lantern Cycle', including *Inauguration of the Pleasure Dome* (1954) and *Lucifer Rising* (1980), both of which are laced with esoteric symbolism, visualizing in rich, hypnotic colour the ceremonial and spiritual aspects of Crowley's occultism. Anger prefigured Alan Moore when he declared in an interview that magic, once integral to daily life, 'was displaced – partly by science', but was now accessible through artistic practice:

> I agree with Crowley's definition that magick is the science of causing change, and whatever causes change is an act of magick. But formal knowledge of magick is not necessary to appreciate my work. My films are not an appeal to the intellect. They are an appeal to the level of dream logic and to the emotions.[15]

Yeats would surely have approved. Anger even visited the abandoned Abbey of Thelema at Cefalù in 1955, hoping to use it as a filming location, but his plans came to nothing.[16]

Arguably the figure who has contributed most to the lasting promotion of magical and literary ideas is the writer Kenneth Grant. As a young man in the early 1940s, Grant got to know the artist Austin Osman Spare (briefly a Probationer in Crowley's A∴A∴) and eventually Crowley himself, who took Grant on as his secretary during the last years of his life in exchange for occult tutelage. Grant began to publish the Typhonian Trilogies, a series of books outlining his interpretations of O. T. O. magic. The first of these was *The Magickal Revival* in 1972. Grant's reason for exposing O. T. O. teachings are distinct from

Regardie's desire to preserve the GD system: 'Unless the requisite contacts on the inner planes are established in the proper manner, no amount of reading will disclose "secrets" that are literally indecipherable and therefore truly occult. The safeguards are both automatic and fool-proof.'[17] In other words, anyone could read them, but only a select few would be able to put them to use. Also unlike Regardie, Grant was adamant that writers of fantastic literature such as Arthur Machen, Algernon Blackwood, Charles Williams and Dion Fortune 'brought powerful influences to bear on the occult scene through their various delineations of the Qliphoth [the negative counterpart to the Kabbalistic Tree of Life]'.[18]

Bizarrely, Grant's theory also ran the other way. He believed that the American horror writer H. P. Lovecraft had contacted certain New England 'cults' who still practised witchcraft from the days of the Salem trials, and had used their information to inform his own supernatural tales.[19] His theory was that Lovecraft did not fully understand what he was channelling, but that his god-like creations Cthulhu, Azathoth and Yog-Sothoth were genuine occult beings who could be used in meditation and invocations. Yog-Sothoth, a primordial entity who appears as a mass of 'iridescent globes' and was first mentioned in the horror novel *The Case of Charles Dexter Ward*, was seen by Grant to represent the Qliphoth. Grant's adoption of Lovecraft's invented pantheon into his Chaos Magic methodology is one of the most compelling examples of how magic and art have interacted in the twentieth century. The occult appeal of Lovecraft's fiction culminated in 1978 with *The Book of Dead Names*, edited by George Hay, which is at once a homage and elaborate joke, claiming to be the genuine 'Necronomicon', a fictional grimoire often referred to by Lovecraft. Introduced by the writer Colin Wilson and with a supplementary essay by the novelist Angela Carter, it includes a section of magic rituals in which the Pentagram of Fire, an invocation once used by GD students, is intended to conjure Yog-Sothoth.[20]

Grant's occult techniques, developed from Crowley and Austin Osman Spare, became what is now called Chaos Magic, a thoroughly postmodern approach to individual magical practice: 'it has no shape, it breeds like a fractal, and mutates as it goes,' wrote Grant Morrison, another comics writer and magician. 'Shattering and binding simultaneously, always up for a laugh, Chaos provides one useful model for the next stage in the collective upgrading of human consciousness.'[21] Is this Crowley's New Aeon 2.0? Chaos magicians advocate for self-fulfilment as a way of gaining control over one's life, or 'making things happen according to your desires', a very different approach to magic than that once practised by the GD.[22]

Chaos also delights in picking up techniques from unlikely sources. The writer William S. Burroughs, a primary figure in the Beat movement of the 1960s, unknowingly became a Chaos magician when he began to employ the now-familiar 'cut-up' technique. First invented by his friend and colleague Brion Gysin (and closely related to the Dadaist 'simultaneous poem' performed in 1916), the 'cut-up' produced a collage effect with the written word, creating random patterns from 'consciously created original parts'.[23] Burroughs also developed the 'playback' technique, a spin on the 'cut-up' that used a tape recorder and a camera as a way of cursing a particular place. It involved making field recordings at the location, inserting 'troubled sounds' such as police sirens and playing it back at the same location. Burroughs performed this technique at a local café whose staff had insulted him: 'Not only did it close down, but the space remained empty for years, unable to be rented for love, or money'.[24] Burroughs's techniques were later developed by Chaos magicians such as David Hines and the musician and performance artist Genesis P. Orridge, who viewed Burroughs and Gysin as unwitting but powerful magicians.[25] Burroughs himself saw his work as possessing 'an element of magical invocation', and he became more involved in occult subcultures as the twentieth century drew on.[26]

In 2002, Alan Moore diagnosed the state of contemporary magic in an unpublished essay titled 'Fossil Angels'. He concluded that ever since science broke from magic to become a modern discipline, magic had become stuck in a nostalgic rut, looking back to a time when it had any real utility in the world:

> Whilst it's difficult to overstate the contributions made to magic as a field by, say, Éliphas Lévi or the various magicians of the Golden Dawn, it's just as hard to argue that these contributions were not overwhelmingly synthetic, in that they aspired to craft a synthesis of previously existing lore, to formalise the variegated wisdoms of the ancients.

The nineteenth-century occult revival had systematized hermetic tradition and used fictional methods such as Bulwer-Lytton's novels, Rosicrucianism and the uncertain origins of the GD's Cipher Manuscripts to link themselves to an ancient pedigree. Moore compares this re-enactment to occultists of the sixteenth century like John Dee, mathematician and advisor to Elizabeth I, who did not feel the need to manufacture a backstory: 'His was a fresh, rip-roaring chapter, written entirely in the present tense, of the ongoing magical adventure', whereas what came after was merely 'an elaborate appendix', a 'bibliography'.

For all Moore's worrying about the custodial impulse in modern magic, the GD and its members remain potent features of his work and continue to exert a hold on his ideas of magic and the imagination. Moore's later work in comics continued to stretch the medium, introducing and promoting occult concepts to a general readership. His thirty-two-issue series *Promethea* (1999–2005) is a visually explosive journey into the world of 'Immateria', a depiction of his concept of a four-dimensional 'Ideaspace'. Through acts of imagination, the protagonist Sophie Bangs invokes and becomes the superhero Promethea, encountering a magical pantheon of past occultists such as Dee, Crowley and the god Thoth as she ascends the Tree of Life. Elsewhere, Moore populated his *Century: 1910* volume of *The League of Extraordinary Gentlemen* series with occultists from literature, including an elderly Zanoni, characters from Machen's *The Three Impostors*

Alan Moore and Kevin O' Neill, *The League of Extraordinary Gentlemen. Century: 1910*, 2009.

and a Crowleyan brotherhood whose members Oliver Haddo (from Maugham's *The Magician*), Simon Iff and Cyril Grey are trying to produce a Moonchild. The opening to his most recent fantasy novel *The Great When* imagines a final meeting between an elderly Crowley and a sickly Dion Fortune as they reminisce about the old days.

Art and magic continue to hybridize into new mediums, playing off one another. For many of the Adepts of the GD the two were indistinguishable: both were capable of bringing about visionary changes in the world, be it from the perspective of a reader, a spectator or a Rosicrucian initiate. In this sense the poet and the occultist share overlapping objectives: both are prophets, claiming access to a state of reality that they consider truth.[27] In the GD this was evident in the symbols of alchemy and Celtic mythology intrinsic to Yeats's verse in the 1890s, in Dion Fortune's novels and Crowley's talismanic first editions. Through its many crises and schisms, the Order and its offshoots acted as a formal space to cultivate and explore art in relation to ritual practice and ancient tradition, providing ready-made networks for artists to both collaborate and inspire. The 'bookishness' that runs inescapably through the history of occultism has meant that as magical practices evolve, art and literature evolve alongside them.

Notes

Introduction: 'A Wild Performance'
1. Christopher McIntosh, *The Rose Cross and the Age of Reason: Eighteenth-century Rosicrucianism in Central Europe and its Relationship to the Enlightenment* (Albany: State University of New York Press, 2011), pp. 24–5.
2. Israel Regardie, *The Golden Dawn: An Account of the Teachings, Rites and Ceremonies of the Order of the Golden Dawn*, vols 1–2 (Saint Paul, MN: Llewellyn Publications, 1978), p. 226.
3. Quoted in Ellic Howe, *The Magicians of the Golden Dawn: A Documentary History of a Magical Order 1887–1923* (London: Routledge & Kegan Paul, 1985), p. 93.
4. Peter Cheeseman, 'Horniman, Annie Elizabeth Fredericka (1860–1937)', *Oxford Dictionary of National Biography* (21 May, 2009).
5. Regardie, *The Golden Dawn*, p. 229.
6. *Ibid.*, p. 236.
7. Quoted in Francis X. King, *The Flying Sorcerer: Being the Magical and Aeronautic Adventures of Francis Barrett, Author of* The Magus (Oxford: Mandrake, 1992), p. 23.
8. Joscelyn Godwin, Christian Chanel, and John P. Deveney, *The Hermetic Brotherhood of Luxor: Initiatic and Historical Documents of an Order of Practical Occultism* (York Beach, ME: Samuel Weiser, 1995), pp. 6–7.
9. Between 1852 and 1869 an 'Order of Rosicrucians' met in Manchester, but this had been literary and antiquarian in nature, without connections to masonry or esoteric subjects. R. A. Gilbert, '"The Supposed Rosy Crucian Society": Bulwer-Lytton and the S.R.I.A.', in *Esotérisme, Gnoses & Imaginaire Symbolique: Mélanges Offerts à Antoine Faivre*, ed., Richard Charon et al. (Leuven: Peeters, 2001), pp. 389–402, p. 397 n20; a constitution published by 'The Society of the Rosy Cross' has been found dating from 1868, but seemed to have been more of a political organization than an occult society.
10. W. B. Yeats, *Autobiographies* (London: Macmillan, 1955), p. 184.
11. H. P. Blavatsky, *The Key to Theosophy*, ed. Josephine Ransom (London: The Theosophical Publishing House, 1948), p. 15; quoted in Jessica L. Harland-Jacobs, *Builders of Empire: Freemasons and British Imperialism, 1717–1927* (Chapel Hill, NC: The University of North Carolina Press, 2007), pp. 5–6
12. Denis Saurat, *Blake & Modern Thought* (London: Constable, 1929), p. 225.
13. V. H. Frater Sapere Aude, 'Historical Lecture', quoted in R. A. Gilbert, *The Golden Dawn: Twilight of the Magicians* (Wellingborough: The Aquarian Press, 1983), p. 102.

14 A. E. Waite, *Shadows of Life and Thought* (Dublin: Bardic Press, 2016), p. 218. The book containing the key was *Polygraphiae* (1518), by the early cryptographer and reputed necromancer Johannes Trithemius.
15 See Howe, *Magicians*, p. 5, and R. A. Gilbert, *The Golden Dawn Companion: A Guide to the hHstory, Structure, and Workings of the Hermetic Order of the Golden Dawn* (Loughborough: Thoth Publications, 2021), p. 9.
16 Edward Bulwer-Lytton (Lord Lytton), *Zanoni* (New York: F. M. Lutton, written in 1842), p. vii.
17 James L. Campbell, *Edward Bulwer-Lytton* (Boston, MA: Twayne Publishers, 1986), p. 109.
18 *Ibid.*, p. 111.
19 Éliphas Lévi, *Transcendental Magic*, trans. A. E. Waite (London: Rider & Co, 1896), p. xix.
20 *Ibid.*, pp. xxiii–xxiv.
21 Christopher McIntosh, 'Éliphas Lévi', in *The Occult World*, ed. Christopher Partridge (London: Routledge, 2014), pp. 220–30 (223).
22 Lévi, *Transcendental Magic*, pp. 122–5.
23 Francis King, *Modern Ritual Magic: The Rise of Western Occultism* (Bridport: Prism Press, 1989), p. 29.
24 *Ibid.*, p. 26; McIntosh, *The Rose Cross and the Age of Reason*, p. 2.
25 Kenneth R. H. Mackenzie, *The Royal Masonic Cyclopaedia of History, Rites, Symbolism, and Biography* (London: Bro. John Hogg, 1877), p. 612.
26 A. E. Waite, *The Brotherhood of the Rosy Cross* (London: W. Rider, 1924), p. 566.
27 Theodor Harmsen, 'Fiction or a Much Stranger Truth: Sources and Reception of the *Geheime Figuren der Rosenkreuze*r – Secret Symbols of the Rosicrucians in the 18th, 19th and 20th Centuries', *Aufklärung und Esoterik: Wege in die Moderne*, vol. 50 (2013), pp. 726–52 (726); Theodor Harmsen, 'The Reception of Jacob Böhme and Böhmist Theosophy in the *Geheime Figuren der Rosenkreuzer*', *Offenbarung und Episteme*, vol. 173 (2012), pp. 183–206 (185); T. M. Greensill, *History of the S.R.I.A.*, 2nd edition (London: Societas Rosicruciana in Anglia, 2003), pp. 69–70.
28 Quoted in Peter Washington, *Madame Blavatsky's Baboon: Theosophy and the Emergence of the Western Guru* (London: Secker & Warburg, 1993), p. 30.
29 *Ibid*, p. 33.
30 Bruce F. Campbell, *Ancient Wisdom Revived: A History of the Theosophical Movement* (Berkeley, CA: The University of California Press, 1980), pp. 53–6.
31 Hodgson even accused HPB of being a Russian spy, a claim which he later withdrew. R. Hodgson, 'Report of the Committee appointed to investigate Phenomena in connection with the Theosophical Society', Society for Psychical Research, December 1885.
32 *Ibid.*, pp. 36–7; S. B. Liljegren, 'Bulwer-Lytton's Novels and Isis Unveiled,' in *Essays and Studies on English Language and Literature*, ed. S. B. Liljegren (Uppsala: Lundequistska Bokhandeln, 1957), p. 8.

33 Quoted in Howe, *Magicians*, p. 31.
34 *Ibid.*, pp. 31–2; Rafal T. Prinke, 'Deeper Roots of the Golden Dawn', *The Hermetic Journal*, vol. 36 (1987), pp. 16–19 (17).
35 Quoted in Howe, *Magicians*, p. 9; quoted in Gilbert, *The Golden Dawn*, Appendix A., p. 95.
36 *Light*, vol. 8, no. 370 (4 February, 1888), p. 55.
37 William Wynn Westcott, M. B., 'A Society of Kabbalists', *Notes and Queries*, vol. 7, no. 163 (9 February 1889), pp. 116–17.
38 W. B. Yeats, *Essays and Introductions* (London: Papermac, 1989), pp. 28–9.
39 The lodge had been named 'Hengist' after a local promontory Hengistbury Head, and bears no relation to the legendary Jutish king. Frederick Holland, who founded a 'Horsa' lodge in 1887, appears not to have known this. P. H. Newnham, *History of the Lodge of Hengist, no. 195, Bournemouth, from 1770 to 1870; a paper* (Bournemouth: 1870), p. 19; p. 31.
40 See Moina Mathers's introduction to S. L. MacGregor Mathers, *Kabbalah Unveiled* (1926); for discussion of ancestry, see S. L. MacGregor Mathers, *The Grimoire of Armadel*, ed. Francis King (London: Routledge & Kegan Paul, 1980), p. 1.
41 *Ibid.*, p. 38.
42 'Notes on Books', *Notes & Queries*, vol. 113, no. 5 (25 February 1888), p. 160; 'The Kabbalah Unveiled', *The Saturday Review of Politics, Literature, Science and Art*, vol. 64, no. 1663 (10 September 1887), pp. 368–9.
43 Mathers, *The Grimoire of Armadel*, p. 4.
44 Janet Sorensen, 'Ossian Poems', in *The Oxford Encyclopedia of British Literature*, ed. David Scott Kastan (Oxford: Oxford University Press, 2006).
45 Quoted in Ithell Colquhoun, *Sword of Wisdom: MacGregor Mathers and 'The Golden Dawn'* (New York: G. P. Putnam's Sons, 1975), p. 97.
46 Yeats, *Autobiographies*, p. 335.
47 The original source for this has not been identified, but the fact is given by Francis King in the introduction to Mathers, *The Grimoire of Armadel*, p. 2, and Ithell Colquhoun in *Sword of Wisdom*, p. 51; Mathers also liked to socialize with writers, and in 1887 was a guest at the house of the Irish novelist and historian J. Fitzgerald Molloy (whose *A Modern Magician* had just been published, its occultist 'Benoni' a weak imitation of Bulwer-Lytton's mage), where he also met George Bernard Shaw. Molloy would enter the GD in 1893, resigning after two years.
48 Quoted in Howe, *Magicians*, p. 12. Letter dated 4 October, 1887.
49 *Ibid.*, p. 12.
50 Anna, Comtesse de Brémont, *Oscar Wilde and his Mother: A Memoir* (London: Everett, 1914), p. 98; Brémont also began the theory that *The Picture of Dorian Gray* was influenced by the GD: 'It was at this point that Oscar Wilde wrote some of his remarkable stories founded on the occult or supernatural … and I have no doubt that his

inspiration was derived from the revelations of his wife's occult studies' (*Ibid.*, p. 99).
51 Quoted in Howe, *Magicians*, p. 64.
52 Ellic Howe, ed., *The Alchemist of the Golden Dawn: The Letters of the Revd W. A. Ayton to F. L. Gardner and Others 1886–1905* (Wellingborough: The Aquarian Press, 1985), p. 57.

Chapter 1 'Metaphors for Poetry'
1 Regardie, *The Golden Dawn*, p. 123.
2 *The English Auden: Poems, Essays and Dramatic Writings 1927–1939*, ed. Edward Mendelson (London: Faber & Faber, 1997), p. 391.
3 Yeats to John O'Leary [week ending 23 July 1892], *The Collected Letters of W. B. Yeats: volume one: 1865–1895*, ed. John Kelly (Oxford: Clarendon Press, 1986), p. 303.
4 Yeats to Israel Regardie (15 March 1935), *The Collected Letters of W. B. Yeats. Electronic edition. Unpublished letters (1905–1939)*, www.nlx.com/collections/130 [accessed 03 April 2025], no. 6201.
5 Yeats, *Autobiographies*, p. 183.
6 R. F. Foster, 'Protestant Magic: W. B. Yeats and the Spell of Irish History', *Proceedings of the British Academy*, vol. 75 (1989), pp. 243–66.
7 'The Poetry of AE', *Daily Express*, Dublin, 3 September 1898 (*UP*, ii, pp. 121–4)
8 R. F. Forster, *W. B. Yeats: A Life: 1: The Apprentice Mage, 1865–1914* (Oxford: Oxford University Press, 1997), pp. 49, 51.
9 G. K. Chesterton, *Autobiography* (London: Hutchinson & Co., 1936), p. 139.
10 Yeats, *Autobiographies.*, p. 150.
11 *Ibid.*, pp. 173–5.
12 *Ibid.*, p. 181.
13 Quoted in full in R. A. Gilbert, *The Golden Dawn and the Esoteric Section* (London: Theosophical History Centre, 1987), p. 22.
14 Richard Ellmann, *Yeats: The Man and the Masks* (London: Faber and Faber, 1969), p. 68. Ellmann includes Yeats's 'Esoteric Sections Journal' in full, pp. 67–9.
15 *Ibid.*, p. 67.
16 *Ibid.*, p. 68.
17 Yeats, *Autobiographies*, pp. 181, 182.
18 W. B. Yeats, 'Irish Fairies, Ghosts, Witches, etc.', *Lucifer*, vol. 3, no. 17 (January 1889), pp. 399–404.
19 W. B. Yeats, *Writings on Irish Folklore, Legend and Myth*, ed. R. Welch (London: Penguin, 1993), p. 66.
20 Yeats to Katherine Tynan [? 22–28 September 1888], *Collected Letters: volume one*, p. 99.
21 Foster, *The Apprentice Mage*, p. 49.
22 Yeats, *Autobiographies*, pp. 182–3.
23 Laurence W. Fennelly, 'W. B. Yeats and S. L. MacGregor Mathers', in *Yeats and the Occult*, ed. George Mills Harper (London: Macmillan, 1976), pp. 285–306 (289).

24 W. B. Yeats, *Memoirs*, ed. Denis Donoghue (London: Macmillan, 1972), p. 26.
25 Yeats, *Autobiographies*, p. 183.
26 Regardie, *The Golden Dawn*, pp. 106–9.
27 Gilbert, *The Golden Dawn*, p. 60.
28 Foster, *The Apprentice Mage*, p. 143; George Mills Harper, *Yeats's Golden Dawn* (London: Macmillan, 1974), p. 40.
29 Yeats, *Autobiographies*, p. 123.
30 Deidre Toomey, 'Gonne, (Edith) Maud (1866–1953), Irish nationalist', *Oxford Dictionary of National Biography* (3 January 2008).
31 Maud Gonne MacBride, *A Servant of the Queen: Reminiscences* (Gerrards Cross: Colin Smythe, 1994), pp. 210–13.
32 Yeats, *Autobiographies*, p. 184.
33 *Ibid.*, p. 186.
34 Yeats, *Memoirs*, p. 27.
35 Foster, *The Apprentice Mage*, p. 129.
36 W. B. Yeats, *The Countess Kathleen and Various Legends and Lyrics* (London: T. Fisher Unwin, 1893), p. 136.
37 Foster, *The Apprentice Mage*, p. 122.
38 Alex Owen, *The Place of Enchantment: British Occultism and the Culture of the Modern* (Chicago, IL: University of Chicago Press, 2004), p. 58.
39 'Lux e Tenebris' was thought to be the motto of a Dr Thiesen of Liège, Belgium, although this has never been confirmed.
40 William Wynn Westcott, *Data of the History of the Rosicrucians* (London: S.R.I.A., 1916).
41 Howe, *Magicians*, pp. 77–8.
42 *Ibid.*, p. 94.
43 See 'The Condition needed for entry into the Second Order' by Sapere Aude (Westcott), Appendix D in Gilbert, *The Golden Dawn*, pp. 126–9.
44 Quoted in Howe, *Magicians*, p. 97.
45 Yeats to Count Plunkett (21 June 1893), *Collected Letters: volume one*, p. 358.
46 Yeats, *Memoirs*, p. 73.
47 Yeats, *Autobiographies*, p. 183.
48 Yeats to Lady Gregory (3 October 1897), *The Collected Letters of W. B. Yeats: volume two: 1896–1900*, ed. Warwick Gould, John Kelly and Deirdre Toomey (Oxford: Clarendon Press, 1997), p. 135.
49 Yeats to Lady Gregory (8 June 1898), *Collected Letters: volume two*, p. 234.
50 Yeats to Lady Gregory (6 December [1898]), *Collected Letters: volume two*, p. 312; Foster, *The Apprentice Mage*, p. 202.
51 Yeats, *Memoirs*, pp. 124–5.
52 Amy M. Clanton, 'Religion as Aesthetic Creation: Ritual and Belief in William Butler Yeats and Aleister Crowley', PhD thesis, University of South Florida (2011), pp. 85–6.
53 Yeats, *Memoirs*, p. 125.
54 Lucy Shepherd Kalogera, 'Yeats's Celtic Mysteries', unpublished thesis 1977, p. 271; p. 270, n52.

55 Yeats to Moina Mathers (*c.* March 20, 1898), *Collected Letters: volume two*, p. 201.
56 W. B. Yeats, *Short Fiction*, ed. G. J. Watson (London: Penguin, 1995), p. ix.
57 *Ibid.*, p. 80.
58 Yeats to John O' Leary (30 May 1897), *Collected Letters: volume two*, p. 104; Yeats to Alice Milligan (23 September 1894), *Collected Letters: volume one*, p. 399.
59 W. B. Yeats, *Mythologies* (London: Macmillan, 1959), p. 1.
60 Yeats, *Short Fiction*, p. 192.
61 Yeats, *Autobiographies*, p. 376; the GD manuscript uses the spelling 'Hodos Chameleonis'.
62 Yeats, *Autobiographies*, p. 270.
63 Yeats to the Editor of *United Ireland* (14 May 1892), *Collected Letters: volume one.*, p. 298.
64 Yeats, *The Speckled Bird*, ed. William H. O'Donnell (Basingstoke: Palgrave Macmillan, 2003), p. 50; Yeats, *Autobiographies*, p. 254.
65 Yeats, *The Speckled Bird*, p. 46.
66 *Ibid.*, p. 47.
67 *Ibid.*, p. 60.
68 *Ibid.*
69 *Ibid.*, p. 70.
70 *Ibid.*, p. 194.
71 Yeats, *Essays and Introductions*, p. 28.
72 Yeats, *The Speckled Bird*, p. 70.
73 *Ibid.*, p. 50.
74 Colquhoun, *Sword of Wisdom*, p. 83.
75 Quoted in Howe, *Magicians*, p. 116.
76 Arthur Versluis, 'Sexual Mysticisms in Nineteenth Century America: John Humphreys Noyes, Thomas Lake Harris, and Alice Bunker Stockham', in *Hidden Intercourse: Eros and Sexuality in the History of Western Esotericism*, ed. Wouter J. Hanegraaff and Jeffrey J. Kripal (New York: Fordham University Press, 2011), pp. 333–54 (342).
77 *Ibid.*, p. 337; *The Unknown World*, vol. 1, no. 1 (15 August 1894), p. 2
78 George Mills Harper, ed., *W. B. Yeats and W. T. Horton: The Record of an Occult Friendship* (London: Macmillan, 1980), p. 95.
79 *Ibid.*
80 W. T. Horton to W. B. Yeats (6 May 1896), *W. B. Yeats and W. T. Horton*, p. 101.
81 Quoted in Howe, *Magicians*, p. 120.
82 *Ibid.*, p. 122.
83 *Ibid.*, p. 121.
84 *Ibid.*, p. 141.
85 *Ibid.*, p. 127.
86 *Ibid.*, p. 129.
87 *Ibid.*, p. 136.
88 Harper, *Yeats's Golden Dawn*, p. 18.
89 Yeats to Lady Gregory (9 February 1899), *Collected Letters: volume two*, p. 357.

90 Ellmann, *Yeats: The Man and the Masks*, p. 1.
91 Yeats, *Essays and Introductions*, pp. 49–50.
92 Yeats, *Memoirs*, p. 27.

Chapter 2 A Gift Given to the Wise

1 Yeats, *The Speckled Bird*, p. 198.
2 Caroline Tully, 'Egyptosophy in the British Museum: Florence Farr, the Egyptian Adept and the *Ka*', in *The Occult Imagination in Britain 1875–1947*, ed. Andrew Radford and Christine Ferguson (London: Routledge, 2017), pp. 131–45 (135).
3 Yeats, *The Speckled Bird*, p. 198.
4 *A Short Enquiry concerning the Hermetic Art, by a Lover of Philalethes.* An Introduction to Alchemy and Notes by S.S.D.D. [Florence Farr] (1894), p. 13.
5 George Bernard Shaw to Florence Farr (8 September 1897), *Florence Farr: Bernard Shaw: W. B. Yeats: Letters*, ed. Clifford Bax (Dublin: Cuala Press, 1941), p. 17.
6 Ibid., p. v.
7 Josephine Johnson, *Florence Farr: Bernard Shaw's New Woman* (Gerrards Cross: C. Smythe, 1975), p. 23.
8 Bax, ed., *Florence Farr: Bernard Shaw: W. B. Yeats: Letters*, p. v.
9 Quoted in Johnson, *Florence Farr*, p. 27.
10 Yeats, *Autobiographies*, p. 121.
11 Ibid., p. 122.
12 Francis King, ed., *Ritual Magic of the Golden Dawn: Works by S. L. MacGregor Mathers and Others* (Rochester, VT: Destiny Books, 1997), pp. 163–4.
13 George Bernard Shaw to Florence Farr (1891), Bax, ed., *Florence Farr*.
14 Bax, ed., *Florence Farr*, p. vi.
15 Mary K. Greer, *Women of the Golden Dawn: Rebels and Priestesses* (Rochester, VT: Park Street Press, 1995), p. 88; Bax, ed., *Florence Farr*, p. ix.
16 George Bernard Shaw, *The Quintessence of Ibsenism* (London: Walter Scott, 1891), pp. 31–45.
17 Shaw to Florence Farr (4 May 1891), Bax, ed., *Florence Farr*, p. 5; (27 April 1893), p. 6.
18 Shaw to Florence Farr (4 May 1891), Bax, ed., *Florence Farr*, p. 6.
19 Yeats, *Memoirs*, p. 27.
20 Quoted in Howe, *Magicians*, p. 93.
21 Ibid., p. 99.
22 Ibid., p. 141.
23 King, *Ritual Magic of the Golden Dawn*, p. 72.
24 George Bernard Shaw, *Plays Unpleasant* (London: Grant Richards, 1898), p. xxiv.
25 Peter Raby, 'Theatre of the 1890s: Breaking down the Barriers', in *The Cambridge Companion to Victorian and Edwardian Theatre* (Cambridge: Cambridge University Press, 2004), pp. 183–206 (199); unsigned notice, *The Daily Telegraph*, 10 December 1892, p. 3.

26 Despite a fascination with the occult, Beardsley was not a part of the GD. Although Ithell Colquhoun speculates that he may have 'sought out something darker in tone' (Colquhoun, *Sword of Wisdom*, p. 145), his mocking responses to Yeats's talk of magic are probably more indicative of his attitude: 'Oh really? How perfectly sweet' (Matthew Sturgis, *Aubrey Beardsley : A Biography* (London: Flamingo, 1999), p. 275).
27 Florence Farr to Shaw (5 December 1905). Quoted in Johnson, *Florence Farr*, p. 63.
28 Ibid., p. 60.
29 Sturgis, *Aubrey Beardsley*, p. 184.
30 Yeats, *Autobiographies*, p. 281.
31 George Moore, *'Hail and Farewell!': Ave* (London: Heinemann, 1911), p. 45.
32 Quoted in Margot Peters, *Bernard Shaw and the Actresses* (New York, NY: Doubleday, 1980), p. 126.
33 Shaw to Henry Arthur Jones (24 December 1894), *Collected Letters: 1874–1897*, ed. Dan H. Laurence (New York: Dodd, Mead & Company, 1965), p. 462.
34 Quoted in Michael Holroyd, *Bernard Shaw: Volume 1: 1856–1898: The Search for Love* (London: Chatto & Windus, 1988), p. 302.
35 William Archer, *The Theatrical 'World' of 1894* (London: Walter Scott, 1895), p. 93.
36 Quoted in Holroyd, *Bernard Shaw: Volume 1*, p. 299.
37 Florence Farr, *The Dancing Faun* (London: Elkin Mathews and John Lane, 1894), pp. 59–60, 61, 17.
38 Johnson, *Florence Farr*, p. 57.
39 Ibid., p. 57.
40 Ian Fletcher, 'Decadence and the Little Magazines', in *Stratford-Upon-Avon Studies* 17: *Decadence and the 1890s* (New York: Holmes & Meier, 1980), pp. 173–202 (192).
41 Sturgis, *Aubrey Beardsley*, p. 78.
42 *The Athenaeum*, no. 3485, 11 August 1894, p. 87.
43 *The Bookman*, July 1894, p. 120.
44 Richard Le Gallienne to Farr (23 September 1895). Quoted in Johnson, *Florence Farr*, p. 64.
45 Gilbert, *The Golden Dawn Companion*, p. 41.
46 Regardie, *The Golden Dawn*, p. 332.
47 Ibid., p. 332.
48 Quoted in Howe, *Magicians*, p. 154. Undated letter to F. L. Gardner, may belong to the period 1895–6.
49 Gilbert, *The Golden Dawn*, p. 50; the notebook containing Farr's transcription and watercolours is held at the Museum of Freemasonry, and also contains 'The Ancient Instructions on Chess men and Tarot' by N.O.M. (Westcott) and other notes.
50 Farr, *A Short Enquiry concerning the Hermetic Art*, p. 11.
51 Farr, *Euphrates, or the Waters of the East by Eugenius Philalethes, 1655, with a commentary by S.S.D. D.* (London: Theosophical Publishing Society, 1896), pp. 3, 7.
52 Ibid., p. 91.

NOTES

53 Eleanor Dobson, *Victorian Alchemy: Science, Magic and Ancient Egypt* (London: UCL Press, 2022), p. 5.
54 Blackden, motto 'Ma Wahanu Thesi' (so far untranslated, presumed Egyptian), had studied at the Royal Academy and during his excavation trips painted many details of the tombs. While in the GD he researched *The Book of the Dead*, believing it to contain initiatory material; his findings were later published in the *Theosophical Review* and *The Occult Review* starting in 1902, and in 1914 by the SRIA. For information on Blackden in Egypt see T. G. H. James, *Howard Carter: The Path to Tutankhamun* (London: Kegan Paul, 1992).
55 Johnson, *Florence Farr*, p. 80.
56 Farr (S.S.D.D.), *Egyptian Magic* (London, 1896), p. 2.
57 *Ibid.*, p. 5.
58 Shaw to Florence Farr (12 October 1896). Bax, ed., *Florence Farr: Bernard Shaw: W. B. Yeats: Letters*, p. 13.
59 Shaw to Florence Farr (14 October 1896), *ibid.*, p. 15.
60 Quoted in Johnson, *Florence Farr*, p. 81.
61 E. A. Wallis Budge, *A Guide to the First, Second and Third Egyptian Rooms*, 3rd edition (London: British Museum, 1924), p. 128.
62 Tully, 'Egyptosophy in the British Museum', p. 135.
63 Quoted in Harper, *Yeats's Golden Dawn*, p. 33.
64 *Ibid.*.
65 Quoted in Greer, *Women of the Golden Dawn*, p. 468.
66 Quoted in Howe, *Magicians*, pp. 107, 106.
67 *Ibid.*, p. 106.
68 Quoted in *ibid.*, pp. 108–9.
69 *The Equinox*, vol. 1, no. 3 (March 1910), p. 182.
70 Compare *Egyptian Magic*, p. 13 with *The Equinox*, vol. 1, no. 3, p. 177.
71 Quoted in *The Magical Mason: Forgotten Hermetic Writings of William Wynn Westcott, Physician and Magus*, ed. R. A. Gilbert (Wellingborough: The Aquarian Press, 1983), p. 8.
72 Quoted in Howe, *Magicians*, p. 169. Undated letter from Westcott to F. L. Gardner.
73 Harper, *Yeats's Golden Dawn*, pp. 221–2.
74 W. B. Yeats, *The Countess Cathleen* (London: T. Fisher Unwin, 1920), p. 102.
75 Foster, *The Apprentice Mage*, p. 209.
76 Moore, *Ave*, pp. 90, 91.
77 Quoted in Johnson, *Florence Farr*, p. 104.
78 Harper, *Yeats's Golden Dawn*, p. 19.
79 Yeats, *Autobiographies*, p. 336.
80 *Ibid.*
81 Harper, *Yeats's Golden Dawn*, pp. 203–4.
82 *Ibid.*, pp. 204–5.
83 *Ibid.*, p. 206.
84 King, *Modern Ritual Magic*, p. 68.
85 Harper, *Yeats's Golden Dawn*, p. 211. Letter to 'Levavi Oculos' from DDCF. 2 April 1900.

86 Yeats to Lady Gregory (25 April 1900), *Collected Letters: volume two*, p. 514.
87 Quoted in Howe, *Magicians*, p. 225.
88 *Ibid.*, p. 224.
89 Quoted in *ibid.*, p. 228.
90 Foster, *The Apprentice Mage*, p. 233.
91 Owen Davies, *Grimoires: A History of Magic Books* (Oxford: Oxford University Press, 2009), p. 173; William Wynn Westcott, *The Chaldæan Oracles of Zoroaster: edited and revised by Sapere Aude, with an introduction by L.O.* (London: Theosophical Publishing Society, 1895), p. 8.
92 Harper, *Yeats's Golden Dawn*, p. 260.
93 *Ibid.*, p. 231.
94 Quoted by Yeats in *Ibid.*, p. 243.
95 Quoted in Howe, *Magicians*, p. 170. 'Statement issued to Adepti by the majority of the Council. February 1901.'
96 Quoted in King, *Modern Ritual Magic*, p. 73.
97 Foster, *The Apprentice Mage*, p. 229.
98 Harper, *Yeats's Golden Dawn*, p. 34.
99 Quoted in Johnson, *Florence Farr*, p. 89.
100 Harper, *Yeats's Golden Dawn*, pp. 38, 230–35.
101 Howe, *Magicians*, pp. 203–4.
102 R. A. Gilbert, *The Golden Dawn Scrapbook: The Rise and Fall of a Magical Order* (York Beach, ME: Samuel Weiser, 1997), p. 7.
103 'The Group as I knew it, and Fortiter,' paper written by Robert Felkin. Quoted in Howe, *Magicians*, p. 251.
104 Quoted in Johnson, *Florence Farr*, p. 92.
105 Yeats, *Autobiographies*, p. 122.

Chapter 3 The Twilight Star

1 Quoted in Gilbert, *The Golden Dawn Scrapbook*, p. 23.
2 Annie Besant, *Esoteric Christianity* (London: The Theosophical Publishing Society, 1905), pp. 36–7.
3 Anna Kingsford and Edward Maitland, *The Perfect Way; or, the Finding of Christ* (London: Hamilton, Adams & Co., 1882), pp. 3; xii.
4 Owen, *The Place of Enchantment*, p. 50.
5 Kathleen Raine, *Yeats, the Tarot and the Golden Dawn* (Dublin: Dolmen Press, 1972), pp. 13–14.
6 Arthur Machen, *Things Near and Far* (London: Martin Secker, 1923), p. 17.
7 R. A. Gilbert, *A. E. Waite: Magician of Many Parts* (Wellingborough: Crucible, 1987), pp. 20–22, 24.
8 Waite, *Shadows of Life and Thought*, pp. 70–1. Waite later corresponded with Bulwer-Lytton's son, Owen Meredith.
9 Gilbert, *A. E. Waite*, p. 76.
10 *Ibid.*, p. 27.
11 Waite, *Shadows of Life and Thought*, p. 48.
12 Robert Browning to A. E. Waite (27 June 1876). Quoted in Gilbert, *A. E. Waite*, p. 33.

13 *Ibid.*, p. 35.
14 Nicola Bown, *Fairies in Nineteenth-century Art and Literature* (Cambridge. Cambridge University Press, 2001), p. 142.
15 Gilbert, *A. E. Waite*, p. 91.
16 A. E. Waite, ed., *Songs and Poems of Fairyland: An Anthology of English Fairy Poetry* (London: Walter Scott, 1888), p. 29.
17 *Ibid.*, p. 420.
18 'Songs and Poems of Fairyland (Book Review)', *The Spectator*, vol. 61, no. 3154 (8 December 1888), p. 1711.
19 'Prince Starbeam, by A. E. Waite (Book Review)', *The Spectator*, vol. 65, no. 3252 (25 October 1890), p. 567.
20 Aleister Crowley, *Moonchild* (London: Sphere, 1972), pp. 147, 164.
21 Éliphas Lévi, *The Mysteries of Magic: A Digest of the Writings of Éliphas Lévi*, ed. A. E. Waite (London: Kegan Paul, Trench, Trübner & Co., 1897), p. 12.
22 Waite, *Shadows of Life and Thought*, p. 98.
23 *Ibid.*, p. 99.
24 A. E. Waite, *The Secret Tradition in Freemasonry* (New York: Rebman, 1911), p. ix.
25 Arthur Machen, *Far Off Things* (London: Martin Secker, 1922), p. 33.
26 *Ibid.*, p. 43.
27 *Ibid.*, p. 126.
28 *Ibid.*, p. 144.
29 Machen, *Things Near and Far*, pp. 21, 16.
30 R. A. Gilbert, ed., *Arthur Machen's Occult Catalogues* (Carlton-in-Coverdale: Tartarus Press, 2019), p. 7.
31 *Ibid.*, p. 59.
32 Waite, *Shadows of Life and Thought*, p. 105.
33 Jerome K. Jerome, *My Life and Times* (London: John Murray, 1983), p. 91.
34 Purefoy Machen, *Where Memory Slept*, ed. Godfrey Brangham (Caerleon: Green Round Press, 1991), p. 61.
35 A. E. Waite, 'The Rosicrucians', *Walford's Antiquarian Magazine and Bibliographic Review*, vol. 11 (January–June, 1887), pp. 97–9, (97).
36 Gilbert, *Arthur Machen's Occult Catalogues*, pp. vi–vii.
37 Machen, *Things Near and Far*, p. 17.
38 Roger Luckhurst, ed., *Late Victorian Gothic Tales* (Oxford: Oxford University Press, 2009), p. 190.
39 Gilbert, *A. E. Waite*, pp. 58, 63, 93, 92.
40 [Obituary of S. L. Macgregor Mathers, unsigned, by A. E. Waite], *The Occult Review*, vol. 29, no. 4 (April 1919), pp. 197, 198.
41 Waite, *Shadows of Life and Thought*, p. 97.
42 A. E. Waite, *The Wordsworth Book of Spells* [*The Book of Ceremonial Magic*, 1911] (Ware: Wordsworth Editions, 1995), p. ix.
43 Waite, *Shadows of Life and Thought*, p. 124.
44 Gilbert, *A. E. Waite*, pp. 109–10.
45 Waite, *Shadows of Life and Thought*, pp. 125–6.
46 John Gawsworth, *The Life of Arthur Machen*, ed. Roger Dobson (Carlton-in-Coverdale: Tartarus Press, 2017), ch. VIII, section 1.

47 Arthur Machen, 'Introduction to *The Great God Pan* (1916)', in *Decadent and Occult Works*, ed. Dennis Denisoff (Cambridge: Modern Humanities Research Association, 2018), pp. 303–7 (303).
48 Luckhurst, *Late Victorian Gothic Tales*, pp. 184, 186.
49 Quoted in Gawsworth, *Life of Arthur Machen*, ch. X, section 1.
50 Luckhurst, *Late Victorian Gothic Tales*, pp. 228–9.
51 Arthur Machen, *The Three Impostors* (London: John Lane, 1895), p. 7.
52 See Arthur Machen and A. E. Waite, *The House of the Hidden Light*, ed. R. A. Gilbert (Carlton-in-Coverdale: Tartarus Press, 2003), p. xviii; Machen, *The Three Impostors*, p. 139.
53 Machen, *The Three Impostors*, p. 144.
54 Yeats, *Short Fiction*, p. 180.
55 Machen and Waite, *The House of the Hidden Light*, p. xix.
56 Godwin et al., *The Hermetic Brotherhood of Luxor*, p. 5.
57 *The Unknown World*, vol. 1, no. 1 (15 August 1894), p. 2.
58 Gilbert, *A. E. Waite*, p. 81.
59 'Resurgam', 'The Rosicrucian Mystery from the standpoint of a Rosicrucian', *The Unknown World*, vol. 1, no. 2 (15 September 1894), p. 86.
60 'Within and Without', *The Unknown World*, vol. 1, no. 4 (15 November 1894), p. 147.
61 R. A. Gilbert, 'Steiger, Isabelle de [*née* Isabelle Lace] (1836–1927), artist and theosophist', *Oxford Dictionary of National Biography* (23 September 2004).
62 Waite, *Shadows of Light and Thought*, p. 141.
63 Gilbert has questioned this line of events, as Robert Palmer Thomas did not join the Order until November 1896.
64 Waite, *Shadows of Light and Thought*, pp. 159–60.
65 Henry Danielson and Arthur Machen, *Arthur Machen: A Bibliography* (London: H. Danielson, 1923), p. 37.
66 Colquhoun, *Sword of Wisdom*, p. 225.
67 Jerome, *My Life and Times*, p. 92.
68 Waite, *Shadows of Life and Thought*, p. 156
69 Machen, *Things Near and Far*, p. 154.
70 *Ibid.*, pp. 137, 148.
71 Regardie, *Golden Dawn*, p. 228.
72 Machen, *Things Near and Far*, p. 151.
73 *Ibid.*
74 *Ibid.*, pp. 151–2.
75 Letter to A. E. Waite (1905), Arthur Machen, *Selected Letters: The Private Writings of the Master of the Macabre*, ed. Godfrey Brangham, Roger Dobson and R. A. Gilbert (Wellingborough: Aquarian Press, 1988), p. 35.
76 Machen, *Things Near and Far*, p. 153.
77 Vincent Starrett, *Born in a Bookshop: Chapters from the Chicago Renaissance* (Norman, OK: University of Oklahoma Press, 1965), pp. 248–9.
78 George Malcom Johnson, 'Blackwood, Algernon Henry (1869–1951), writer of supernatural fiction', *Oxford Dictionary of National Biography* (23 September 2004).

79 Algernon Blackwood, letter to Vera Wainwright (14 March 1943).
80 MacBride, *A Servant of the Queen*, p. 215.
81 Algernon Blackwood, 'The Little People & Co.', in *The Lure of the Unknown: Essays on the Strange* (Dublin: Swan River Press, 2022) pp. 39–49 (42).
82 Diary, 7 December 1902 (copyright R. A. Gilbert). Quoted in Gilbert, *A. E. Waite*, p. 114.
83 Diary, 10 January, 1903. *Ibid.*
84 Gilbert, *A. E. Waite*, pp. 85–6.
85 Machen's Welsh name for his Tosspots was 'Sasiwn Cwrw Dda' ('The Society of Good Beer Drinkers'), and he referred to it in letters as 'S∴C∴D∴'.
86 Arthur St John Adcock, *The Glory that was Grub Street* (New York: Stokes, 1928), p. 218.
87 Machen & Waite, *The House of the Hidden Light*, pp. v, xxxiv.
88 *Ibid.*, p. 5.
89 Diary, 12 March 1903. Quoted in *ibid.*, p. xxvi.
90 Waite, *Shadows of Life and Thought*, p. 182.
91 Danielson and Machen, *Arthur Machen: A Bibliography*, p. 36; Waite, *Shadows of Life and Thought*, p. 167.
92 Gilbert, *A. E. Waite*, p. 116.
93 Diary, 21 March 1903. Quoted in *ibid.*, p. 116.
94 Quoted in *ibid.*, p. 117.
95 Waite, *Shadows of Life and Thought*, p. 228.
96 Letter to Brodie-Innes (18 November 1903). Quoted in Howe, *Magicians*, p. 255.
97 Quoted in Gilbert, *A. E. Waite*, pp. 118, 119.
98 Letter to A. E. Waite (1907), Machen, *Selected Letters*, p. 43.
99 *The Letters of Evelyn Underhill*, ed. Charles Williams (London: Longmans, Green and Co., 1943), p. 8.
100 Evelyn Underhill, *The Column of Dust* (London: Methuen, 1909), p. 10.
101 Evelyn Underhill, *Mysticism: A Study of the Nature and Development of Man's Spiritual Consciousness* (New York, NY: E. P. Dutton & Co., 1912), p. 178.
102 *Ibid.*
103 *Ibid.*, p. 151.
104 Arthur Machen, 'What is Mysticism? Bringing Humanity to Exquisite Perfection', *Evening News* (London), 4 March 1913, p. 4; *The Letters of Evelyn Underhill*, p. 140.
105 Gilbert, *A. E. Waite*, p. 74.
106 A E. Waite, *Strange Houses of Sleep* (London: P. S. Welby, 1906), p. 140.
107 Arthur Machen, *The Secret of the Sangraal, & Other Writings* (Carlton-in-Coverdale: Tartarus Press, 2007), p. 149.
108 Aiden Reynolds and William Charlton, *Arthur Machen: A Short Account of his Life and Work* (London: The Richards Press, 1963), p. 118.
109 Arthur Machen, *The Grande Trouvaille: A Legend of Pentonville* (London: The First Edition Bookshop, 1923), unpaginated.

NOTES

Chapter 4 Babe of the Abyss

1. Quoted in Aleister Crowley, *The Confessions of Aleister Crowley: An Autohagiography*, ed. John Symonds and Kenneth Grant (London: Arkana Books, 1989), p. 196.
2. *Ibid.*, p. 194.
3. Anthony Powell, *To Keep the Ball Rolling: The Memoirs of Anthony Powell. Volume II: Messengers of the Day* (London: Heinemann, 1978), p. 82.
4. Maurice Richardson, *Fits & Starts: Collected Pieces* (London: Michael Joseph, 1979), pp. 116–17.
5. Richard Kaczynski, *Perdurabo: The Life of Aleister Crowley* (Berkeley, CA: North Atlantic Books, 2010), p. 22.
6. John Symonds, *The Great Beast: The Life of Aleister Crowley* (London: Rider and Company, 1951), p. 15; Gary Lachman, *Aleister Crowley: Magick, Rock and Roll, and the Wickedest Man in the World* (New York: Penguin, 2014), p. 41.
7. Kaczynski, *Perdurabo*, p. 41.
8. Lachman, *Aleister Crowley*, p. 51.
9. *Ibid.*, p. 52.
10. Kaczynski, *Perdurabo*, p. 54.
11. Davies, *Grimoires*, p. 180.
12. Kaczynski, *Perdurabo*, p. 38; Sturgis, *Aubrey Beardsley*, p. 19.
13. Joseph Bristow, 'Aleister Crowley's Poetic Fin de Siècle: Swinburne's Legacy, Decadent Drag, and Spiritual Sex Magick', *Victorian Literature and Culture*, vol. 49, no. 4 (2021), pp. 777–805 (789).
14. Aleister Crowley, *The Collected Works of Aleister Crowley, vol. 1* (Inverness: Society for the Propagation of Religious Truth, 1905), p. 5; Crowley inscribed a copy of *Aceldama* to Beardsley, one of two editions bound in vellum. See Timothy d'Arch Smith, *The Books of the Beast* (Mandrake Press, 1991), p. 23.
15. Crowley, *Collected Works*, vol. 1, p. 5.
16. Crowley, *Confessions*, pp. 144, 143.
17. Aleister Crowley, *White Stains: The Literary Remains of George Archibald Bishop, a Neuropath of the Second Empire* [Leonard Smithers, May 1898].
18. Crowley, *Confessions*, p. 139.
19. Gilbert, *A. E. Waite*, p. 83.
20. Crowley, *Collected Works*, vol. 1, pp. 29, 35.
21. Crowley, *Confessions*, p. 534.
22. 'Z. Symbolism of the Temple, Candidate, and Ritual of the Neophyte Grade'. See Regardie, *The Golden Dawn*, pp. 43, 479.
23. d'Arch Smith, *Books of the Beast*, p. 14.
24. Crowley, *Confessions*, pp. 179, 166.
25. Yeats to John Quinn (21 March [1915]), *Collected Letters of W. B. Yeats. Electronic edition. Unpublished Letters*, no.2619.
26. Crowley to Gerald Yorke (27 March 1946), Yorke Collection.
27. Crowley, *Confessions*, pp. 179, 181, 182.
28. Aleister Crowley, *The Drug and Other Stories*, ed. William Breeze (Ware: Wordsworth Editions, 2010), p. 126.
29. Symonds, *The Great Beast*, p. 30.

30 Kaczynski, *Perdurabo*, p. 85.
31 *Ibid.*, p. 51.
32 *Ibid.*, p. 256.
33 Crowley, *Confessions*, p. 80.
34 *Ibid.*, p. 235.
35 *Ibid.*
36 *Ibid.*, p. 393.
37 *Ibid.*, p. 394.
38 *Ibid.*, p. 620.
39 Richard Kaczynski, *Friendship in Doubt: Aleister Crowley, J. F. C. Fuller, Victor B. Neuburg, and British Agnosticism* (New York: Oxford University Press, 2024), pp. 79–80.
40 Kaczynski, *Perdurabo*, p. 184.
41 Crowley, *Confessions*, p. 572.
42 James Machin, 'Aleister Crowley and Occult Meaning', in *The Palgrave Handbook of Contemporary Gothic*, ed. Clive Bloom (London: Macmillan, 2020), pp. 321–35 (329).
43 Aleister Crowley, 'The Terror', *The International*, vol. 11, no. 2 (1917), p. 384.
44 *The Equinox*, vol. I, no. 5 (March 1911), p. 150.
45 *Ibid.*, p. 136.
46 Waite was also subject to an obituary by Crowley in vol. X, notable for the fact that Waite was still alive (Crowley had done the same for his uncle in a previous issue).
47 *The Equinox*, vol. I, no. 3 (March 1910), p. 330.
48 *Ibid.*, p. 268.
49 *The Equinox*, vol. I, no. 2 (September 1909), pp. 109–10.
50 P. R. Stephensen, *The Legend of Aleister Crowley*, 3rd edition (Phoenix, AZ: Falcon Press, 1983), pp. 70–2.
51 *Review of Reviews*, vol. 39, no. 232 (April 1909), p. 374.
52 *The Equinox*, vol. I, no. 2 (September 1909), pp. 241, 239, 290.
53 Crowley, *Moonchild*, p. 110.
54 S. L. MacGregor Mathers to J. Brodie-Innes (8 October 1909); Gilbert, *The Golden Dawn Companion*, p. 52.
55 Summary of Brodie-Innes's reply follows the typescript of the above letter.
56 Quoted in Kaczynski, *Perdurabo*, p. 207.
57 '"The Dead Cat": Publishing the Secrets of the Rosicrucian Order', *Croydon Chronicle and East Surrey Advertiser* (26 March 1910), p. 4.
58 Quoted in King, *Modern Ritual Magic*, pp. 119, 122.
59 Kaczynski, *Perdurabo*, p. 224.
60 Quoted in *ibid.*, p. 228.
61 Aleister Crowley, 'The "Rosicrucian" Scandal', Hermetic Library website <hermetic.com/crowley/the-rosicrucian-scandal/index> [accessed 4 January 2025].
62 Kaczynski, *Perdurabo*, p. 259.
63 Louis Marlow, *Seven Friends* (London: The Richards Press, 1953), pp. 39–64.

64　W. Somerset Maugham, *The Magician: A Novel, together with a Fragment of Autobiography* (New York, NY: Arno Press, 1977), p. x.
65　Crowley, *Confessions*, p. 571.
66　Oliver Haddo [Aleister Crowley], 'How to Write A Novel! After W. S. Maugham', *Vanity Fair*, vol. 81 (30 December, 1908), pp. 838–40 (838).
67　Crowley, *Confessions*, p. 572.
68　*The Magical Record of the Beast 666: The Diaries of Aleister Crowley 1914–1920*, ed. John Symonds and Kenneth Grant (London: Duckworth, 1972), pp. 51–67.
69　Kaczynski, *Perdurabo*, pp. 305, 309.
70　Crowley, *Confessions*, p. 777.
71　*Ibid.*, p. 817; Kaczynski, *Perdurabo*, p. 310.
72　Crowley, *Moonchild*, p. 161.
73　*Ibid.*, p. 143.
74　*Ibid.*, p. 187.
75　*Ibid.*, p. 173.
76　*Ibid.*, p. 111.
77　Kaczynski, *Perdurabo*, p. 311.
78　Quoted in *ibid.*, p. 340.
79　William Buehler Seabrook, quoted in *ibid.*, p. 331.
80　Symonds, *The Great Beast*, p. 151.
81　Quoted in Kaczynski, *Perdurabo*, p. 363.
82　Symonds, *The Great Beast*, p. 155.
83　Mary Butts, *The Journals of Mary Butts*, ed. Nathalie Blondel (New Haven, CT: Yale University Press, 2002), pp. 181, 186.
84　Aleister Crowley, *The Diary of a Drug Fiend* (London: Collins, 1922), p. v.
85　*Ibid.*, p. 308.
86　*Ibid.*, p. 364.
87　Kaczynski, *Perdurabo*, p. 386.
88　Crowley, *Confessions*, p. 917.
89　Phil Baker, *City of the Beast: The London of Aleister Crowley* (London: Strange Attractor Press, 2022), p. 122.
90　Craig Munro, *Wild Man of Letters: The Story of P. R. Stephensen* (Melbourne: Melbourne University Press, 1984), p. 89.
91　Quoted in *ibid.*, p. 93.
92　Quoted in Phil Baker, *The Devil is a Gentleman: The Life and Times of Dennis Wheatley* (Sawtry: Dedalus, 2009), p. 301.

Chapter 5　'The Spell of Sound'

1　Yeats to Lady Gregory (25 April 1900), *Collected Letters: volume two*, p. 514.
2　W. T. Horton, *A Book of Images*, introduction by W. B. Yeats (London: The Unicorn Press, 1898), p. 16.
3　'Manuscript papers of Florence Farr concerning philosophy and mysticism' (*c.* 1900–1904). Museum of Freemasonry.
4　*Ibid.*

5 Florence Farr and O. Shakespear, *The Beloved of Hathor and The Shrine of the Golden Hawk* (n.p.p: [1902]).
6 W. B. Yeats, *Uncollected Prose*, vol. 2, ed. John P. Frayne and Colton Johnson (London: Macmillan, 1975), p. 266.
7 'At Stratford-on-Avon', *The Speaker: The Liberal Review* (11 May 1901), p. 158.
8 Foster, *The Apprentice Mage*, p. 257.
9 Quoted in Johnson, *Florence Farr*, p. 101.
10 Yeats, letter to A. E.
11 Yeats, 'Speaking the Psaltery', *Essays and Introductions*, p. 13.
12 Yeats, 'Bardic Ireland', *Uncollected Prose*, vol. 1, pp. 163–6 (164). See also Ambrose Ih-Ren Mong, 'Yeats and Bardic Tradition', *Canadian Journal for Irish Studies*, vol. 20, no. 1 (July 1994), pp. 89–101.
13 Yeats to Florence Farr (29 January 1901), *The Collected Letters of W. B. Yeats: volume three: 1901–1904*, ed. John Kelly and Ronald Schuchard (Oxford: Clarendon Press, 1994), p. 26.
14 Foster, *The Apprentice Mage*, pp. 257–8.
15 Yeats to Lady Gregory (20 January 1902), *Collected Letters: volume three*, p. 149.
16 Waite, *Shadows of Life and Thought*, p. 184.
17 Elizabeth Foley O'Connor, *Pamela Colman Smith: Artist, Feminist & Mystic* (Liverpool: Liverpool University Press, 2021), pp. 23–5, 45.
18 *Ibid.*, pp. 7–8.
19 Pamela Colman Smith, 'Two Negro Stories from Jamaica', *The Journal of American Folklore*, vol. 9, no. 35 (October – December 1896), p. 278.
20 Pamela Colman Smith, letter to Albert Bigelow Paine (17 March 1901), quoted in Joan Coldwell, 'Pamela Colman Smith and the Yeats Family', *The Canadian Journal of Irish Studies* vol. 3, no. 2 (November 1977), pp. 27–34 (29).
21 *Ibid.*, p. 28.
22 Pamela Colman Smith, letter to Albert Bigelow Paine (19 December 1901), quoted in *ibid.*, p. 29.
23 Gilbert, *The Golden Dawn Companion*, p. 186 (the motto is recorded on the Order Roll incorrectly as 'Quod Tibbi id allium'); O'Connor, *Pamela Colman Smith*, p. 184.
24 Yeats to Lady Gregory (9 December 1902), *Collected Letters: volume three*, p. 271.
25 *The Green Sheaf*, vol. II (London, 1903).
26 Owen, *The Place of Enchantment*, p. 24.
27 Quoted in Simon Wilson, 'Wilde, Beardsley, Salomé and Censorship', *The Wildean*, vol. 51 (July 2017), pp. 45–82 (48).
28 Greer, *Women of the Golden Dawn*, p. 320.
29 'The Rites of Astaroth', *The New Age*, vol. 1, no. 19 (5 September 1907), pp. 294–5.
30 'Marie Corelli and the Modern Girl', *The New Age*, vol. 1, no. 14 (1 August 1907).
31 Johnson, *Florence Farr*, p. 149.
32 Quoted in Crowley, *Confessions*, p. 544.

33 Johnson, *Florence Farr*, p. 174.
34 Quoted from an advertisement in *The Freewoman*, vol. 1, no. 26 (16 May 1912).
35 *Ibid.*
36 Quoted in Johnson, *Florence Farr*, p. 180.
37 *Ibid.*, p. 182.
38 O'Connor, *Pamela Colman Smith*, p. 102.
39 The Hon. Mrs. Forbes-Sempill, 'Music Made Visible: An Unmusical Artist's Lightning Impressions Recorded While Listening to Music', *The Illustrated London News* (12 February 1927), p. 260.
40 Lady Archibald Campbell, 'Faerie Ireland', *The Occult Review*, vol. 6, no. 5 (November 1907), pp. 259–74 (266).
41 O'Connor, *Pamela Colman Smith*, p. 150.
42 Yeats to Charles Elkin Mathews and Others (17 March 1903), *Collected Letters: volume 3*, p. 328
43 William Rothenstein, 'Three Impressions', *The Arrow* (Dublin, 1939), pp. 16–17.
44 Melinda Boyd Parsons, 'Pamela Colman Smith and Alfred Stieglitz', *History of Photography*, vol. 20, no. 4 (Winter 1996), pp. 285–92 (285).
45 Pamela Colman Smith, undated letter to Alfred Stieglitz [1908]. Quoted in *ibid.*, p. 290.
46 James Huneker, [untitled review], *New York Sun* (15 January 1907).
47 'Als ik kan, notes: reviews', *The Craftsman*, vol. 9 (March 1907), p. 769.
48 Parsons, 'Pamela Colman Smith and Alfred Stieglitz', p. 285.
49 Waite, *Shadows of Life and Thought*, p. 184.
50 Gilbert, *A. E. Waite*, p. 138; Waite, *Shadows of Life and Thought*, p. 194.
51 Lévi, *Transcendental Magic*, p. 3.
52 Juliette Wood, 'The Celtic Tarot and the Secret Tradition: A Study in Modern Legend Making ', *Folklore*, vol. 109 (1998), pp. 15–24 (15); McIntosh, 'Éliphas Lévi', pp. 220–30 (225).
53 A. E. Waite, *The Pictorial Key to the Tarot* (New York: S. Weiser, 1975), p. 4.
54 Waite, *Shadows of Life and Thought*, p. 185.
55 Pamela Colman Smith, letter to Alfred Stieglitz (19 November 1909), quoted in O'Connor, *Pamela Colman Smith*, p. 175.
56 *Ibid.*
57 'Notes of the Month', *The Occult Review*, vol. 10, no. 6 (December 1909), p. 301.
58 See Gillian Furlong, 'An Early Supporter of Women's Rights', in *Treasures from UCL* (London: UCL Press, 2015), pp. 172–5.
59 J. B. Yeats, *Letters to his Son W. B. Yeats and Others*, ed. Joseph Hone (London: Faber & Faber, 1944), p. 162.
60 Harper, *Yeats's Golden Dawn*, p. 126.
61 Virginia Moore, *The Unicorn: William Butler Yeats' Search for Reality* (New York: Macmillan, 1954), p. 170.
62 Quoted in Ellmann, *Yeats: The Man and the Masks*, p. 259.
63 Foster, *W. B. Yeats: A Life: II: The Arch-poet, 1915–1939* (Oxford: Oxford University Press, 2003), p. 23.

64 Yeats to Agnes Tobin (4 June [1915]). *Collected Letters of W. B. Yeats. Electronic edition. Unpublished Letters*, no. 2656.
65 Quoted in George Mills Harper and Walter Kelly Hood (ed.), *A Critical Edition of Yeats's* A Vision *(1925)* (London: Macmillan, 1987), p. xiv.
66 Foster, *The Arch-poet*, p. 106; George's motto was 'Nemo Sciat' ('Nobody must know'), and she entered the Second Order in 1916.
67 Foster, *The Arch-poet*, p. 106.
68 Ronald Schuchard, 'Yeats and Spirituality', *The Princeton University Library Chronicle*, vol. 59, no. 3 (April 1998), pp. 321–49 (341); W. B. Yeats, *A Vision* (New York: Macmillan, 1938), p. 8.
69 Yeats to Lady Gregory (4 January [1918]). *Collected Letters of W. B. Yeats. Electronic edition. Unpublished Letters*, no. 3384.
70 Harper and Hood, *A Critical Edition*, pp. xxiv–xxv.
71 Yeats, *A Vision*, pp. xii, 12, 15.
72 Hazard Adams, *The Book of Yeats's Vision: Romantic Modernism and Antithetical Tradition* (Ann Arbour, MI: The University of Michigan Press, 1995), p. 121.
73 *Ibid.*, p. 180.
74 *Ibid.*, p. 2.
75 *Ibid.*, p. 162.
76 *Ibid.*, p. 161.
77 Yeats, *A Vision* (1938), p. 8.
78 *Ibid.*, p. 25.
79 W. B Yeats, *A Vision: An Explanation of Life Founded upon the Writings of Giraldus and upon Certain Documents Attributed to Kusta Ben Luka* (London: T. Werner Laurie, 1925), p. ix.
80 Yeats, *Autobiographies*, p. 187.
81 Quoted in Harper, *Yeats's Golden Dawn*, p. 146.
82 Harper and Hood, *A Critical Edition*, p. xliv.
83 From an early draft, quoted in *ibid.*, p. xlv; Yeats, *A Vision* (1925), pp. ix–x. After Locke's death, Horton 'saw her in apparition and attained through her certain of the traditional experiences of the saint'.
84 Yeats, *A Vision* (1925), pp. ix–x; Harper and Hood, *A Critical Edition*, p. xlvi; T. H. Pattinson had been a member of the S.R.I.A. when he joined Isis-Urania in 1888, the same year becoming Imperator of the Horus Temple at Bradford. See Gilbert, *The Golden Dawn Companion*, p. 32.
85 Yeats, *A Vision*, p. 255.
86 *Ibid.*, p. 253.
87 Yeats, *Autobiographies*, p. 576.
88 Yeats to Olivia Shakespear (13 October 1929); Yeats to George Yeats (28 October 1929).
89 *Ibid.*

Chapter 6 Metaphysical Thrillers

1. *The Oxford Book of English Mystical Verse*, ed. D. H. S. Nicholson and A. H. E. Lee (London: Oxford University Press, 1917), pp. v–vi.
2. Grevel Lindop, *Charles Williams: The Third Inkling* (Oxford: Oxford University Press, 2015), p. 56.
3. Gilbert, *A. E. Waite*, p. 139.
4. Waite, *Shadows of Life and Thought*, pp. 229, 142, 183.
5. Charles Williams, *The Image of the City and Other Essays*, selected by Anne Ridler with an introduction (Oxford: Oxford University Press, 1958), p. xxiv.
6. Alice Mary Hadfield, *Charles Williams: An Exploration of his Life and Work* (Oxford: Oxford University Press, 1983), p. 4.
7. Charles Williams to Lewis Chase (23 July 1931). Quoted in Lindop, *Charles Williams*, p. 191.
8. Quoted in Peter Sutcliffe, *The Oxford University Press: An Informal History* (Oxford: Oxford University Press, 1978), p. 203.
9. Commonplace Book, Bodleian, MS Eng. E. 2012 [p. 124].
10. See, for example, D. H. S. Nicholson, *Some Characteristics of the Mystical Church* (London: The Theosophical Publishing Society, 1912), with an introduction by A. E. Waite.
11. Nicholson and Lee, *The Oxford Book of English Mystical Verse*, p. 522.
12. Lindop, *Charles Williams*, p. 84.
13. A. E. Waite to Charles Williams (14 July 1917). uoted in *ibid.*, p. 57
14. Aren Roukema, 'A Veil that Reveals: Charles Williams and the Fellowship of the Rosy Cross', *Journal of Inklings Studies*, vol. 5, no. 1 (2015), pp. 22–71 (42).
15. Williams to John Pellow (undated, [1922]). Quoted in Lindop, *Charles Williams*, p. 86.
16. Alan Richardson, *Priestess: The Life and Magic of Dion Fortune* (Wellingborough: The Aquarian Press, 1987), p. 28.
17. Unsigned, 'Atlantean Memories', *Inner Light*, vol. 2, no. 8 (May 1929).
18. Violet M. Firth, *More Violets: A Child's Thoughts on Nature in Verse and Prose* (England: Jarrold and Sons, [1920]), p. 3.
19. *Ibid.*, p. 51.
20. Dion Fortune, *Psychic Self Defence* (Wellingborough: The Aquarian Press, 1957), pp. 12, 16.
21. Quoted in Gareth Knight, *Dion Fortune and the Inner Light* (Loughborough: Thoth Publications, 2000), p. 71.
22. Fortune, *Psychic Self Defence*, p. 9.
23. Dion Fortune, *Sane Occultism and Practical Occultism in Daily Life* (Wellingborough: The Aquarian Press, 1987), pp. 14–15.
24. King, *Modern Ritual Magic*, p. 111.
25. Dion Fortune, 'Ceremonial Magic Unveiled', *The Occult Gazette* (January 1933), reproduced in *Rites of Isis and of Pan*, ed. Gareth Knight, p. 83.
26. Lindop, *Charles Williams*, p. 64.
27. *Ibid.*, p. 65.
28. Commonplace Book, Bodleian, MS Eng. E. 2012.

29 Lindop, *Charles Williams*, p. 93; Gilbert, *A. E. Waite*, p. 149.
30 Anonymous [A. E. Waite], *The Third Order of the Rosy Cross: World of Formation Part II. The Pontifical Ceremony of Admission to the Grade of Adeptus Minor, 5=6* (privately printed [London], 1917), p. 55.
31 Gilbert, *A. E. Waite*, p. 142.
32 Williams, *The Image of the City*, p. xxv.
33 A. E. Waite, 'On Ceremonial Union', in *The Hermetic Papers of A. E. Waite: the Unknown Writings of a Modern Mystic*, ed. R. A. Gilbert (Wellingborough: The Aquarian Press, 1987), p. 189.
34 Lindop, *Charles Williams*, pp. 102, 133
35 Williams to Phyllis Jones (undated [1927]). Quoted in *ibid.*, p. 134.
36 A. E. Waite, diary (11 April 1901). Quoted in Gilbert, *A. E. Waite*, p. 67.
37 Lindop, *Charles Williams*, p. 246.
38 Charles Williams, *Shadows of Ecstasy* (London: Faber and Faber, 1948), p. 11.
39 John Heath-Stubbs, *Literary Essays*, ed. A. T. Tolley (Manchester: Carcanet, 1998), p. 139.
40 Lindop, *Charles Williams*, p. 213.
41 T. S. Eliot to Charles Williams (7 October 1934). Quoted in *ibid.*, pp. 214–15.
42 Knight, *Dion Fortune and the Inner Light*, p. 42.
43 Dion Fortune, *The Secrets of Dr Taverner* (Wellingborough: The Aquarian Press, 1989), p. 29.
44 *Ibid.*, p. 10.
45 *Ibid.*, p. 32.
46 Knight, *Dion Fortune and the Inner Light*, p. 75.
47 Quoted in *ibid.*, p. 91.
48 Roma A. King, Jr., *The Pattern in the Web: The Mythical Poetry of Charles Williams* (Kent, OH: Kent State University Press, 2013), p. 3.
49 Charles Williams and C. S. Lewis, *Arthurian Torso: Containing the Posthumous Fragment of the Figure of Arthur* (London: Oxford University Press, 1948), p. 13.
50 *TLS*, 17 December 1938, p. 804; *Blackfriars*, vol. 20, no. 228 (March 1939), pp. 236–7 (237).
51 Charles Williams, *Taliessin through Logres* (London: Oxford University Press, 1969), pp. 8, 4.
52 Gilbert, *A. E. Waite*, p. 149.
53 Charles Williams, *Poetry at Present* (Oxford: The Clarendon Press, 1930), pp. 59, 61.
54 Ottoline Morrell to Charles Williams (12 December 1933). Quoted in Lindop, 'Charles Williams and W. B. Yeats', *Yeats Annual*, vol. 21 (2018), pp. 317–54 (326).
55 *The Letters of Evelyn Underhill*, pp. 12–13.
56 Quoted in Richardson, *Priestess*, p. 117.
57 *Ibid.*, p. 117.
58 King, *Modern Ritual Magic*, p. 157.
59 Fortune, *The Esoteric Orders and their Work* (Wellingborough: The Aquarian Press, 1982), pp. 62–3.

60 Dion Fortune, *The Sea Priestess* (Wellingborough: The Aquarian Press, 1989), pp. 25–7.
61 Dion Fortune, 'Ceremonial Magic Unveiled', p. 83.
62 *Ibid.*
63 King, *Modern Ritual Magic*, p. 157. The Inner Light also maintained a 'semi-amicable' relationship with the Stella Matutina, p. 157.
64 Fortune to Israel Regardie (1 November 1932). Quoted in Knight, *Dion Fortune and the Inner Light*, p. 198.
65 Dion Fortune, *Glastonbury: Avalon of the Heart* (York Beach, ME: Samuel Weiser, 2000), pp. 2, 4, 9.
66 Ronald Hutton, *The Triumph of the Moon* (London: Yale University Press, 1999), p. 183.
67 Quoted in Richardson, *Priestess*, p. 209.
68 Dion Fortune, *Dion Fortune's Rites of Isis and of Pan*, ed. Gareth Knight (Cheltenham: Skylight Press, 2013)
69 *Ibid.*, p. 96.
70 *Ibid.*, p. 100.
71 *Ibid.*
72 Hutton, *Triumph of the Moon*, p. 183.
73 Dion Fortune, *The Winged Bull* (Wellingborough: The Aquarian Press, 1971), p. 84.
74 Dion Fortune, *The Goat-Foot God* (Wellingborough: The Aquarian Press, 1989), p. 36.
75 *Ibid.*, p. 55.
76 Georgia Van Raalte, 'Literary Initiation in the Occult Novels of Dion Fortune' (unpublished doctoral thesis, University of Surrey, 2022), p. 52.
77 Knight, *Dion Fortune and the Inner Light*, p. 304.
78 Dion Fortune, *Aspects of Occultism* (Wellingborough: The Aquarian Press, 1973), p. 78.
79 *Selected Letters of Philip Larkin: 1940–1985*, ed. Anthony Thwaite (London: Faber, 1992), p. 79.
80 Quoted in Lindop, *Charles Williams*, pp. 369, 398.
81 Charles Williams, *The Region of the Summer Stars* (Oxford: Oxford University Press, 1950), p. 36; Williams, *The Image of the City*, p. 148.
82 Hadfield, *Charles Williams*, p. 217.
83 *Letters to Lalage: The Letters of Charles Williams to Lois Lang-Sims*, ed. Glen Cavaliero (Kent, OH: Kent State University Press, 1989), p. 32.
84 Quoted in Knight, *Dion Fortune and the Inner Light*, p. 245
85 Fortune, *Aspects of Occultism*, p. 87.
86 Fortune, *Psychic Self Defence*, pp. 203–4.
87 *Ibid.*, p. 70.
88 Francis King and Isabel Sutherland, *The Rebirth of Magic* (London: Corgi, 1982), pp. 149–50.
89 Quoted in Alan Richardson, *Aleister Crowley and Dion Fortune: The Logos of the Aeon and the Shakti of the Age* (Woodbury, MN: Llewellyn Publications, 2009), p. 32.

90 *Ibid.*, p. 36.
91 Kaczynski, *Perdurabo*, p. 530; inscription quoted in Knight, *Dion Fortune and the Inner Light*, p. 238.
92 Richardson, *Aleister Crowley and Dion Fortune*, p. 34.

'An Elaborate Appendix'
1 Alan Moore and Steve Moore, 'The Moon and Serpent Grand Egyptian Theatre of Marvels', *KAOS 14*, ed. Joe Biroco (London: Kaos-Babylon Press, 2002), pp. 187–94 (192).
2 Lance Parkin, *Magic Words: The Extraordinary Life of Alan Moore* (London: Aurum Press, 2013), p. 278.
3 Eddie Campbell, *Eddie Campbell's Egomania*, no. 2 (Paddington, QLD: Antelope Pineapple Pty Ltd, 2002), pp. 2–5.
4 Moore and Moore, 'The Moon and Serpent', pp. 194, 187.
5 Parkin, p. 44.
6 *Ibid.*, p. 280.
7 Gilbert, *The Golden Dawn Companion*, p. 217.
8 Kaczynski, *Perdurabo*, p. 432.
9 Christopher A. Plaisance, 'Israel Regardie and the Psychologization of Esoteric Discourse', *Correspondences*, vol. 3 (2015), pp. 5–54 (11).
10 Israel Regardie, *What You Should Know about the Golden Dawn* (Phoenix, AZ: Falcon Press, 1983), pp. 36, 39.
11 Colquhoun, *Sword of Wisdom*, p. 21.
12 Henrik Bogdan, 'The Babalon Working 1946: L. Ron Hubbard, John Whiteside Parsons, and the Practice of Enochian Magic', *Numen*, vol. 63, no. 1 (2016), pp. 12–32 (13).
13 Quoted in *ibid.*, p. 27.
14 *Ibid.*, p. 20.
15 Quoted in Alice L. Hutchinson, *Kenneth Anger: A Demonic Visionary* (London: Black Dog Publishing, 2004), p. 115.
16 Dave Evans, *The History of British Magick after Crowley* ([UK]: Hidden Publishing, 2007), p. 5.
17 Kenneth Grant, *Nightside of Eden* (London: Frederick Muller, 1977), p. xi.
18 *Ibid.*, p. 127.
19 *Ibid.*, p. 128.
20 John L. Steadman, *H. P. Lovecraft and the Black Magickal Tradition: The Master of Horror's Influence on Modern Occultism* (San Francisco, CA: Weiser Books, 2015), p. 79.
21 Phil Hine, *Prime Chaos: Adventures in Chaos Magic*, introduction by Grant Morrison (Tempe, AZ: New Falcon Publications, 1999), p. 11.
22 Genesis P. Orridge, 'Magick Squares and Future Beats: The Magickal Processes and Methods of William S. Burroughs and Brion Gysin', in *Book of Lies: The Disinformation Guide to Magick and the Occult*, ed. Richard Metzger (San Francisco, CA: Disinformation Books, 2014), n.p.
23 Edward S. Robinson, *Shift Linguals: Cut-up Narratives from William S. Burroughs to the Present* (Amsterdam: Rodopi, 2011), p. 25.

24 Orridge, 'Magick Squares'.
25 *Ibid.*
26 Quoted in *My Kind of Angel: i.m. William Burroughs*, ed. Rupert Loydell (Exeter: Slide Publications, 1998), p. 42.
27 Leon Surette, *The Birth of Modernism: Ezra Pound, T. S. Eliot, W. B. Yeats, and the Occult* (Montreal: McGill-Queen's University Press, 1993), p. 281.

Bibliography

Adams, Hazard, *The Book of Yeats's Vision: Romantic Modernism and Antithetical Tradition* (Ann Arbour, MI: The University of Michigan Press, 1995)
Adcock, Arthur St John, *The Glory that was Grub Street* (New York, NY: Stokes, 1928)
Allderidge, Patricia H., 'Dadd, Richard (1817–1886), painter', *Oxford Dictionary of National Biography*, 23 September 2004 <doi.org/10.1093/ref:odnb/37337>
'Als ik kan, notes: reviews', *The Craftsman*, vol. 9 (March 1907), p. 769
Archer, William, *The Theatrical 'World' of 1894* (London: Walter Scott, 1895)
Ashley, Mike, *Starlight Man: The Extraordinary Life of Algernon Blackwood* (Eureka: Stark House Press, 2019)
The Athenaeum, 3485 (11 August 1894)
Baker, Phil, *The Devil is a Gentleman: The Life and Times of Dennis Wheatley* (Sawtry: Dedalus, 2009)
—, *Austin Osman Spare: The Life and Legend of London's Lost Artist* (London: Strange Attractor Press, 2011)
—, *City of the Beast: The London of Aleister Crowley* (London: Strange Attractor Press, 2022)
Bax, Clifford, ed., *Florence Farr: Bernard Shaw: W. B. Yeats: Letters* (Dublin: Cuala Press, 1941)
Besant, Annie, *Esoteric Christianity* (London: The Theosophical Publishing Society, 1905)
Blackburn, Simon, ed., *The Oxford Dictionary of Philosophy*, 3rd edition (Oxford: Oxford University Press, 2016)
Blackfriars, vol. 20, no. 228 (March 1939), pp. 236–7
Blackwood, Algernon, *The Lure of the Unknown: Essays on the Strange* (Dublin: Swan River Press, 2022)
Blavatsky, H. P., *Isis Unveiled: A Master-key to the Mysteries of Ancient and Modern Science* (London: Bernard Quaritch, 1877)
—, *The Key to Theosophy*, ed. Josephine Ransom (London: The Theosophical Publishing House, 1948)
Bogdan, Henrik, 'The Babalon Working 1946: L. Ron Hubbard, John Whiteside Parsons, and the Practice of Enochian Magic', *Numen*, vol. 63, no. 1 (2016), pp. 12–32
Brémont, Anna de, Comtesse, *Oscar Wilde and his Mother: A Memoir* (London: Everett, 1911)
Briggs, Katherine, *The Fairies in English Tradition and Literature* (Chicago, IL: University of Chicago Press, 1969)
Bristow, Joseph, 'Aleister Crowley's Poetic Fin de Siècle: Swinburne's

Legacy, Decadent Drag, and Spiritual Sex Magick', *Victorian Literature and Culture*, vol. 49, no. 4 (2021), pp. 777–805

Bown, Nicola, *Fairies in Nineteenth-century Art and Literature* (Cambridge: Cambridge University Press, 2001)

Budge, E. A. Wallis, *A Guide to the First, Second and Third Egyptian Rooms*, 3rd edition (London: British Museum, 1924)

Bulwer-Lytton, Edward (Lord Lytton), *Zanoni* (New York, NY: F. M. Lutton, [written 1842])

Butts, Mary, *The Journals of Mary Butts*, ed. Nathalie Blondel (New Haven, CT: Yale University Press, 2002)

Campbell, Lady Archibald, 'Faerie Ireland', *The Occult Review*, vol. 6, no. 5 (November 1907), pp. 259–74

Campbell, Bruce F., *Ancient Wisdom Revived: A History of the Theosophical Movement* (Berkeley, CA: The University of California Press, 1980)

Campbell, Eddie, *Eddie Campbell's Egomania* no. 2 (Paddington, QLD: Antelope Pineapple Pty Ltd, 2002)

Campbell, James L., *Edward Bulwer-Lytton* (Boston, MA: Twayne Publishers, 1986)

Chajes, J. H., 'Kabbalah Practices / Practical Kabbalah: The Magic of Kabbalistic Trees', *Aries*, vol. 19, no. 1 (2019), pp. 112–45

Cheeseman, Peter, 'Horniman, Annie Elizabeth Fredericka (1860–1937)', *Oxford Dictionary of National Biography*, 21 May 2009 <doi.org/10.1093/ref:odnb/33993>

Clanton, Amy M., 'Religion as Aesthetic Creation: Ritual and Belief in William Butler Yeats and Aleister Crowley', PhD thesis, University of South Florida, 2011

Clarke, Peter B., ed., *Encyclopedia of New Religious Movements* (London: Routledge, 2006)

Clawson, Mary Ann, *Constructing Brotherhood: Class, Gender, and Fraternalism* (Princeton, NJ: Princeton University Press, 1989)

Coldwell, Joan, 'Pamela Colman Smith and the Yeats Family', *The Canadian Journal of Irish Studies*, vol. 3, no. 2 (November 1977), pp. 27–34

Colquhoun, Ithell, *Sword of Wisdom: MacGregor Mathers and 'The Golden Dawn'* (New York: G. P. Putnam's Sons, 1975)

Crowley, Aleister, *White Stains: The Literary Remains of George Archibald Bishop, a Neuropath of the Second Empire* [Leonard Smithers, May 1898]

—, *In Residence: A Don's Guide to Cambridge* (Cambridge: Elijah Johnson, 1904)

—, *The Collected Works of Aleister Crowley*, vol. 1 (Inverness: Society for the Propagation of Religious Truth, 1905)

—, ed., *The Equinox: The Review of Scientific Illuminism* vol. 1, no. 1–10 (1910–13)

—, 'The "Rosicrucian" Scandal', 1911, Hermetic Library website, hermetic.com/crowley/the-rosicrucian-scandal/index [accessed 4 January 2025]

—, *The Diary of a Drug Fiend* (London: Collins, 1922)

—, *The Magical Record of the Beast 666: The Diaries of Aleister Crowley 1914–1920*, eds. John Symonds and Kenneth Grant (London: Duckworth, 1972)

—, *Moonchild* (London: Sphere, 1972)

—, *The Confessions of Aleister Crowley: An Autohagiography*, ed. John Symonds and Kenneth Grant (London: Arkana Books, 1989)

—, *The Drug and Other Stories*, ed. William Breeze (Ware: Wordsworth Editions, 2010)

The Daily Telegraph (10 December 1892)

'The Dancing Faun [review]', *The Bookman* (July 1894), p. 120

Danielson, Henry, and Arthur Machen, *Arthur Machen: A Bibliography* (London: H. Danielson, 1923)

D'Arch Smith, Timothy, *The Books of the Beast* (Mandrake Press, 1991)

Davies, Owen, *Grimoires: A History of Magic Books* (Oxford: Oxford University Press: 2009)

'"The Dead Cat": Publishing the Secrets of the Rosicrucian Order', *Croydon Chronicle and East Surrey Advertiser* (26 March 1910), p. 4

Dobson, Eleanor, *Victorian Alchemy: Science, Magic and Ancient Egypt* (London: UCL Press, 2022)

Doyle White, Ethan, 'Lucifer Over Luxor: Archaeology, Egyptology, and Occultism in Kenneth Anger's Magick Lantern Cycle', *Present Pasts* vol. 7, no. 1/2 (2016), pp. 1–10

Eckhartshausen, Carl von, *The Cloud upon the Sanctuary*, trans. Isabelle de Steiger (London: George Redway, 1896)

Ellmann, Richard, *Yeats: The Man and the Masks* (London: Faber and Faber, 1969)

[The Equinox, unsigned review] *Review of Reviews*, vol. 39, no. 232 (April 1909), p. 374

Evans, Dave, *The History of British Magic after Crowley* ([UK]: Hidden Publishing, 2007)

Farr, Florence, *The Dancing Faun* (London: Elkin Mathews and John Lane, 1894)

—, *A Short Enquiry concerning the Hermetic Art, by a Lover of Philalethes*, (London: Theosophical Publishing Society, 1894)

—, *Euphrates, or the Waters of the East by Eugenius Philalethes, 1655, with a Commentary by S.S.D.D.* (London: Theosophical Publishing Society, 1896)

— [S.S.D.D.], *Egyptian Magic* (London, 1896)

—, 'Manuscript papers of Florence Farr concerning philosophy and mysticism' (*c.* 1900–1904), Museum of Freemasonry

—, and O. Shakespear, *The Beloved of Hathor and The Shrine of the Golden Hawk* (n.p.p: [1902])

—, 'Marie Corelli and the Modern Girl', *The New Age*, vol. 1, no. 14 (1 August 1907)

—, 'The Rites of Astaroth', *The New Age*, vol. 1, no. 19 (5 September 1907)

—, *The Solemnization of Jacklin* (London: 1912)

Firth, Violet M., [Dion Fortune], *More Violets: A Child's Thoughts on Nature in Verse and Prose* (England: Jarrold and Sons, [1920])

Fletcher, Ian, 'Decadence and the Little Magazines', in *Stratford-Upon-Avon Studies 17: Decadence and the 1890s* (New York: Holmes & Meier, 1980), pp. 173–202

Forbes-Sempill, The Hon. Mrs, 'Music Made Visible: An Unmusical Artist's Lightning Impressions Recorded While Listening to Music', *The Illustrated London News* (12 February 1927), p. 260

Fortune, Dion, 'Atlantean Memories', *Inner Light*, vol. 2, no. 8 (May 1929)

—, *Psychic Self Defence* (Wellingborough: Aquarian Press, 1957)

—, *The Winged Bull* (Wellingborough: Aquarian Press, 1971)

—, *Aspects of Occultism* (Wellingborough: Aquarian Press, 1973)

—, *The Esoteric Orders and their Work* (Wellingborough: Aquarian Press, 1982)

—, *Sane Occultism and Practical Occultism in Daily Life* (Wellingborough: Aquarian Press, 1987)

—, *The Goat-Foot God* (Wellingborough: Aquarian Press, 1989)

—, *The Sea Priestess* (Wellingborough: Aquarian Press, 1989)

—, *The Secrets of Dr Taverner* (Wellingborough: Aquarian Press, 1989)

—, *Glastonbury: Avalon of the Heart* (York Beach, ME: Samuel Weiser, 2000)

—, *Dion Fortune's Rites of Isis and of Pan*, ed. Gareth Knight (Cheltenham: Skylight Press, 2013)

Foster, R. F., 'Protestant Magic: W. B. Yeats and the Spell of Irish History', *Proceedings of the British Academy*, vol. 75 (1989), pp. 243–66

—, *W. B. Yeats: A Life. I: The Apprentice Mage, 1865–1914* (Oxford: Oxford University Press, 1997)

—, *W. B. Yeats: A Life. II: The Arch-poet, 1915–1939* (Oxford: Oxford University Press, 2003)

Freeman, Nick, 'Wilde's Edwardian Afterlife: Somerset Maugham, Aleister Crowley, and *The Magician*', *Literature and History*, vol. 16, no. 1 (2007), pp. 16–29

The Freewoman, vol. 1, no. 26 (16 May 1912)

Furlong, Gillian, *Treasures from UCL* (London: UCL Press, 2015)

Gan, Richard, Susan Snell, and David Peabody, 'Robert Wentworth Little: A Duplicitous Freemason, Wordsmith and Mystic, Part 1', *Ars Quatuor Coronatorum*, vol. 130 (2017), pp. 1–24

Gawsworth, John, *The Life of Arthur Machen*, ed. Roger Dobson (Carlton-in-Coverdale: Tartarus Press, 2017)

Gilbert, R. A., *The Golden Dawn: Twilight of the Magicians* (Wellingborough: Aquarian Press, 1983)

—, *A. E. Waite: Magician of Many Parts* (Wellingborough: Crucible, 1987)

—, *The Golden Dawn and the Esoteric Section* (London: Theosophical History Centre, 1987)

—, *The Golden Dawn Scrapbook: The Rise and Fall of a Magical Order* (York Beach, ME: Samuel Weiser, 1997)

—, '"The Supposed Rosy Crucian Society": Bulwer-Lytton and the S.R.I.A.', in *Esotérisme, Gnoses & Imaginaire Symbolique: Mélanges Offerts à Antoine Faivre*, ed., Richard Charon et al. (Leuven: Peeters, 2001), pp. 389–402

—, 'Mathers, Samuel Liddell (1854–1918), occultist', *Oxford Dictionary of National Biography*, 23 September 2004 <doi.org/10.1093/ref:odnb/53858>

—, 'Steiger, Isabelle de [*née* Isabelle Lace] (1836–1927), artist and theosophist', *Oxford Dictionary of National Biography*, 23 September 2004 <doi.org/10.1093/ref:odnb/53851>
—, ed., *Arthur Machen's Occult Catalogues* (Carlton-in-Coverdale: Tartarus Press, 2019)
—, *The Golden Dawn Companion: A Guide to the History, Structure, and Workings of the Hermetic Order of the Golden Dawn* (Loughborough: Thoth Publications, 2021)
Godwin, Joscelyn, Christian Chanel, and John P. Deveney, *The Hermetic Brotherhood of Luxor: Initiatic and Historical Documents of an Order of Practical Occultism* (York Beach, ME: Samuel Weiser, 1995)
Gould, Warwick, and Marjorie Reeves, *Joachim of Fiore and the Myth of the Eternal Evangel* (Oxford: Oxford University Press, 2001)
Graf, Susan Johnston, *Talking to the Gods: Occultism in the Work of W. B. Yeats, Arthur Machen, Algernon Blackwood, and Dion Fortune* (Albany, NY: State University of New York Press, 2015).
Grant, Kenneth, *Nightside of Eden* (London: Frederick Muller, 1977).
Grant, Marion, 'Advertising Women's Entrepreneurship in *The Green Sheaf*: Pamela Colman Smith and the *Fin-de-Siècle* Marketplace', *Nineteenth-Century Gender Studies*, vol. 18, no. 2 (Summer 2022), n.p.
Greensill, T. M., *History of the S.R.I.A.*, 2nd edition (London: Societas Rosicruciana in Anglia, 2003)
Greer, Mary K., *Women of the Golden Dawn: Rebels and Priestesses* (Rochester, VT: Park Street Press, 1995)
Haddo, Oliver [Aleister Crowley], 'How to Write A Novel! After W. S. Maugham', *Vanity Fair*, 30 December 1908, pp. 838–40
Hadfield, Alice Mary, *Charles Williams: An Exploration of his Life and Work* (Oxford: Oxford University Press, 1983)
Harland-Jacobs, Jessica L., *Builders of Empire: Freemasons and British Imperialism, 1717–1927* (Chapel Hill, NC: The University of North Carolina Press, 2007)
Harmsen, Theodor, 'The Reception of Jacob Böhme and Böhmist Theosophy in the *Geheime Figuren der Rosenkreuzer*', *Offenbarung und Episteme*, vol. 173 (2012), pp. 183–206
—, 'Fiction or a Much Stranger Truth: Sources and Reception of the *Geheime Figuren der Rosenkreuzer* – Secret Symbols of the Rosicrucians in the 18th, 19th and 20th Centuries', *Aufklärung und Esoterik: Wege in die Moderne*, vol. 50 (2013), pp. 726–52
Harper, George Mills, *Yeats's Golden Dawn* (London: Macmillan, 1974)
—, ed., *Yeats and the Occult* (London: Macmillan, 1976)
—, ed., *W. B. Yeats and W. T. Horton: The Record of an Occult Friendship* (London: Macmillan, 1980)
—, and Walter Kelly Hood, ed., *A Critical Edition of Yeats's* A Vision *(1925)* (London: Macmillan, 1987)
Heath-Stubbs, John, *Literary Essays*, ed. A. T. Tolley (Manchester: Carcanet, 1998)
Hine, Phil, *Prime Chaos: Adventures in Chaos Magic*, introduction by Grant Morrison (Tempe, AZ: New Falcon Publications, 1999).

Hockley, Frederick, *The Rosicrucian Seer: Magical Writings of Frederick Hockley*, ed. John Hammill (Wellingborough: Aquarian Press, 1986)

Holroyd, Michael, *Bernard Shaw: Volume 1: 1856–1898: The Search for Love* (London: Chatto & Windus, 1988)

Horton, W. T., *A Book of Images*, introduction by W. B. Yeats (London: The Unicorn Press, 1898)

Howe, Ellic, ed., *The Alchemist of the Golden Dawn: The Letters of the Revd W. A. Ayton to F. L. Gardner and Others 1886–1905* (Wellingborough: Aquarian Press, 1985)

—, *The Magicians of the Golden Dawn: A Documentary History of a Magical Order 1887–1923* (London: Routledge & Kegan Paul, 1985)

Huneker, James, [untitled review], *New York Sun*, 15 January 1907

Hutchinson, Alice L., *Kenneth Anger: A Demonic Visionary* (London: Black Dog Publishing, 2004)

Hutton, Ronald, *The Triumph of the Moon* (London: Yale University Press, 1999)

James, T. G. H., *Howard Carter: The Path to Tutankhamun* (London: Kegan Paul, 1992)

Jerome, Jerome K., *My Life and Times* (London: John Murray, 1983)

Johnson, George Malcom, 'Blackwood, Algernon Henry (1869–1951), writer of supernatural fiction', *Oxford Dictionary of National Biography*, 23 September 2004 <doi.org/10.1093/ref:odnb/31913>

Johnson, Josephine, *Florence Farr: Bernard Shaw's New Woman* (Gerrards Cross: C. Smythe, 1975)

'The Kabbalah Unveiled', *The Saturday Review of Politics, Literature, Science and Art*, vol. 64, no. 1663 (10 September 1887), pp. 368–9

Kaczynski, Richard, *Perdurabo: The Life of Aleister Crowley* (Berkeley, CA: North Atlantic Books, 2010)

—, *Friendship in Doubt: Aleister Crowley, J. F. C. Fuller, Victor B. Neuburg, and British Agnosticism* (New York: Oxford University Press, 2024)

Kalogera, Lucy Shepherd, 'Yeats's Celtic Mysteries', PhD thesis, Florida State University, 1977

King, Francis, *Modern Ritual Magic: The Rise of Western Occultism* (Bridport: Prism Press, 1989)

—, ed., *Ritual Magic of the Golden Dawn: Works by S. L. MacGregor Mathers and Others* (Rochester, VT: Destiny Books, 1997)

King, Francis, and Isabel Sutherland, *The Rebirth of Magic* (London: Corgi, 1982)

King, Jr, Roma A., *The Pattern in the Web: The Mythical Poetry of Charles Williams* (Kent, OH: Kent State University Press, 2013)

Kingsford, Anna, and Edward Maitland, *The Perfect Way; or, the Finding of Christ* (London: Hamilton, Adams & Co., 1882)

Knight, Gareth, *Dion Fortune and the Inner Light* (Loughborough: Thoth Publications, 2000)

Lachman, Gary, *Aleister Crowley: Magick, Rock and Roll, and the Wickedest Man in the World* (New York: Penguin, 2014)

Larkin, Philip, *Selected Letters of Philip Larkin: 1940–1985*, ed. Anthony Thwaite (London: Faber, 1992)

Lévi, Éliphas, *Transcendental Magic*, trans. A. E. Waite (London: Rider & Co, 1896)
—, *The Mysteries of Magic: A Digest of the Writings of Éliphas Lévi*, ed. A. E. Waite (London: Kegan Paul, Trench, Trübner & Co., 1897)
Liljegren, S. B., 'Bulwer-Lytton's Novels and Isis Unveiled', in *Essays and Studies on English Language and Literature*, ed. S. B. Liljegren (Uppsala: Lundequistska Bokhandeln, 1957)
Lindop, Grevel, *Charles Williams: The Third Inkling* (Oxford: Oxford University Press, 2015)
—, 'Charles Williams and W. B. Yeats', *Yeats Annual*, vol. 21 (2018), pp. 317–54
Loydell, Rupert, ed., *My Kind of Angel: i.m. William Burroughs* (Exeter: Slide Publications, 1998)
Luckhurst, Roger, ed., *Late Victorian Gothic Tales* (Oxford: Oxford University Press, 2009)
MacBride, Maud Gonne, *A Servant of the Queen: Reminiscences* (Gerrards Cross: Colin Smythe, 1994)
Machen, Arthur, *The Three Impostors* (London: John Lane, 1895
—, *Hieroglyphics* (London: Grant Richards, 1902)
—, *The House of Souls* (London: E. Grant Richards, 1906)
—, 'What is Mysticism? Bringing Humanity to Exquisite Perfection', *Evening News* (London), 4 March 1913, p. 4
—, *Far Off Things* (London: Martin Secker, 1922)
—, *The Grande Trouvaille: A Legend of Pentonville* (London: The First Edition Bookshop, 1923)
—, *Things Near and Far* (London: Martin Secker, 1923)
—, *Selected Letters: The Private Writings of the Master of the Macabre*, ed. Godfrey Brangham, Roger Dobson and R. A. Gilbert (Wellingborough: Aquarian Press, 1988)
—, and A. E. Waite, *The House of the Hidden Light*, ed. R. A. Gilbert (Carlton-in-Coverdale: Tartarus Press, 2003)
—, *The Secret of the Sangraal, & Other Writings* (Carlton-in-Coverdale: Tartarus Press, 2007)
—, *Decadent and Occult Works*, ed. Dennis Denisoff (Cambridge: Modern Humanities Research Association, 2018)
Machen, Purefoy, *Where Memory Slept*, ed. Godfrey Brangham (Caerleon: Green Round Press, 1991)
Machin, James, 'Aleister Crowley and Occult Meaning', in *The Palgrave Handbook of Contemporary Gothic*, ed. Clive Bloom (London: Macmillan, 2020), pp. 321–35
Mackenzie, Kenneth R. H., *The Royal Masonic Cyclopaedia of History, Rites, Symbolism, and Biography* (London: Bro. John Hogg, 1877)
Maitland, Edward, *Annie Besant: Her Life, Letters, Diary, and Work* (London, 1913).
Marlow, Louis, *Seven Friends* (London: The Richards Press, 1953).
Mathers, S. L. MacGregor, trans., *The Kabbalah Unveiled* (London: Kegan Paul, Trench and Turner, 1926)

—, trans., *The Grimoire of Armadel*, ed. Francis King (London: Routledge & Kegan Paul, 1980)

Maugham, W. Somerset, *The Magician: A Novel, together with a Fragment of Autobiography* (1908; New York, NY: Arno Press, 1977)

McIntosh, Christopher, *The Rose Cross and the Age of Reason: Eighteenth-century Rosicrucianism in Central Europe and its Relationship to the Enlightenment* (Albany, NY: State University of New York Press, 2011)

Molloy, J. Fitzgerald, *A Modern Magician*, 3 vols (London: Ward & Downey, 1887)

Mong, Ambrose Ih-Ren, 'Yeats and Bardic Tradition', *Canadian Journal for Irish Studies*, vol. 20, no. 1 (July 1994), pp. 89–101

Moore, Alan, and Steve Moore, 'The Moon and Serpent Grand Egyptian Theatre of Marvels', *KAOS 14*, ed. Joe Biroco (London: Kaos-Babylon Press, 2002), pp. 187–94

Moore, Alan, J. H. Williams III, and Mick Gray, *Promethea* (La Jolla, CA: America's Best Comics, 1999–2005)

Moore, George, *'Hail and Farewell!': Ave* (London: Heinemann, 1911)

Moore, Virginia, *The Unicorn: William Butler Yeats' Search for Reality* (New York, NY: Macmillan, 1954)

Morrisson, Mark S., 'Apocalypse 1917: Esoteric Modernism and the War in Aleister Crowley's *Moonchild*', *Modernist Cultures*, vol. 12, no. 1 (2017), pp. 98–119

Munro, Craig, *Wild Man of Letters: The Story of P. R. Stephensen* (Melbourne: Melbourne University Press, 1984)

Newnham, P. H., *History of the Lodge of Hengist, no. 195, Bournemouth, from 1770 to 1870; a paper* (Bournemouth: 1870)

Nicholson, D. H. S., and A. H. E. Lee, eds, *The Oxford Book of English Mystical Verse* (London: Oxford University Press, 1917)

'Notes of the Month', *The Occult Review*, vol. 10, no. 6 (December 1909), p. 301

'Notes on Books,' *Notes & Queries*, vol. 113, no. 5 (25 February 1888), p. 160

O'Connor, Elizabeth Foley, *Pamela Colman Smith: Artist, Feminist & Mystic* (Liverpool: Liverpool University Press, 2021)

Önnerfors, Andreas, *Freemasonry: A Very Short Introduction* (Oxford: Oxford University Press, 2017)

Orridge, Genesis P., 'Magick Squares and Future Beats: The Magickal Processes and Methods of William S. Burroughs and Brion Gysin', in *Book of Lies: The Disinformation Guide to Magick and the Occult*, ed. Richard Metzger (San Francisco, CA: Disinformation Books, 2014).

Owen, Alex, *The Place of Enchantment: British Occultism and the Culture of the Modern* (Chicago, IL: University of Chicago Press, 2004)

Parkin, Lance, *Magic Words: The Extraordinary Life of Alan Moore* (London: Aurum Press, 2013)

Parsons, Melinda Boyd, 'Pamela Colman Smith and Alfred Stieglitz', *History of Photography*, vol. 20, no. 4 (Winter 1996), pp. 285–92

Partridge, Christopher, ed., *The Occult World* (Abingdon: Routledge, 2015)

Peters, Margot, *Bernard Shaw and the Actresses* (New York, NY: Doubleday, 1980)

Plaisance, Christopher A., 'Israel Regardie and the Psychologization of Esoteric Discourse', *Correspondences*, vol. 3 (2015), pp. 5–54
Powell, Anthony, *To Keep the Ball Rolling: The Memoirs of Anthony Powell. Volume II: Messengers of the Day* (London: Heinemann, 1978)
'Prince Starbeam, by A. E. Waite (Book Review)', *The Spectator*, 25 October 1890, p. 567
Prinke, Rafal T., 'Deeper Roots of the Golden Dawn', *The Hermetic Journal*, vol. 36 (1987), pp. 16–19
Raby, Peter, 'Theatre of the 1890s: Breaking Down the Barriers', in *The Cambridge Companion to Victorian and Edwardian Theatre* (Cambridge: Cambridge University Press, 2004), pp. 183–206
Raine, Kathleen, *Yeats, the Tarot and the Golden Dawn* (Dublin: Dolmen Press, 1972)
Ransome, Arthur, *Bohemia in London* (New York: Dodd, Mead & Company, 1907)
Regardie, Israel, *The Golden Dawn: An Account of the Teachings, Rites and Ceremonies of the Order of the Golden Dawn*, vols 1-2 (Saint Paul, MN: Llewellyn Publications, 1978)
—, *What You Should Know about the Golden Dawn* (Phoenix, AZ: Falcon Press, 1983)
Reynolds, Aiden, and William Charlton, *Arthur Machen: A Short Account of his Life and Work* (London: The Richards Press, 1963)
Richardson, Alan, *Priestess: The Life and Magic of Dion Fortune* (Wellingborough: Aquarian Press, 1987)
—, *Aleister Crowley and Dion Fortune: The Logos of the Aeon and the Shakti of the Age* (Woodbury, MN: Llewellyn Publications, 2009)
Richardson, Maurice, *Fits & Starts: Collected Pieces* (London: Michael Joseph, 1979)
Robinson, Edward S., *Shift Linguals: Cut-up Narratives from William S. Burroughs to the Present* (Amsterdam: Rodopi, 2011)
Rose, Phyllis, *Alfred Stieglitz: Taking Pictures, Making Painters* (New Haven, CT: Yale University Press, 2019)
Rothenstein, William, 'Three Impressions', *The Arrow* (Dublin, 1939), pp. 16–17
Roukema, Aren, 'A Veil that Reveals: Charles Williams and the Fellowship of the Rosy Cross', *Journal of Inklings Studies*, vol. 5, no. 1 (2015), pp. 22–71
Saurat, Denis, *Blake & Modern Thought* (London: Constable, 1929)
Scholem, Gershom, 'Knorr von Rosenroth, Christian', *Encyclopaedia Judaica*, vol. 12 (2007), pp. 240–41
Schuchard, Ronald, 'W. B. Yeats and the London Theatre Societies', *The Review of English Studies*, vol. 29, no. 6 (November 1978), pp. 415–46
—, 'An Attendant Lord: H. W. Nevinson's Friendship with W. B. Yeats', *Yeats Annual*, vol. 7 (1990), pp. 90–130
—, 'Yeats and Spirituality', *The Princeton University Library Chronicle*, vol. 59, no. 3 (April 1998), pp. 321–49
Shaw, George Bernard, *Plays: Pleasant and Unpleasant* (Chicago, IL: H. S. Stone, 1898)

—, *The Quintessence of Ibsenism* (London: Walter Scott, 1891)
ben Simeon, Abraham, of Worms, *The Book of the Sacred Magic of Abra-melin the Mage*, trans. S. L. MacGregor Mathers (New York: Dover, 1975).
Smith, Pamela Colman, 'Two Negro Stories from Jamaica', *The Journal of American Folklore*, vol. 9, no. 35 (October–December 1896), p. 278
—, ed., *The Green Sheaf*, vols 1–13 (1903–4)
'Songs and Poems of Fairyland (Book Review)', *The Spectator*, 8 December 1888
Sorensen, Janet, 'Ossian Poems', in *The Oxford Encyclopedia of British Literature*, ed. David Scott Kastan (Oxford: Oxford University Press, 2006)
Starrett, Vincent, *Born in a Bookshop: Chapters from the Chicago Renaissance* (Norman, OK: University of Oklahoma Press, 1965)
Steadman, John L., *H. P. Lovecraft and the Black Magickal Tradition: The Master of Horror's Influence on Modern Occultism* (San Francisco, CA: Weiser Books, 2015)
Steele, Tom, *Alfred Orage and the Leeds Arts Club, 1893–1923* (Aldershot: Scolar Press, 1990)
Stephenson, P. R., *The Legend of Aleister Crowley*, 3rd edition (Phoenix, AZ: Falcon Press, 1983)
Sturgis, Matthew, *Aubrey Beardsley: A Biography* (London: Flamingo, 1999)
Surette, Leon, *The Birth of Modernism: Ezra Pound, T. S. Eliot, W. B. Yeats, and the Occult* (Montreal: McGill-Queen's University Press, 1993)
Sutcliffe, Peter, *The Oxford University Press: An Informal History* (Oxford: Oxford University Press, 1978)
Symonds, John, *The Great Beast: The Life of Aleister Crowley* (London: Rider and Company, 1951)
The Theosophical Review, vol. 36, no. 216 (August 1905), p. 551
Times Literary Supplement, 17 December 1938, p. 804
Toomey, Deidre, 'Gonne, (Edith) Maud (1866–1953), Irish nationalist', *Oxford Dictionary of National Biography*, 3 January 2008 <doi.org/10.1093/ref:odnb/37465>
Trexler, Adam, 'Crafting a *New Age*: A. R. Orage and the Politics of Craft', *The Journal of Modern Craft*, vol. 4, no. 2 (July 2011), pp. 161–82
Tryphonopoulos, Demetres, 'The History of the Occult Movement', in *Literary Modernism and the Occult Tradition*, ed. Leon Surrette and Demetres Tryphonopoulos (Orona, ME: The National Poetry Foundation, 1996), pp. 19–49
Tully, Caroline, 'Egyptosophy in the British Museum: Florence Farr, the Egyptian Adept and the *Ka*', in *The Occult Imagination in Britain 1875–1947*, ed. Andrew Radford and Christine Ferguson (London: Routledge, 2017), pp. 131–45
Underhill, Evelyn, *The Column of Dust* (London: Methuen, 1909)
—, *Mysticism: A Study of the Nature and Development of Man's Spiritual Consciousness* (New York: E. P. Dutton & Co., 1912)

—, *The Letters of Evelyn Underhill*, ed. Charles Williams (London: Longmans, Green and Co. 1943)
Urban, Eusebio [William Q. Judge], 'The Dweller of the Threshold', *The Path*, vol. 9, no. 3 (1888), pp. 281–4
van Raalte, Georgia, 'Literary Initiation in the Occult Novels of Dion Fortune', PhD thesis, University of Surrey, 2022
Versluis, Arthur, 'Sexual Mysticisms in Nineteenth Century America: John Humphreys Noyes, Thomas Lake Harris, and Alice Bunker Stockham', in *Hidden Intercourse: Eros and Sexuality in the History of Western Esotericism*, ed. Wouter J. Hanegraaff and Jeffrey J. Kripal (New York: Fordham University Press, 2011), pp. 333–54
Waite, A. E., *The Unknown World*, vol. 1, no. 1 to vol. 2, no. 5 (August 1894–June 1895)
—, 'The Rosicrucians', *Walford's Antiquarian Magazine and Bibliographic Review*, vol. 11 (January–June 1887), pp. p97–9
—, ed., *Songs and Poems of Fairyland: An Anthology of English Fairy Poetry* (London: Walter Scott, 1888)
—, *Strange Houses of Sleep* (London: P. S. Wellby, 1906)
—, *The Wordsworth Book of Spells* [*The Book of Ceremonial Magic*, 1911] (Ware: Wordsworth Editions, 1995)
—, *The Secret Tradition in Freemasonry* (New York: Rebman, 1911)
—, *The Third Order of the Rosy Cross: World of Formation Part II. The Pontifical Ceremony of Admission to the Grade of Adeptus Minor, 5=6* (privately printed [London], 1917)
—, [unsigned obituary of S. L. MacGregor Mathers], *The Occult Review*, vol. 29, no. 4 (April 1919), p. 197
—, *The Brotherhood of the Rosy Cross* (London: W. Rider, 1924)
—, *The Pictorial Key to the Tarot* (New York: S. Weiser, 1975)
—, *Hermetic Papers of A. E. Waite: The Unknown Writings of a Modern Mystic*, ed. R. A. Gilbert (Wellingborough: Aquarian Press, 1987)
—, *Shadows of Life and Thought* (Dublin: Bardic Press, 2016)
Wallis, R. T., *Neoplatonism* (London: Duckworth, 1972)
Washington, Peter, *Madame Blavatsky's Baboon: Theosophy and the Emergence of the Western Guru* (London: Secker & Warburg, 1993)
Westcott, William Wynn, *The Chaldæan Oracles of Zoroaster: edited and revised by Sapere Aude, with an introduction by L.O.* (London: Theosophical Publishing Society, 1895)
—, *Data of the History of the Rosicrucians* (London: S.R.I.A., 1916)
Williams, Charles, 'Commonplace Book', 1912–23, Bodleian, MS Eng. E. 2012
—, *Poetry at Present* (Oxford: Clarendon Press, 1930)
—, *War in Heaven* (London: Victor Gollancz, 1930)
—, *The Greater Trumps* (London: Victor Gollancz, 1932)
—, *Shadows of Ecstasy* (London: Faber, 1948)
—, and C. S. Lewis, *Arthurian Torso: Containing the Posthumous Fragment of the Figure of Arthur* (London: Oxford University Press, 1948)
—, *The Region of the Summer Stars* (Oxford: Oxford University Press, 1950)

—, *The Image of the City and Other Essays*, selected by Anne Ridler with an introduction (Oxford: Oxford University Press, 1958)

—, *Taliessin through Logres* (London: Oxford University Press, 1969)

—, *Letters to Lalage: The Letters of Charles Williams to Lois Lang-Sims*, ed. Glen Cavaliero (Kent, OH: Kent State University Press, 1989)

Williams, Mark, *Ireland's Immortals: A History of the Gods of Irish Myth* (Princeton, NJ: Princeton University Press, 2016)

Wilson, Simon, 'Wilde, Beardsley, Salomé and Censorship', *The Wildean*, vol. 51 (July 2017), pp. 45–82

Wood, Juliette, 'The Celtic Tarot and the Secret Tradition: A Study in Modern Legend Making', *Folklore*, vol. 109 (1998), pp. 15–24

Yeats, J. B., *Letters to his Son W. B. Yeats and Others*, ed. Joseph Hone (London: Faber & Faber, 1944)

Yeats, W. B., 'Irish Fairies, Ghosts, Witches, etc.', *Lucifer*, vol. 3, no. 17 (January 1889), pp. 399–404

—, *The Wanderings of Oisin and Other Poems* (London: Kegan Paul, Trench & Co., 1889)

—, *The Countess Kathleen and Various Legends and Lyrics* (London: T. Fisher Unwin, 1893)

—, and Edwin Ellis, *The Works of William Blake: Poetic, Symbolic, and Critical*, 3 vols (London: Bernard Quaritch, 1893)

—, 'At Stratford-on-Avon', *The Speaker: The Liberal Review* (11 May 1901), p. 158

—, *The Countess Cathleen* (London: T. Fisher Unwin, 1920)

—, *A Vision: An Explanation of Life Founded upon the Writings of Giraldus and upon Certain Documents Attributed to Kusta Ben Luka* (London: T. Werner Laurie, 1925)

—, *Autobiographies: Reveries over Childhood and Youth and the Trembling of the Veil* (New York: Macmillan, 1927)

—, *A Vision* (New York: Macmillan, 1938)

—, *Autobiographies* (London: Macmillan, 1955)

—, *Memoirs*, ed. Denis Donoghue (London: Macmillan, 1972)

—, *Uncollected Prose*, 2 vols, ed. John P. Frayne and Colton Johnson (London: Macmillan, 1970–75)

—, *Essays and Introductions* (London: Papermac, 1989)

—, *Writings on Irish Folklore, Legend and Myth*, ed. R. Welch (London: Penguin, 1993)

—, *Short Fiction*, ed. G. J. Watson (London: Penguin, 1995)

—, *The Speckled Bird*, ed. William H. O'Donnell (Basingstoke: Palgrave Macmillan, 2003)

Picture Credits

Black and white illustrations
2 Harold B. Lee Library, Brigham Young University, Provo, Utah (NC 1115 .H7)
6 From the British Library archive, London
13 Private collection
22 Wellcome Library, London (2002007145)
25 Harold B. Lee Library, Brigham Young University, Provo, Utah (BF 1879 .T2 C6 1896)
35 Private collection
40 Published by Dolmen Press, Dublin
50 Private collection
65 Division of Rare and Manuscript Collections, Cornell University Library. Bernard F. Burgunder Collection of George Bernard Shaw (4617)
71 Bridgeman Images
76 Hamilton College Library Digital Collections, Clinton, New York (BF1001 .U6)
79, 84 Private collection
85 TopFoto/Fortean
88 Bettmann/Getty Images
98 Photos courtesy Tartarus Press
102 John M. Kelly Library, University of Toronto
112 Private collection
116 From the British Library archive
119 Hamilton College Library Digital Collections, Clinton, New York (BF1001 .U6)
135 Charles Walker Collection/Alamy Stock Photo
140, 146, 147, 153 Private collection
166 Harold B. Lee Library, Brigham Young University, Provo, Utah (NC 1115 .H7)
169 Abbey Theatre Archives
173 Shakespeare Birthplace Trust
174 Centre for Digital Humanities at Toronto Metropolitan University
181 Beinecke Rare Book and Manuscript Library, Yale University, New Haven. Alfred Stieglitz/Georgia O'Keeffe Archive (YCAL MSS 85)
182 Photo The Metropolitan Museum of Art/Art Resource/Scala, Florence. © Marius de Zayas
199 Photo courtesy Editorial La Felguera, Madrid
214 Facsimile Dust Jackets LLC, www.dustjackets.com. © Estate of Lanta Spurrier

PICTURE CREDITS

222 Courtesy New Falcon Publications. © United States Ecclesiastical Society and Seminary
230 © Alan Moore and Kevin O'Neill, permission granted by Knockabout

Colour plates
I Bridgeman Images
II Bridgeman Images
III Museum of Freemasonry, London (GD 8/4/4a-e)
IV Museum of Freemasonry, London (GD 2/3/1/1)
V Private collection
VI, VII From the British Library archive
VIII Hamilton College Library Digital Collections, Clinton, New York (BF1001 .U6)
IX Private collection. 'The Mail Car' © 2025 Estate of Jack B Yeats. All rights reserved, DACS
X Private collection
XI Contraband Collection/Private collection/Alamy Stock Photo. © Estate of Beresford Egan
XII Facsimile Dust Jackets LLC, www.dustjackets.com
XIII National Library of Ireland, Dublin
XIV Victoria and Albert Museum, London. Given by Gwen John (E.289-1925)
XV Lebrecht History/Bridgeman Images
XVI Museum of Freemasonry, London. GD 9/2/2
XVII, XVIII Mary Evans Picture Library/ Harry Price Library of Magical Literature, University of London. © J. F. C. Fuller
XIX Ordo Templi Orientis
XX Bridgeman Images
XXI Private collection
XXII Whitney Museum of American Art, New York. Gift of Mrs Sidney N. Heller (60.42l)
XXIII Beinecke Rare Book and Manuscript Library, Yale University, New Haven. Cary Collection of Playing Cards (ENG38)
XXIII (bottom right) Private collection

Acknowledgments

This is not the first history of the Hermetic Order of the Golden Dawn by any means; neither is it a complete history. It is rather an attempt to say something about the literature and art produced by members of this now-famous secret society. I advise readers wishing to know more about Mathers's Order and its operations to seek out *The Magicians of the Golden Dawn: A Documentary History of a Magical Order 1887–1923* by the printer and historian Ellic Howe, whose access to private archives and commitment to distinguishing fact from fiction (wherever possible) laid the groundwork for later studies by R. A. Gilbert, Francis King, George Mills Harper, Mary K. Greer, Alex Owen and others. Gilbert's *The Golden Dawn: Twilight of the Magicians*, *The Golden Dawn Companion* and *Scrapbook* are also essential. Like many before me, I am not an occultist or a practitioner of magic, merely an ex-literature student who wishes to understand how ritual played a part in the lives of artists.

My thanks first of all go to the team at Thames & Hudson: Ben Hayes, for taking a chance on an unusual proposal, my editor Kate Edwards, Nikos Kotsopoulos, India Jackson, Rowena Alsey and Celia Falconer. To Jonathan Pelham for the extraordinary cover. I am supremely grateful to Carolyne Larrington and Grevel Lindop, who read early chapter drafts and whose comments helped shape them into something readable. To Sam Collinson and Amy Ebrey for help with the Latin mottos. To Alan Moore for permission to quote from 'Fossil Angels'. Thanks also to Richard Parkinson, Andrew Radford, Matthew J. A. Green, R. A. Gilbert, Stuart D. Lee, the staff at the Library of Freemasonry and the Weston Library at Oxford, the administrators of the International Association for the Preservation of Spiritualist and Occult Periodicals website (without whom my life would have been twice as difficult), and to my agent Catherine Cho.

ACKNOWLEDGMENTS

Outside of the book-writing world, thank you to Sarah, Lauren and Matt at the Queen's College Library. To my parents for their ever-present support, and my brothers for their company on walks around occult London. To Janna, Nahum and Amos: this is what I've been doing after you go to bed! Don't read it quite just yet. To my wife Damaris, for everything you do, and finally to Anfinn, who grew at the same time as this book.

Index

Italic page numbers indicate illustrations; **bold** entries refer to colour plates

A
A∴A∴ (Argenteum Astrum) 144–5, 150, 152, 156, 163, 164, 226
  see also Crowley, Aleister
Abbey of Thelema *see* Thelema
Africanus, Leo 186
Alchemy 17
  and Farr 72–3, 178
  in fiction 49, 51, 52, 114, 117, 118, 126
  and GD 10, 39, 201, 223, 225, 231
  and Machen 105, 107, 108, 109
  and W. A. Ayton 29, 97, 170
  and Waite 104, 105, 109, 110
Alpha et Omega (A∴O∴) 164, 200, 225
  in America 223–4
  and Fortune 209, 211
  and Moina Mathers 200, 209
Amoun Temple *see* Stella Matutina
Anger, Kenneth 226
Archer, Ethel 145
Arms and the Man see Shaw, George Bernard
Arthurian legend 105
  Company of Avalon 206
  in fiction 129, 203, 212
  Fortune and Glastonbury 206, 211
  and Machen 126, 130, 213
  in poetry 192, 194–5, 207–8, 212
  in ritual 52, 53, 95, 165
  and Waite 130, 131, 183, 192
Avenue Theatre 66–7, 72, 82, **XIV**
Ayton, Rev W. A.
  as alchemist 97, 170
  and Independent and Rectified Rite 128, 164
  and Isis-Urania 28–9, 62, **XX**
  and Yeats 41

B
Barrett, Francis 10, 107
Bates, Emily Katherine 113
Beardsley, Aubrey 64, 136–7, 138
  and the Avenue Theatre 66, **XIV**
  Keynotes 68–9, *116*, 117, **VI**, **VII**
Bedford Park (Chiswick) 32, 60–1, 64, 113
Bennett, Allan
  and Annie Horniman 56, 63
  and Crowley 141, 142–3, 154, 158
  and Farr 78–81
  in *A Vision* 189
Berridge, Edward 55, 56, 62, 63, 111, 118, 120, 154, 158
Besant, Annie 33, 97–9, 176, 198
Blackden, M. W. 73, 87, 123, 126
  and Waite 127, 128, 164
Blackwood, Algernon *6*, 124, 148, 205, 213
Blake, William 31, 33, 36, 43, 138, 176, 180, 188
Blavatsky, Helena 18–19, 28, 33–7, *35*, 73, 100, 106, 109, 176
Bodley Head (publishers) *see* Lane, John
Böhme, Jakob 99, 107, 188
Brémont, Anna Elizabeth 28
British Museum 14, 24, 32, 100, 109, 141
  the Egyptian gallery 73–4, 75–6, 91
  in fiction 52, 215;
  and Mathers 28, 38, 110
Broad Sheet (periodical) 175
  see also Smith, Pamela Colman
Brodie-Innes, John W. 29, 77, 81, 90, 92, 125, 151, 213, 215

INDEX

and Alpha et Omega 200
and Crowley 148–9, 151
and Waite 127–8
Browning, Robert 101
Builders of the Adytum
  (B.O.T.A.) 224
Bullock, Percy 72, 87, 90, 125, 127
Bulwer-Lytton, Edward 14–15, 16,
  18–19, 20, 21, 24, 100, 134, 229
Burroughs, William S. 228
Butts, Mary 161–2

C

Celtic tradition
  'Bardic Ireland' 170
  Celtic Mysteries 46–8, 52, 57,
    83, 168
  in fiction 49, 51, 52, 120
  folklore 36, 48, 120, 179
  and Fortune 197, 211–12
  Irish literary revival 37, 43, 45,
    49, 51, 82, 83, 176
  and Mathers 21, 29, 45, 54
  and Smith 179
  and Williams 195
Cipher Manuscripts *see* Hermetic
  Order of the Golden Dawn
Colquhoun, Ithell 225
Companions of the Co-inherence
  217
  see also Williams, Charles
Constant, Alphonse Louis (Éliphas
  Lévi) 15–16, 20, *25*, 26, 38, 73,
  100, 104, 107, III, 183, **XV**
Crowley, Aleister 88, 132–63, *140*,
  164, 165, 211, 218–19, 225
  and the A∴A∴ 144–5, 212, **XVII**,
    XVIII, XIX
  Abbey of Thelema 160–1
  and *Abra-Melin* 134, 142
  and Bennett 78, 141, 154
  Equinox (periodical) 79, 80, 104,
    146, *147*, 149–55, 224, **X**;
  fictional representations of 122,
    156, 158–60, 163, 215, 229, 231
  and GD 31, 87–9, 132, 134, 136
  journalism 148, 155, 156–7
  and magic 157, 159, 219, 221, 226
  and Mathers 132, 143, 149, 158
  Moonchild 21, 104, 158–60,
    204, 213, **XI**
  opinion of GD members 120–1,
    139, 141, 148–9, 158
  poetry 136–9, 141, 195
  Rites of Eleusis 212, 223
  and Rose Edith Kelly 143, 155
  short stories 142, 145, 148

D

Dadd, Richard 101
Decadence 69, 117, 132, 134, 136–7
Dee, John 45, 142, 229
Dickson, Carnegie 191, 201
Dolmetsch, Arnold 168, 170, 177
Dunsany, Edward John Moreton
  Drax Plunkett (Lord Dunsany)
  148, 212

E

Egan, Beresford **XI**
Egyptian religion: *The Book of the
  Dead* 80, 92
  and Crowley 143
  the Chantress 75–7, 95
  and Farr 59, 73–5, 212
  and GD ritual 43, 44, 78, 80–1,
    220
  and Mathers 43–4, 57, 83
  and theosophy 19, 165, 176–7
Eliot, T. S. 12, 204
Ellis, Edwin 33, 43, 195
Equinox (periodical) *see* Crowley,
  Aleister
Evans, Thomas 211–12
  see also Fortune, Dion

F

fairies 36, 55, 101–3, *102*, 197
Farr, Florence 29, 59–96, *65*, 141,
  164–91
  Avenue Theatre 66–7, 72
  as Chief Adept 81, 86, 91–2
  The Dancing Faun 67–9, 70, 115,
    177, 178, **VI**
  Egyptian Magic 73–5, 212
  Egyptian plays 165–7, 176–7

and Isis-Urania 41, 45, 61, 62–4,
    70–2, 81–2, 86–7, 90–5, 139, 141
and Mathers 77, 81, 86–7
and the *New Age* 165, 177–8
and the psaltery 168–70 *169*, 176,
    177, 179, 180
and Shaw 60–2, 67, 74–5
and the Sphere groups 77–82,
    90–1, 120
on the stage 60–2, 64, 66–7, 82–3
and theosophy 37, 95–6, 176–7
and Yeats 36, 59–62, 66, 82–3,
    92–3, 167–70, 189, 190
Felkin, Robert 81, 125, 164, 185, 223
Fellowship of the Rosy Cross
    (F∴R∴C∴) 193, 196, 201–2,
    204, 208
    see also Waite, A. E.
Fellowship of the Three Kings 168,
    175
Forest Hill (Mathers' lodgings) 9,
    29, 38, 41–3, 62, 63, 111
Fortune, Dion (Violet Mary Firth)
    192–219, 196–7, *199*, 212, 224, **XII**
    and Alpha et Omega 200–1, 209
    The Cosmic Doctrine 206, 209
    and Crowley 219, 231
    Fraternity of the Inner Light
        210–11, 212
    and Glastonbury 206, 211
    Magical Battle of Britain 217–18
    occult thrillers 213, *214*, 215–16
    and psychology 198–200, 205,
        210, 213
    theory of literature 212–13, 215–16
    and theosophy 198, 209
    and trance mediumship 206,
        209–10
Fraternity of the Inner Light 209,
    210–12, 213, 217–18, 223
    see also Fortune, Dion
freemasonry 10, 16–17, 152, 205
    and GD members 10, 12, 21, 29,
        72, 193
    grade structure and rituals 14,
        26, 97, 127
    Mark Masons' Hall 61, 124
    see also SRIA

Fryer-Fortescue, Ethel 175, 179
Fuller, J. F. C. 144, 150, 178, 219

G

Gardner, Frederick Leigh 73, 75,
    78, 81, 134
Golden Dawn (GD) *see* Hermetic
    Order of the Golden Dawn
Gonne, Maud
    and the GD 41, 57, 124
    and nationalist politics 46, 92
    and Yeats 41, 45, 46–7, 48, 82, 83
Grant, Kenneth 219, 226–7
Gregory, Augusta (Lady Gregory)
    46, 47, 48, 57, 87, 165, 170, 175,
    186, 187
Green Sheaf (periodical) *174*, 175–6,
    179–80, 184
    see also Smith, Pamela Colman
grimoire 10, 11, 51, 52, 107, 111, 134,
    221, 227
    The Magus (Francis Barrett) 10, 107
    Key of Solomon 22, 23–4
    *Book of the Sacred Magic of Abra-
        Melin the Mage* 134, *135*
    Kabbalah Unveiled 23, 38, 99, 111,
        143, 156

H

Hamilton, Lillias 197–8
Harris, Thomas Lake *see*
    Brotherhood of the New Life
Hermetic Brotherhood of Luxor
    10, 73, 117
Hermetic Order of the Golden
    Dawn (GD)
    Cipher Manuscripts 12, 14–15, 20,
        24, 108, 124, 128, 141, 193, 229
    Flying Rolls 45, 61, 63, 70, 201,
        224, 225
    foundation 19–20, 24–9, 150, **IV**
    grade structure 26–7, 31, 122, 164
    initiation into 8–9, 27–8, 30,
        38, 41, 61, 95, 121, 201–2
    mottos 27, 38, 61, 111, 136, 175
    Second Order 27, 39, 43–5, 55, 63,
        77–8, 89–90, 94, 150–1, 185,
        XVI

INDEX

secrets published 150–1, 210, 224–5
Hermetic Society 23, 29, 32, 38, 39
Hirsig, Leah 160–1, 162
Hockley, Frederick 14, 20, 108
Hogg, Amelia *see* Machen, Arthur
Horlick's Magazine 126, 129, 145
Horniman, Annie 8–9, 28, 46, 66, 77
   bankrolling the Matherses 9, 43, 54, 66
   and the GD crisis 54–7, 83, 90–4
   in Isis-Urania 9, 57, 62, 63
Horos scandal 95, 195
Horton, W. T. 2, 50, 55, 165, *166*, *174*, 176, 186, 189, 190
Howe, Ellic 14, 225
Hubbard, L. Ron 225–6
Huddleston, Dorothy Purefoy *see* Machen, Arthur
Hunter, Dorothea 46, 48, 87, 165, 189–90
Hunter, Edmund 46, 53, 87, 89, 165
Hyde-Lees, Georgina ('Georgie') 186–7
see also Yeats, W. B.

I

Independent and Rectified Rite (Independent and Rectified R. R. et A. C.) 99, 128, 164, 165
   and its dissolution 193
   and Lee and Nicholson 195
   and Smith 175
Inklings 217
Isis-Urania Temple *see* Hermetic Order of the Golden Dawn

J

Jennings, Hargrave 20, 106, 107, 109
Jerome, Jerome K. 108, 121
Jones, George Cecil 134, 154, 164

K

kabbalah 7, 15, 20, 73
   and esoteric Christianity 43, 193, 201–2

and Farr 97, 178
and Fortune 211, 218
and the GD 10, 47, 97, 183, 213
Kabbalah Unveiled 23, 38, 99, 111, 143, 156
and Regardie 211, 224
Tree of Life (diagram) 26, 27, 47, 81, 91, 92, 139, 227
Kelly, Edward 45, *112*, 142
Kelly, Rose Edith *see* Crowley, Aleister
Kingsford, Anna 23, 34, 38, 99
see also Hermetic Society

L

Lakeman, Ada *see* Waite, A. E.
Lane, John 64
   and the Bodley Head 64, 68, 175
   and *Keynotes* 68–9, 115
   The Yellow Book 69, 136, 176
Lawrence, D. H. 12, 163, 215
Le Gallienne, Richard 68, 69, 115
Lee, Rev A. H. E. 192, 195, 196, 201, 203
Lévi, Éliphas *see* Constant, Alphonse Louis
Lewis, C. S. 207–8, 217
Light (periodical) 20, 110, 117, 130, 212
Little, Robert Wentworth *see* SRIA
Lovecraft, H. P. 227
Loveday, Charles 206, 209
Lucifer (periodical) *see* Theosophical Society
Lumley Brown, Margaret 216, 218

M

Machen, Arthur 97–131, *98*, 105–10, 113–17, 126–7, 196–7, 219, 223
   and Amy Hogg 110, 113, 120–1
   The Great God Pan 68, 69, 109, 114–15, 118, 195, 213, **VIII**
   and the Independent and Rectified Rite 128–9
   in Isis-Urania 99, 121–4
   and occultism 106–8, 130
   Rabelaisian Order of Tosspots 125

The Three Impostors 115, *116*, 117
and Underhill 129–30
and Waite 108, 118, 121, 125–6, 128–9 130, 131
Mackenzie, Kenneth R. H. 14, 16, 17, 19–20, 29, 108
magic 15–16, 19, 37, 94, 122, 129–30, 159
  chaos magic 227
  invisibility 142
  invocation of spirits 78–81, *112*, 141
  Lesser Ritual of the Pentagram 39, 202–3
  scrying 77, 142
  sex magic 144, 152, 162, 218, 225
  Sphere groups 77–82, 90–1, 120
  visions 47–8, 63–4, 176, 179
  and Yeats 21, 30–1, 33, 34, 37, 42, 46, 51, 58
Maitland, Edward 23, 29, 99, 118
Mansfield, Katherine 155, 177
Martyn, Edward 52, 82, 83, 170
Mathers, Moina (Mina Bergson) 62, *84*, 187, **I**
  and Alpha et Omega 200, 209, 210, 224
  as artist and designer 7, 26, 48, *135*
  and Mathers 24, 28–9, 43
  and Yeats 45, 48, 57, 189
Mathers, Samuel Liddell MacGregor 7–8, 9, 21, *22*, 29, 43, *85*, 110–11, 225, **I**
  and Crowley 89, 132–3, 134, 141, 142–3, 149, 151–5, 163
  and Farr 62, 72, 77, 81, 86–7
  in fiction 49, 52, 54, 158, 215
  and freemasonry 22–3
  and GD rituals 14, 24, 26–8, 39, 91, 97, 225
  as Imperator 31, 54, 55–7, 81
  Kabbalah Unveiled 23, 38, 99, 143
  Key of Solomon 23–4
  Rites of Isis 83, *85*, 223
  and the Second Order 7–9, 43–4, 45, **II**
  and Yeats 31, 37, 38, 41–2, 51, 57, 87–8, 165, 189, 190
  see also Mathers, Moina
Mathews, Elkin 64, 83, 175 *see also* John Lane
Maugham, W. Somerset 155–6
Mead, G. R. S. 176, 201, 225
Modernism 12, 177–8, 180, *181*, *182*, 183, 216
Moon and Serpent Grand Egyptian Theatre of Marvels *see* Moore, Alan
Moore, Alan 220–1, 223, 226, 228–31, *230*
Moore, Steve 221
Moriarty, Theodore 205, 206; *see also* Fortune, Dion
Morrell, Ottoline 204, 208
mysticism 97, 99, 114, 129–30, 201
  in art 175, 180
  and Fortune 210
  in poetry 192–3, 195
  and Thomas Lake Harris 55, 99
  and Waite 110, 127, 164
  and Yeats 31, 37, 90, 168, 188
  see also occultism

N

Neo-Platonism 73, 114, 215
Neuburg, Victor 144–5
New Age (periodical) 165, 177–8, 195
Nicholson, D. H. S. 192, 195, 196, 201, 203

O

O. T. O. (Ordo Templi Orientis) 152, 157, 219, 226–7
Occult Review (periodical) 129–30, 155, 177, 178, 184, 210–11
occultism 11–12, 109, 200, 210
  in fiction 114–15, 117, 124, 129, 158–60, 204
  and psychology 198–200, 205, 210, 213
  revival 10, 15, 23, 31, 97–9, 229
  see also magic
Orage, A. R. *see New Age*

276

INDEX

Oxford Book of English Mystical Verse 192, 193, 195
OUP (Oxford University Press) 192, 193, 194, 202–3, 208, 217
see also Williams, Charles

P

Paget, Dorothy 66, 83, 179
Paget, Henrietta (Henrietta Farr) 60, 66, 95
Parsons, Jack 225–6
Pollexfen, George 41, 47–8
Pollitt, Herbert 136–7
Powell, Anthony 133, 163

R

Redway, George (bookseller) 23, 106–8, 109, 110, 114, 134
Regardie, Israel 31, 211, *222*, 224, 227
Richardson, Maurice 133
Rosenkreutz, Christian *see* Rosicrucianism
Rosher, Charles 78, 80, 81, 136, 141
Rosicrucianism
  and Bulwer-Lytton 20, 229
  in fiction 49
  and freemasonry 14, 16–18, 193, 223 (*see also* SRIA)
  and the GD 7–8, 38, 44
  Hargrave Jennings and 20, 106, 107, 109
Russell, George (AE) 46, 47, 49, 175

S

Savoy (periodical) 49, 138, 176
Shakespear, Olivia 165–7, 178, 187
Shaw, George Bernard 64
  Arms and the Man 65, 67, 75
  and Farr 60, 61–2, 64, 67, 68
  and magic 60, 74–5
  the *New Age* 165, 177–8, 195
  see also Farr, Florence
Simpson, Elaine 63, 89, 132
Sinnett, A. P. 32, 100, 106, 110, 113
Smith, Pamela Colman 164–91,

165, 168, 170–5, *173*, 177, *181*, *182*, **IX, XXI, XXII**
  and Alfred Stieglitz 180, 183, 184
  Green Sheaf 174, 175–6, 179, 184
  and Independent and Rectified Rite 175, 185
  and Isis-Urania 170, 175
  and the Ryder-Waite tarot 183–4, **XXIII**
  and Yeats 172, 180
Smithers, Leonard (publisher) 138
Spare, Austin Osman 145, 226, 227
Sphere groups; *see* Farr, Florence
spiritualism 11, 100, 103, 109, 110, 129
  and Blavatsky 18, 19
  and Yeats 32, 186–9
  see also Light (periodical)
Sprengel, [Anna] 12, 27, 28, 77, 95, 191, 220, 223
  as fictional character 27, 51
  and Westcott 12–14, 20, 86, 87
SRIA (Societas Rosicruciana in Anglia) 10, *13*, 26, 97, 99, 106
  and Bulwer-Lytton 18
  and the GD 28
  and Mathers 23
  and Waite 111, 127
  see also Rosicrucianism
Steiger, Isabelle de 76, 118, *119*, 134, **VIII**
Stella Matutina 31, 151, 201, 223
  Amoun Temple 185, 187, 191
  formation 164, 185
  and Fortune 210, 211
  rituals published 224
  and Yeats 31, 165, 191
  see also Felkin, Robert
Stephensen, P. R. 162–3
Stevenson, Robert Louis 114, 115, 171
Stieglitz, Alfred 180, 183, 184
Stoker, Bram 149, 172, 206
Swedenborg, Emanuel 55, 99, 170, 188
Swinburne, Algernon Charles 137, 138, 143

INDEX

T
tarot 23, 165, 176, 204, 224, 225
  and the GD 26, 63, 122, 183
  Ryder-Waite deck 183–5, **XXIII**
  Thoth Tarot 219
Terry, Ellen 171, 172, *173*, 179
Thelema 143–4, 160
  Abbey of Thelema 160–2
  see also Crowley, Aleister
Theosophical Society 10, 18, 19, 28, 100, 109
  and Blackwood 124
  and the Esoteric Section 33–4, 37, 42, 58
  and Farr 96, 176–7
  and Fortune 198, 209
  Lucifer 35, 36, 74, 106, 111, 117
  see also Blavatsky, Helena
theosophy 23, 32–3, 73, 124, 176
  and Christianity 17, 209, 210
  and George Redway 106, 109
  see also Theosophical Society
Thomas, Robert Palmer 93, 94, 120, 127
Todhunter, John 32, 41, 61, 66–7, 95, 113, 176

U
Underhill, Evelyn 129–30, 192, 195, 208–9
Unknown World (periodical) 55, 76, 117–20, *119*, 127, 145, **VII**
  see also Waite, A. E.

V
Vaughan, Thomas 72–3, 107, 110

W
Waddell, Leila 152, *153*
Waite, A. E. 14, 29, 97–131, *98*, 183–4, 210, 219
  Book Black Magic and of Pacts 112, 122, 134, 149
  and Crowley 134, 142, 158
  and Éliphas Lévi 15, 100, 104, 111
  and esoteric Christianity 99, 109, 164, 193
  Fellowship of the Rosy Cross 192, 193, 202, 208
  and freemasonry 17, 111, 127
  Independent and Rectified Rite 127–8, 164
  and Isis-Urania 111, 113, 120, 124
  and Machen 99, 108–9, 115, 118, 121, 126–7, 129, 130
  as a poet 101–3, *102*, 126, 195
  and spiritualism 100, 109
  Unknown World 55, 76, 117–20, *119*, 145, **VII**
  and Williams 192–3, 196, 201, 208
Watkins, J. M. (bookseller) 90, 195
Westcott, William W. *13*, 20, 72, 81, 110, 158, **III**
  and the Cipher Manuscripts 12–14, 20, 23, 87
  Collectanea Hermetica 59, 72–4, 90, 118, 201
  and Mathers 23, 24–8, 86
  GD organization and teachings 26–7, 44, 45, *71*, 91, 150, 201
  and Waite 111, 120
Wheatley, Dennis 163
Wilde, Constance 28, 114
Wilde, Oscar 28, 67, 69, 113–14, 177
Wilkinson, Louis 155
Williams, Charles 192–219, *193*, 194, 201, 203–4
  Companions of the Co-inherence 217
  and the Fellowship of the Rosy Cross 193, 196, 201, 202–4, 208
  and the Inklings 217
  and T. S. Eliot 204
  and Underhill 129
  and Waite 192–3, 208
  and Yeats 192, 195, 208
Williams, Florence (Florence Conway) *see* Williams, Charles
Woodford, Rev A. F. A. 12, 14, 20, 24
Woodman, William Robert 24, 27, 31, 87

Y
Yeats, W. B. 10, 29, 30–58, *31–2*, 58, 115, 117, 164–91, 219, **V**

and Blackwood 124
and Blake 31, 33, 36
and Farr 36, 41, 59, 60, 82, 92–3, 167–70
in fiction 142, 149, 158
and Gonne 41, 45, 46–7, 57
and Horton 2, *50*, 55, 165, *166*
and Irish nationalism 43, 46, 51–2, 83, 92, 188
and Irish tradition 37, 46, 48, 170, 176
and Isis-Urania 30–1, 38–42, *40*, 43–5, 92–6, **XIII**
magic and poetry 31, 54, 58, 155, 191, 231
and Mathers 21, 23, 24, 28, 38, 45, 54, 165, 189–90
Order of Celtic Mysteries 46–8
and Smith 172–3, 175–6, 180
The Speckled Bird (unfinished novel) 21, 51, 52–4, 55, 59, 90, 92
and spiritualism 186, 187
and Stella Matutina 165, 185–6, 191
and theosophy 32, 33–6; *A Vision* 187–91, 208
and Williams 192, 195, 208
Yorke, Gerald 99, 125

Z
Zanoni see Bulwer-Lytton, Edward